CAR(
TRAVEL

MW00677765

CULLASAJA FALLS, WESTERN NORTH CAROLINA

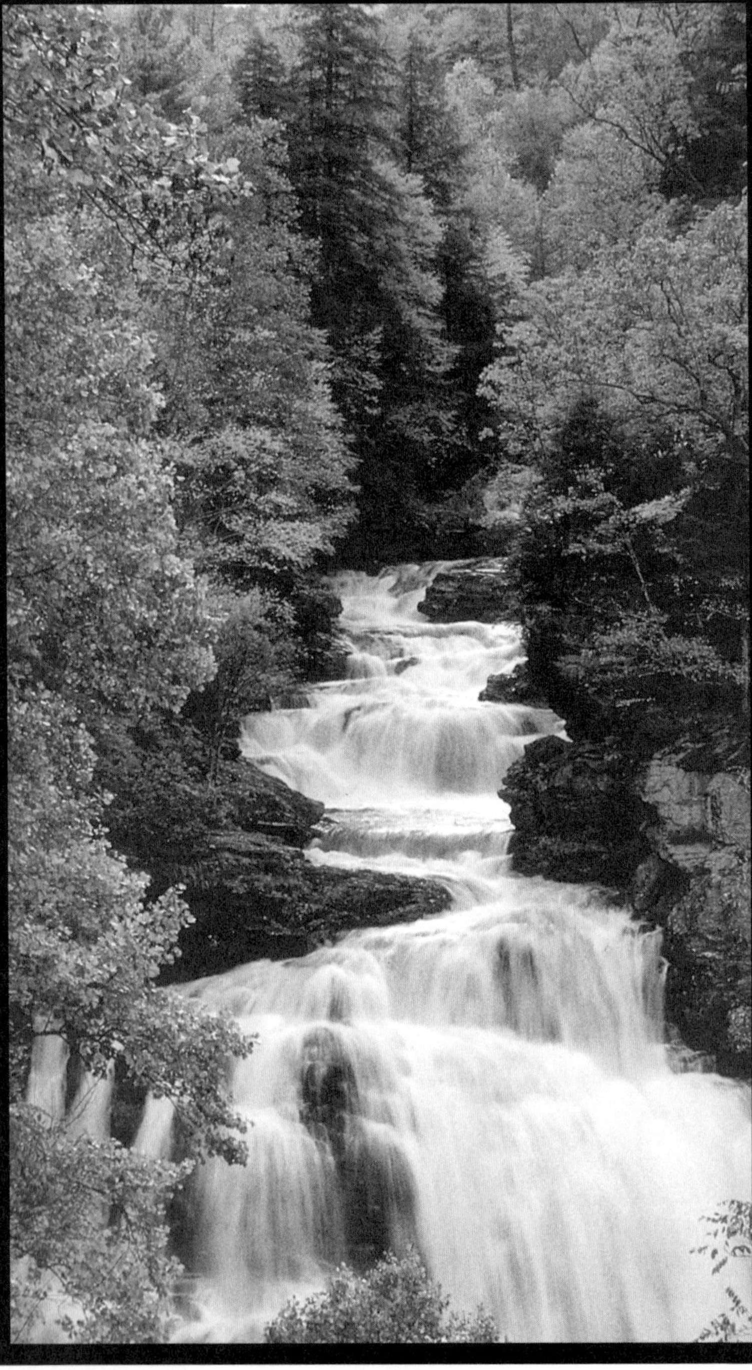

© John MacLean

CAROLINAS
TRAVEL ✦ SMART®

Second Edition

Frances Creswell Helms

John Muir Publications
Santa Fe, New Mexico

John Muir Publications, P.O. Box 613, Santa Fe, New Mexico 87504

Printed in the United States of America.
Second edition. First printing September 1999.

ISSN 1094-4222
ISBN 1-56261-516-5

Editor: Peg Goldstein
Graphics Editor: Ann Silvía
Production: Kathleen Sparkes, White Hart Design
Design: Marie J.T. Vigil
Cover design: Janine Lehmann
Map style development: American Custom Maps—Jemez Springs, NM
Map illustration: Kathleen Sparkes, White Hart Design
Printing: Publishers Press
Front cover photos: small—© John Elk III (Charleston, South Carolina)
                    large—© Robb Helfrick (Blue Ridge Parkway, Western North Carolina)
Back cover photo: © Robb Helfrick (Cape Hatteras Lighthouse, Cape Hatteras National Seashore,
                  North Carolina)

Distributed to the book trade by
Publishers Group West
Berkeley, California

CAROLINAS TRAVEL•SMART: A GUIDE THAT GUIDES

Most guidebooks are primarily directories, providing information but very little help in making choices—you have to guess how to make the most of your time and money. *Carolinas Travel•Smart* is different: By highlighting the very best of the region and offering various planning features, it acts like a personal tour guide rather than a directory.

TAKE THE STRESS OUT OF TRAVEL

Sometimes traveling causes more stress than it relieves. Sorting through information, figuring out the best routes, determining what to see and where to eat and stay—all this can make a vacation feel daunting rather than fun. Relax. We've done a lot of the legwork for you. This book will help you plan a trip that suits you—whatever your time frame, budget, and interests.

SEE THE BEST OF THE REGION

Author Frances Helms has lived in the Carolinas most of her life. She has hand-picked every listing in this book, and she gives you an insider's perspective on what makes each one worthwhile. So while you will find many of the big tourist attractions listed here, you'll also find lots of smaller, lesser known treasures, such as the Wright Brothers Memorial in Kill Devil Hills and the World's Largest Chair in Thomasville. And each sight is described so you'll know what's most—and sometimes least—interesting about it.

In selecting the restaurants and accommodations for this book, the author sought out unusual spots with local flavor. While in some areas of the region chains are unavoidable, wherever possible the author directs you to one-of-a-kind places. We also know that you want a range of options: One day you may crave fresh seafood, while the next day you would be just as happy (as would your wallet) with barbecue hash. Most of the restaurants and accommodations listed here are moderately priced, but the author also includes budget and splurge options, depending on the destination.

CREATE THE TRIP YOU WANT

We all have different travel styles. Some people like spontaneous weekend jaunts, while others plan longer, more leisurely trips. You may want to cover as much ground as possible, no matter how much time you have. Or maybe you would prefer to focus your trip on one part of the state or on some special interest, such as history, nature, or art. We've taken these differences into account.

Though the individual chapters stand on their own, they are organized in a geographically logical sequence, so that you could conceivably fly into Charlotte, drive chapter by chapter to each destination in the book, and end up close to where you started. Of course, you don't have to follow that sequence, but it's there if you want a complete picture of the region.

Each destination chapter offers ways of prioritizing when time is limited: In the Perfect Day section, the author suggests what to do if you have only one day to spend in the area. Also, every Sightseeing Highlight is rated, from one to four stars: ★★★★—or "must see"—sights first, followed by ★★★ sights, then ★★ sights, and finally ★—or "see if you have time" sights. At the end of each sight listing is a time recommendation in parentheses. User-friendly maps help you locate the sights, restaurants, and lodging of your choice.

And if you're in it for the ride, so to speak, you'll want to check out the Scenic Routes described at the end of several chapters. They take you through some of the most scenic parts of the region.

In addition to these special features, the appendix has other useful travel tools:

- The Planning Map and Mileage Chart help you determine your own route and calculate travel time.
- The Special Interest Tours show you how to design your trip around any of six favorite interests.
- The Resource Guide tells you where to go for more information about national and state parks, individual cities and counties, local bed-and-breakfasts, and more.

HAPPY TRAVELS

With this book in hand, you have many reliable recommendations and travel tools at your fingertips. Use it to make the most of your trip. And have a great time!

WHY VISIT THE CAROLINAS?

Life is different in the Carolinas: slower, richer, and extremely well mannered. If you smile and wave at strangers here, those strangers will smile and wave in return. And if you ask someone's help, you will get it almost instantly. Carolinians pride themselves on their friendliness and their hospitality. That they also love their homeland is evidenced by the oft-posed query, "If this isn't God's country, why did He make the sky Carolina blue?" Your best response to this is to smile appreciatively, even if you know better. Or think you know better.

You probably studied the Carolinas in school. Both states are integral to the history of the United States. North Carolina is the site of the "Lost Colony," an abiding mystery of settlers who disappeared, never to be seen or heard from again. The colonists included Virginia Dare, the first English child born in the New World. South Carolina is the site of Charleston, one of the nation's oldest and most beautiful cities.

You have probably heard of the battles of Cowpens and Kings Mountain and the shots fired on Fort Sumter. You are most likely familiar with Francis Marion, Andrew Jackson, John C. Calhoun, Wilma Rudolph, Ava Gardner, George Rogers, Doc Watson, Dale Earnhardt, and Strom Thurmond—Carolinians all, although probably never before mentioned in the same sentence. You may own a Pawleys Island hammock or a Jugtown vase, you may drive a Spartanburg BMW or wear clothing designed by Alexander Julian, you may display a blanket woven by a Cherokee or dress your beds with linens from Burlington, Cannon, or a host of other Carolina textile companies.

But the Carolinas' people and products are easily overshadowed by the state's main attraction: their scenic beauty. From the southern Appalachians in the west to the Atlantic coastline in the east, North and South Carolina are full of incomparable vistas. Depending on the season, they may be clothed in snow or rhododendron, painted with a blazing palette in autumn, or lightly pasteled in spring. Sunrise over the Carolina shores and sunset over the Carolina mountains leave little to be desired by even the most well-traveled soul.

And whether your interests are defined by the rolling dunes of a resort island, the greens of a championship golf course, the footprints of history, or the blueprints of the future, the Carolinas beckon irresistibly. Even better, the states are easily accessible and extremely affordable.

HISTORY

The name *Carolina* is derived from Carolana, a section of the New World named in honor of King Charles I of England, who granted the land to Sir Robert Heath in 1629. Charles II renamed the area Carolina and granted it to eight nobles, known as the lords proprietors, in 1663.

The human history of what is today North and South Carolina extends back 11,000 years, however, to when the first Native Americans migrated into the region, settled, and began to develop individual tribes. By end of the fifteenth century, when Europeans arrived, the area was home to a wide variety of Native American cultures.

Spaniards tried to establish a colony on Winyah Bay in South Carolina in 1526. The French nearly managed a permanent settlement in 1562, when Huguenots landed near present-day Beaufort. The first English attempt at colonizing North Carolina came in 1585 on Roanoke Island. None of these efforts proved successful, however.

It remained for the lords proprietors to establish the first permanent European settlement in the Carolinas. The English arrived at Albemarle Point in South Carolina in 1670, and, 10 years later, moved across the Ashley River to the present site of Charleston. The city quickly grew to become a major seaport and trading center, as well as a social center for colonists who moved inland and established rice, indigo, and cotton plantations.

In the beginning of the eighteenth century, the English presence in North Carolina began to assert itself with the establishment of a colonial governor's palace in New Bern. The British crown soon removed the lords proprietors, however, and assumed governance itself. The English yoke quickly began to wear heavily on the colonists and, in 1775, Carolinians were ready to revolt. They did so by penning the Mecklenburg Declaration of Independence in Charlotte a full year before the national document was signed by all of the colonies.

During the Revolutionary War, more than 200 battles and skirmishes were fought in the Carolinas. The battles of Cowpens and Kings Mountain turned the tide of the war in the South, spurring British troops to Yorktown, Virginia, where they surrendered.

But peace was not to last. In December 1860 the Ordinance of Secession was passed in Charleston, and South Carolina became the first state to secede from the Union. Just a few months later, Southern forces fired on Fort Sumter in Charleston, and the Civil War had begun. The Carolinas suffered fiercely over the next four years, as families were decimated, crops were destroyed, and homes were burned.

It was not until the 1880s, when the textile industry began to flourish, that the Carolinas began their slow steps to recovery. And it was not until the end of World War II that the states began to pull themselves out of great economic depression—not the depression caused by the crash on Wall Street in 1929 but the depression caused by lingering and compounded effects of the Civil War. (Visitors will hear older Carolinians refer to the conflict as the War Between the States.)

In the 1960s, during the Civil Rights movement, integration was accomplished if not easily at least quietly in the Carolinas. White Carolinians did not display massive resistance to integration as did their neighbors in Virginia. No public officials blocked black children from doorways. Only one famous confrontation occurred—at the Woolworth sit-ins in Greensboro. There, the world watched as a small group of African Americans quietly demanded service, day after day, at an all-white lunch counter. White Carolina eventually capitulated, and the protesters left a lasting impression on the state and the nation. Today, the counter where the protest occurred is part of a museum devoted to the Civil Rights movement.

By the end of the Vietnam War, the Carolinas' economy had changed: Cotton was no longer king, and agriculture was no longer the leading occupation of the states' residents. The mills were still here, but so too were dyeing and finishing plants. Industry diversified, and foreign investment boomed. Today you'll still find extensive apple and peach orchards here—Spartanburg County in South Carolina ships more peaches each year than the entire state of Georgia—but you'll also see giant research centers and an enviable economy boasting one of the lowest unemployment rates in the nation.

The states composing the Sun Belt, the Carolinas included, have become the focus of economic development and migration from other states. The number of Carolina residents who were born elsewhere is on the upswing. Word of all the Carolinas have to offer has spread and is spreading still. Tourism, for very good reasons, is a leading industry.

CULTURES

The earliest settlers of the Carolinas, of course, were Native Americans. They came from many tribes—chief among them were the Cherokee, the Lumbee, and the Catawba. They are still here, although in lesser numbers. The Catawba have a reservation in York, South Carolina; the Cherokee in Cherokee, North Carolina.

Most of the Indian inhabitants of the Carolinas were moved to Oklahoma in the 1830s for resettlement. In fact, it was in the Carolinas that the infamous "Trail of Tears" had its beginning. The relocation is recalled today through the outdoor drama *Unto These Hills*, which plays every summer in Cherokee.

The English, Spanish, and French all took stabs at colonizing the Carolinas, with the English winning out. From the very beginning of European settlement in South Carolina, black servants and slaves—some from the Caribbean Islands, specifically Barbados, and others directly from Africa—were brought into the colony to clear the land and work the crops. Slavery would do much to shape the history and culture of the state.

It helped establish an agricultural economy and also fomented what became derogatorily known as "plantation mentality"—the notion of whites as superior, blacks as inferior. For much of its early history, South Carolina was a black majority community, yet the white man remained firmly in control. In North Carolina in the 1700s, a third of the population was enslaved by just 10 percent of the residents.

But some larger cities, especially Charleston, had sizable populations of blacks who had bought their freedom and earned their living as artisans, craftsmen, and business owners. The contributions of the Carolinas' blacks—slaves and free—became integral to the states' economy and culture, influencing areas such as the visual arts,

By the mid-1700s, German, Scotch-Irish, and Welsh settlers, very different from the English landed aristocracy, had moved into the tidewater area of South Carolina. These groups also moved into North Carolina, with the English, Germans, and Scotch-Irish being dominant. Their heritage and traditions maintained dominance for nearly 200 years.

In North Carolina a large contingent of Moravians, a Protestant sect that formed in Moravia and Bohemia in the mid-1400s, founded the town of

Bethabara in the 1750s. Before reaching North Carolina, the group had first settled in Savannah, Georgia, and then Pennsylvania, where they founded the city of Bethlehem in the 1740s. The Moravians brought their heavily Germanic lifestyle and cuisine to the region. Costumed living-history interpreters in Historic Bethabara Park and Old Salem now give visitors insight into Moravian life in the 1700s.

Links to the past here are strong. In the mountains of North Carolina, where some communities have remained isolated by choice as well as nature, the influence of Old English can still be heard in speech. In the lowcountry, or tidewater area, of South Carolina, a number of black Americans speak the Gullah dialect, a combination of an African language and English. These blacks, known as Geechees, maintain folk traditions, such as weaving baskets from sweetgrass, and hand their skills down from family to family, generation to generation.

Until the 1970s, most people who lived in the Carolinas were born in the Carolinas. In more recent times, Greenville, South Carolina, has experienced a large influx of Hispanics. Many were originally Mexican migrant workers, who followed the crops north, stopping in South Carolina for the peaches and North Carolina for the apples, eventually choosing to stay. Both states, over the past 20 years, have received significant numbers of Cambodians, Laotians, and Vietnamese from war-torn countries.

Modern Europeans are arriving in increasing numbers. Foreign companies such as Michelin, BMW, Hoechst, and Honda now do business here and have also enriched the region's cultural diversity.

THE ARTS

You'll find folk and fine artists at work throughout the Carolinas, with exhibit areas ranging from garish roadside stands to softly lighted museums. Artwork encompasses whirligigs and whammy-diddles, baskets, oil and pastel paintings, pottery, sculpture, decorative clothing, and imaginative but serviceable furniture.

The music of the Carolinas spans from opera—one of the first operas in America was performed in Charleston—to bluegrass. In the 1930s Charleston's Cabbage Row was the inspiration for George Gershwin's Catfish Row in *Porgy & Bess*. The Spoleto Festival U.S.A., featuring classical music and jazz, ballet and drama, is held annually in Charleston, while North Carolina's Maggie Valley is the stomping ground for cloggers, banjo pickers, and the music of the hills.

Carolina musicians such as Chubby Checker, James Brown, Dizzy Gillespie, Randy Travis, the Marshall Tucker Band, the Blue Ridge Quartet, the Cornelius Brothers and Sister Rose, and Hootie and the Blowfish have made their marks on the world in genres including country, jazz, rock 'n' roll, Southern rock, gospel, and soul. Even Carolina beaches have their own sound. You can't do the shag, South Carolina's state dance, to anything but Carolina beach music.

The states celebrate their traditions with a wide variety of festivals, from the Chit'lin' Strut in Salley, South Carolina, in November and the National Hollerin' Contest in Spivey's Corner, North Carolina, in June, to the Apple Festival in Hendersonville, North Carolina, in September and the Peach Festival in Gaffney, South Carolina, in July. In between you will find festivals dedicated to azaleas, roses, Scots and Native American ancestry, ramps, kudzu, poke sallet (wild greens), veterans of "the Mighty Moo" (USS *Cowpens*), and every facet of the arts.

Historical reenactments include the annual "Over the Mountain March," based on a Revolutionary War march that originated in Tennessee, wound through the North Carolina mountains and the South Carolina foothills, camped at the Cowpens, and ended at Kings Mountain, where the mountain men made the difference in the colonial forces. Many historic sights offer interpreters—from those who reenact the lives of early Native Americans to those who give tours of colonial and antebellum homes.

CUISINE

Southern cooking has its origin in the Carolinas, and some dishes—such as the lowcountry's chicken bog, a fowl-based gumbo of sorts—are found nowhere else. Grits are on every breakfast menu, and livermush (scrapple is the closest comparison) is a favorite.

If you're lucky enough to get invited to a Carolinian's home for Sunday dinner, odds are that your plate will hold either fried chicken accompanied by mashed potatoes and milk gravy or baked ham and potato salad. And you will soon learn that fried chicken can taste a hundred different ways, depending on which "old family recipe" is employed in its preparation. If you want to try cooking it yourself, the recommended method is to dredge skinned and freshly washed chicken pieces in liberally seasoned flour (salt, black pepper, and sugar) and place them in vegetable shortening already heated to medium high in a cast-iron frying pan. When the pieces brown on both sides, turn the heat to medium low or low and patiently cook until done. (You can speed the process by covering the pan for a couple of minutes, but if you keep it there too long, the crust will get soggy instead of crisp—a no-no.)

Restaurants try to emulate the taste produced by this method, and while some serve excellent fried chicken, it's never as good as homemade. For one thing, it's illegal to use cast-iron pots and pans for commercial food preparation.

Ham, too, can have many tastes. It can be served baked, fried, glazed, barbecued, with dumplings or without, with pineapple and raisin sauce, or with red-eye gravy, depending on whether it's a smoke-cured, fresh, or country ham. There's not much anyone can do to ruin ham, so it's always a good, safe menu choice.

The more adventuresome diner is encouraged to visit a fish camp, which might be called a fish house or seafood restaurant in other locales. But other locales don't provide the same atmosphere. Carolina fish camps usually are rustic-looking restaurants where the food is more important than the decor, lines are long, and you get more than you can possibly eat. While Calabash, North Carolina, is the seafood capital of the Carolina coast—with more than 30 restaurants offering a variety of freshly caught and wonderfully prepared seafood—the inland eateries are a special treat.

Tradition has it that fish camps arose from fishermen's desire to enjoy their catches while camped at a river. Since the fishermen often didn't want to cook themselves, and since those who had had little or no luck fishing still wanted to join their fellow sportsmen at a meal, enterprising restaurateurs stepped in to obtain the catch of the day.

Fish camps most frequently offer catfish (fried, baked, broiled; salt-and-peppered, Cajun style, or plain; small, medium, or large; whole or filets), perch, flounder, shrimp, oysters, and lobster. Those who aren't fish lovers can order chicken or steak. Though "seafood restaurants" might offer mahi-mahi, cod, and more exotic selections, fish camps offer "all you can eat" choices, which pricier seafood restaurants seldom do.

Another Carolina specialty is barbecue. Lexington, North Carolina, calls itself the "Barbecue Capital of the World," and, indeed, the Lexington No. 1 Bar-B-Q has catered a meal at the White House. But you will find barbecue treasures across the states. A word of caution: South Carolinians prefer barbecue hash, which may be a combination of pork, chicken, and even beef or venison and differs greatly from the hickory-smoked, chopped-pork variety. Check to be sure which kind you are ordering.

You'll find people arguing over whether barbecue sauce should be mustard- or tomato-based and whether red slaw or white slaw is the better complement. (Pick the tomato-based sauce for pork or beef, but try mustard-based for chicken; order the red slaw on sandwiches.) Maurice's Piggy Park in Columbia, South Carolina, has a wonderful mustard-based sauce.

Fresh, locally grown vegetables are available in the Carolinas throughout much of the year. Tomatoes—sliced, fried, stewed and baked—are a staple, as are squash, corn, sweet potatoes, cucumbers, cabbage, okra, onions, green beans, crowder peas, green peas, pinto beans, lima beans, carrots, and peppers. Almost any vegetable will grow in Carolina soil, which ranges from rich black in the mountains to bright red in the piedmont to white in the coastal plains.

You won't see orange groves here, but you will see acres of peaches and apples, strawberries and peanuts, watermelons and cantaloupes. Blueberries will grow with little care, blackberries are abundant in the wild, and muscadines, grapes, plums, pears, and cherries flourish. Pecan and black walnut trees are plentiful, as are the nuts.

FLORA AND FAUNA

The seasons of the year are clearly marked by the flora of the Carolinas. Spring is hailed by rhododendron and mountain laurel in the west and daffodils and azaleas everywhere else. Summer finds acres of marigolds and cornflowers dotting the countryside, while roses climb everywhere. Fall brings asters and mums; winter, hardy holly berries and mistletoe, with dainty camellias announcing the approach of yet another spring.

Trees, too, trace the seasons: buds and blossoms in spring; glossy green leaves in summer; brilliant reds, yellows, and oranges in fall (North Carolina offers a toll-free Leaf Hotline to update visitors on the best times to catch the peak color in the mountains); and elegant bare branches in winter. North Carolina's official tree is the longleaf pine, which keeps its needles year-round; South Carolina's is the palmetto, which grows best in the area's warmer climes. Both states boast quantities of cedar and fir and varieties of pine.

The northern state's flower is the dogwood—from a tree that proliferates in the wild throughout both states. The southern state's flower is the yellow jasmine, which also grows abundantly. Among the more unusual of South Carolina's flora (maybe it's also fauna) is the Venus's-flytrap, a carnivorous plant that is native to the state.

In both states the Department of Transportation participates in the National Wildflower Project. Major highways are bordered by wildflowers of all colors and varieties, adding beauty to the monotony of the interstate systems.

Fauna in North and South Carolina varies according to topography. Deer are abundant nearly everywhere and, in recent years, have become somewhat of a menace to homeowners and drivers alike. The Wildlife Commission has allowed extra hunting days in an effort to control the deer population. Wild turkeys, waterfowl, doves, and pheasants are plentiful and also draw many hunters. While fox hunting is not as big a sport in the Carolinas as it is in neighboring Virginia, dogs are used to hunt other quarry: opossums and raccoons, referred to locally as possums and coons.

The mountains are home to bears and bobcats, which sometimes make their way to the piedmont. Snakes are found in all regions; poisonous varieties include copperheads, rattlesnakes, and cottonmouth water moccasins. Alligators sometimes make their presence known along the coast. This habit is especially disconcerting to golfers, who have come upon this unexpected water hazard at more than a few championship courses.

Numerous varieties of fish are found in rivers, lakes, and streams throughout the states. These range from rainbow trout in the mountains to catfish, crappie, and bream in the piedmont to flounder and perch along the coast. You can go crabbing along the intercoastal waterways or deep-sea fishing off the coast.

Mosquitoes can be a nuisance in low-lying areas in summer, so be sure to bring repellent. Yellow jackets and other wasps, bumblebees and dirt daubers are plentiful, and only the latter pose no danger of stinging. You should especially beware of wasps at heavily used roadside picnic areas. If you are allergic, be sure to bring your antidote.

Birds are plentiful, colorful, and musically talented, and birding is a popular pastime in all areas of the states. The state bird of North Carolina is the cardinal; South Carolina is represented by the less brilliantly hued Carolina wren. You will also find bluebirds—the Audubon Society has marked a Bluebird Trail (a line of bluebird houses) through the Carolinas—and hummingbirds, mockingbirds, and bobwhites. A few larger lawns even sport elegant strolling peacocks.

The Nature Conservancy is hard at work in the Carolinas. The organization seeks to protect stands of virgin timber and wetlands so that future generations may continue to enjoy the beauty that has been here since the beginning of time.

LAY OF THE LAND

The Carolinas are divided into roughly three sections: the mountains, the piedmont, and the coastal plains. The only regions unique to a particular state are the Sandhills in North Carolina and the lowcountry in South Carolina.

North Carolina is bordered on the east by 300 miles of sandy beaches, islands, and inlets, including the massive Albemarle and Pamlico Sounds. The piedmont, in more recent years referred to as the heartland, is composed of gently rolling plains punctuated with numerous lakes. Western North Carolina is bounded by two ranges of the southern Appalachians, the Blue Ridge Mountains and the Great Smoky Mountains, with peaks exceeding 6,000 feet. Mount Mitchell, 6,684 feet above sea level in North Carolina's Smokies, is the tallest mountain east of the Mississippi. The state has numerous major rivers, including the French Broad, the Yadkin, and the Catawba.

South Carolina is fortunate to have an incomparable strand of beaches ranging from the northeastern tip to the southeastern border with Georgia. It also boasts a collection of resort islands, as well as an intracoastal waterway. The enormous Santee Cooper country offers lakes and rivers, two of which empty into the Atlantic at Charleston. The piedmont is essentially flat but well forested, and its foothills offer vistas of the not-too-distant Blue Ridge.

Gold was first discovered in North America near Concord, North Carolina, and was mined in North and South Carolina. The North Carolina mountains are noted for sapphire deposits, and other precious stones have been found there. Granite and limestone are quarried in both states, and mica is mined.

North Carolina has underground caves and caverns, and South Carolina has marshlands and swamps. If you don't like a particular terrain, drive a few miles: It will change!

OUTDOOR ACTIVITIES

If you can do it anywhere, you can do it in the Carolinas. Of course, bullfighting hasn't caught on here yet, but few other outdoor sports are lacking.

The Appalachian Trail offers the most all-inclusive hiking experience in North Carolina. You'll also find nature trails tucked away in national forests and military parks, on historic estates, and in brand-new developments in both North and South Carolina. Hunting, fishing, hang gliding, and horseback riding are available nearly everywhere, as are tennis and swimming. Only hunting and fishing require licenses, which are easily available and reasonably priced. You can fly-fish for trout in mountain streams or go surf fishing along the coast. You can scuba dive, surfboard, water-ski, and snow ski. Ice rinks are few and far between, but a determined vacationer can find them. You can rock climb, bike, and try white-water rafting and kayaking in both states. And you can golf to your heart's content. The designer championship courses in Southern Pines, North Carolina, and on Hilton Head, South Carolina, alone could keep a golfer from ever wanting to go home.

PLANNING YOUR TRIP

Before you set out on your trip, you'll need to do some planning. Use this chapter in conjunction with the tools in the appendix to answer some basic questions. First of all, when are you going? You may already have specific dates in mind; if not, various factors will probably influence your timing. Either way, you'll want to know about local events, the weather, and other seasonal considerations. This chapter discusses all of that.

How much should you expect to spend on your trip? This chapter addresses various regional factors you'll want to consider in estimating your travel expenses. How will you get around? Check out the section on local transportation. If you decide to travel by car, the Planning Map and Mileage Chart in the appendix can help you figure out exact routes and driving times, while the Special Interest Tours provide several focused itineraries. The chapter concludes with some reading recommendations, both fiction and nonfiction, to give you various perspectives on the region. If you want specific information about individual cities or counties, use the Resource Guide in the appendix.

HOW MUCH WILL IT COST?

You can spend as much or as little in the Carolinas as you would elsewhere, but here, with a little advance planning and a few bouts of frugality, you will get more for your money. Unless you intend to camp and carry and prepare your own food, you can expect to spend a minimum of $175 per day for food, lodging, and gas for a family of four (two adults, two children sharing a room). Depending on your taste and means, you can spend much, much more.

Attractions such as admissions to theme parks, shows, exhibitions, and other activities are extra. Your best bet is to plan what you want to see and do and budget accordingly, allowing a little extra for a few irresistible urges that are sure to arise. For example, you might intend to spend the day drowsing in the sun at Myrtle Beach and feed the kids hot dogs for supper, but the call of Medieval Times, a sumptuous banquet coupled with fantastic entertainment, might quash those intentions—as well as empty your purse unexpectedly.

As you plan your itinerary, ask tour, travel, and hotel staff about packages built around your special interests—anything from outlet shopping to history. Golf packages proliferate in the Sandhills and along the Grand Strand but can be found at nearly every destination in this guide. Golfers will find greens fees amazingly reasonable for the quality of courses in the Carolinas. Golfers with an affinity for history will remember that Charleston was the site of America's first golf course—the South Carolina Golf Club and Charleston Green was founded in 1786—and all golfers will know that both Carolinas are golf heavens.

The North Carolina mountains have become year-round destinations, and prices, while still not exorbitant, reflect their popularity. You can expect motel or hotel rooms to range upward from $50 per night, but many include a free continental breakfast. You might plan to visit a deli, buy the makings of a picnic lunch, and use one of many roadside tables, where you can enjoy freshly made sandwiches and an incomparable view at the same time. You might choose to have supper at a family restaurant, where buffet-style meals begin at $6.99 per person, or you might opt for a more exclusive establishment, where entrees start at $15 and everything else costs extra.

Winter in the mountains doesn't allow for as many picnics but makes up for it with ski packages that include almost everything but a change of underwear. North Carolina ski resorts have become nearly as popular as many New England destinations, the primary difference being the artificially made snow that provides the base, especially early in the season.

The piedmont portions of both states offer meal, accommodation, and attraction prices in very reasonable ranges. The Carolinas' largest theme park, Paramount's Carowinds, which includes a huge water park, is open late March through early October (the water park opens later and closes earlier). One-day admission costs $20 for seniors and children and $32 for everyone else; two-day admission is a bigger bargain, and the park honors season tickets issued by its sister parks, including Paramount's Kings Dominion in Virginia. Discount tickets frequently are available in area fast-food restaurants and grocery stores, so be sure to ask if any promotions are available and how you might take advantage of them.

CLIMATE

In South Carolina, especially from Columbia to Charleston, people are fond of explaining, "It's not the heat, it's the humidity." It certainly is. But only in late summer. Usually.

In antebellum days, lowcountry planters went upcountry to escape mosquitoes and malaria during the unbearable summers. They sat on verandahs and drank iced tea and mint juleps, slept under draped mosquito netting, and kept servants busy waving massive fans. Today Carolinians have appliances that help them keep cool and comfortable, but they still must use common sense. Jog or play tennis, if you must, in July and August, but stick to the early mornings or late evenings. Enjoy pools and beaches at mid-morning and mid-afternoon and seek indoor shelter from the sun at noon. But the heat won't prohibit a leisurely walk through a national forest or military park with heavy shade from trees overhead, or a round of golf, especially if you take a cart.

Temperatures average in the high 80s to low 90s in summer and the mid-40s in winter. But single-digit lows and 100-plus highs aren't unheard of. The extremes rarely last long, however, which spells good news for visitors and residents alike. Heavy snow in winter is rare enough to delight even the most jaded resident, but travelers should know that snow removal isn't as quick as it is in states to the north.

Where clothing is concerned, use common sense. Pack for whatever type of vacation you have planned. In summer bring plenty of shorts and T-shirts for play and lightweight and loose dresses and suits for dressing up. In winter bring heavy woolens or furs and coats and gloves. In spring and fall, play it safe by packing extra jackets and sweaters for cool mornings and evenings. Don't be too surprised, though, if early October brings a frost and freeze warning and late January brings a balmy breeze. There are reasons why the weather is considered a suitable topic of conversation in this area of the country, and it always holds a few surprises.

WHEN TO GO

It doesn't take much brain power to realize that beaches are crowded in summer and ski slopes draw their biggest numbers in winter. If you want sun and fun—Myrtle Beach bills itself as "the Sun and Fun Capital of the World"—you will find it in abundance from mid-May through Labor Day along the Grand

Strand. If you are a bit hardier, you might consider joining the Canadians who begin flocking to South Carolina's beaches as early as March and assuredly in April, when prices are still at off-season lows and flags bearing the maple leaf fly everywhere.

A trip to the beach can be a bargain at any time of the year if you return relaxed and refreshed. People who visit the beach year-round say that "wave therapy" is invaluable and that the beach can refresh in winter as well as in summer—you just have to wear more clothes. Beachside accommodations may be as low as $30 (per room, not per person) a night in January and rise to more than $200 in July.

Calendars of events, available from both states, will help you decide when you want to visit according to your interests. For example, Orangeburg in Pee Dee Country, South Carolina, hosts the Grand American Coon Hunt every January. It is the nation's largest field trial for coon dogs (qualifiers go on to the World Coon Hunt) and also offers bench shows and other events for spectators.

March brings the Canadian-American Days Festival to Myrtle Beach and includes sporting events, concerts, and historical tours, all to entertain Canadians on spring break. The spring also brings steeplechase and harness racing, from the Blockhouse in North Carolina to Aiken and Camden in South Carolina.

April welcomes the annual North Carolina Azalea Festival to Wilmington and the annual Dogwood Festival to Fayetteville. Hot-air balloon enthusiasts won't want to miss Freedom Weekend Aloft, held annually the last full weekend (Friday through Monday) in May in Greenville, South Carolina. The event features big-name entertainment, a crafts show, amusement rides, daily races of more than 100 hot-air balloons, and a gigantic fireworks finale.

The Spoleto Festival U.S.A. is held annually the last week in May and the first week in June in Charleston. This famous international festival, the American counterpart to the one in Spoleto, Italy, showcases world-renowned performers in drama, dance, music, and art. For information, contact Spoleto Festival U.S.A., P.O. Box 157, Charleston, South Carolina 29402; 843/722-2764.

The Southern 500 in Darlington, South Carolina, takes place Labor Day weekend and tops all other events in the NASCAR Winston Cup division. Also in September is the King Mackeral Tournament held in Wrightsville Beach, near Wilmington.

Fall and winter bring such events as Plantation Days in Charleston in November and the Christmas Candlelight Tours in Columbia in December. Whenever you plan to visit the Carolinas, you will find something exciting going on. To find out specifics, request a free annual calendar of events from the North Carolina Travel and Tourism Division, Department of Commerce, 301 North Wilmington Street, Raleigh, NC 27626-2825 or call toll-free in the United States and Canada, 800/VISIT-NC. South Carolina's annual calendar of events is included in the *South Carolina Travel Guide*, available free from the South Carolina Department of Parks, Recreation and Tourism, P.O. Box 71, Columbia, SC 29202, 803/734-0122.

TIME AND DAYLIGHT

Both North and South Carolina are entirely within the eastern standard time zone, and all locales in both states observe daylight saving time, which extends from the first Sunday in April to the last Sunday in October.

In midsummer, night does not fall until past nine o'clock, so travelers who plan to camp will have ample time to pitch their tents after late arrivals at their destinations. Sunrise is usually before seven o'clock in summer, making for long days that can be as leisurely or as action-packed as you wish.

TRANSPORTATION

If you fly into Charlotte, you will be almost in the center of the two Carolinas. The city has the largest international airport in the Carolinas, with over 150 daily flights serving more than 150 cities in the United States, Europe, Mexico, and the Caribbean. But Greenville-Spartanburg, Raleigh-Durham, and Columbia are other favorite arrival/departure points.

All the usual rental car companies—Hertz, Avis, National, Budget, Alamo, Thrifty, Dollar—operate out of area airports. It is wise to book your rental car in advance, to avoid standing in line only to learn that your five-person family will have to squeeze into a subcompact car. Remember to inquire about discounts such as those from AAA, airline frequent flyer programs, and travel promotions.

Whether you are driving a rental or your own car, you will have your choice of highways for ease and convenience and byways for scenic beauty and exploration. The Carolinas are served by two north/south interstate highways: I-95 in the east and I-85 in the states' central portions. North Carolina's I-40 traverses east/west, as does South Carolina's I-26.

The scenic highway routes suggested in this guide may be augmented as your time allows by opting for state highways or even county roads. All are passable in all seasons by regular passenger vehicles. The only exception is found in the North Carolina mountains, where occasional heavy snowfalls in winter may close less well-maintained roads to all but four-wheel-drive vehicles. You will also find some islands along the coast inaccessible except by ferry or water taxi.

Amtrak offers service to and from numerous locations in the Carolinas and can be a relaxing way to travel. Inquire about regional specials when booking your trip. For information and reservations 24 hours a day, call 800/872-7245.

CAMPING, LODGING, AND DINING

All the major chains are represented in nearly every suggested destination in this guide, and they can generally be depended on for good service. Because they are so universal in their amenities and prices, they are mentioned here only if few or no suitable alternatives are available. This guide instead features locally owned and operated accommodations or those that are unique or offer the true flavor of your destination.

If you want a different kind of lodging, both states offer a wonderful selection of bed-and-breakfasts and historic inns. The Vintage Inn in Abbeville, South Carolina, successfully blends old and new in an elegantly restored 1870s Victorian house with a wraparound porch sporting wicker furniture. The master suite offers a Jacuzzi for two. The cost ranges from $65 to $125 per night. Even more elegant is Litchfield Plantation on Pawleys Island. The house, built about 1750, has four suites overlooking either the Avenue of Live Oaks or ancient rice fields, and room or suite rates range from $75 to $150.

The Grove Park Inn Resort, popular with the southern gentry since 1913, brought F. Scott Fitzgerald, Woodrow Wilson, Henry Ford, and Thomas Edison to Asheville. Accommodations in this combination of rustic charm and luxury, featuring a 120-foot great hall flanked with 12-foot fireplaces, will cost you $140 to $265 per night. Grove Park has several fine restaurants and moderately priced cafés. Sunday brunch at $26 per person in the inn's Blue Ridge Dining Room is an Asheville tradition, so you will want to make reservations early. Equally popular is the $32 Friday night seafood buffet. Dining on the verandah is an unforgettable experience.

You won't find anything in the true budget range on Hilton Head Island, but you will find family packages offered at some of the world's finest resorts. Call 800/444-4772 for the Hilton Head Accommodations and Golf Hotline, a free island-wide reservation network that offers to match your requirements for homes, villas, and golf and tennis packages. You may also visit the island's home page at www.digitel.net/HiltonHeadVacations/.

Camping is an attractive possibility throughout the Carolinas, and some camps cater to special interests, including RV owners, Harley riders, and

Christian families. Many offer pools and are near restaurants if no restaurant is on-site. State parks offer cabins and campsites in both Carolinas, but you must reserve these accommodations well in advance (reservations are accepted beginning in January). Campsites range from $10 to $20 per night; cabins from $35 to $90. The scenery, whether rugged mountains, quiet forests, or breezy beaches, is unmatchable.

RECOMMENDED READING

A visit to any public library will yield a treasure trove of books about North and South Carolina. You might begin with the text most familiar to native South Carolinians, Mary Simms Oliphant's *The History of South Carolina* (Laidlaw Brothers, 1977), an engaging narrative that has been widely used in the state's public schools. A second volume describing the state's colorful past and an array of influential characters is *The South Carolina Story* by Anne Riggs Osborne (Sandlapper Publishing, 1988). Another easy but fascinating read is *South Carolina Indian Lore* by Bert W. Bierer (Bierer/State Printing Company, 1972), which reveals the early world of the state's major Indian tribes—the Cherokee, Upper Creek, Lower Creek, Chickasaw, Savanah, and Catawba—as well as smaller groups such as the Appalachia, Peedee, Winyah, Waccamaw, Yemassee, Palachocola, Tuscorora, Notchee, and Utchee. The book features early hand-drawn maps and black-and-white photographs of relics and sites.

Lore of a later age and a different culture is revealed through the text and photographs in *South Carolina's Low Country—A Past Preserved* by Catherine Campani Messmer (Sandlapper Publishing, 1988). Messmer's writing is conversational in tone and acquaints readers with the families who left indelible stamps on the area's rice, indigo, and cotton plantations.

South Carolina in the Modern Age by Walter B. Edgar (University of South Carolina Press, 1992) tells how South Carolina disappeared from the national scene after losing an entire generation of young white men and nearly all of its capital wealth during the Civil War. The book provides this information as background but focuses on the third century of the state's history, beginning with the rise of populist governor "Pitchfork" Ben Tillman in the 1890s and ending with the Sun Belt industrial development of the 1990s. Edgar, who has taught South Carolina history at the University of South Carolina since the 1970s, offers an insider's view of the state, which is too often confused with its neighbor to the north.

That neighbor to the north is revealed in two recommended books: *North Carolina: Portrait of the Land and Its People* by John Rucker (American Geographic

Publishing, 1989) and *North Carolina Illustrated, 1524–1894* edited by H. G. Jones (University of North Carolina Press, 1983). The first volume is 112 pages of simple text and gorgeous color photos. The second book is 482 pages long with more than 1,150 black-and-white photographs. This title provides a fascinating, in-depth, and slightly academic look at North Carolina. The definitive volume on the state, however, is *North Carolina Through Four Centuries* by William S. Powell (University of North Carolina Press, 1989). Photos are few, but the text is voluminous and the author adept at painting pictures with words. Also recommended is *Western North Carolina Since the Civil War* by Ina Woestemeyr Van Noppen and John J. Van Noppen (Appalachian Consortium Press, 1973), which tells how the mountain people have preserved their culture while inspiring business and industry.

People specifically interested in the Cherokee Indians will find moving accounts of their history in *Cherokee Sunset: A Nation Betrayed* by Samuel Carter III (Doubleday & Company, 1976) and *The Cherokee Indian Nation: A Troubled History* by Duane H. King (University of Tennessee Press, 1979). Both books offer small collections of black-and-white photographs, as well as compelling narratives.

Many books discuss the historic sights mentioned in this guide. Among the most recent is the 1997 publication *Reynolda: A History of an American Country Home* by Barbara Mayer. Here readers learn the story of Katharine and R. J. Reynolds (of North Carolina tobacco fame).

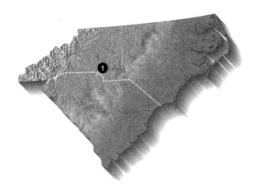

1
CHARLOTTE

Charlotte has grown over the past 40 years—from a sleepy, medium-size southern city to a fast-growing, leading-edge industrial, banking, and sporting center of more than a million people. What once was Douglas Field, with a handful of runways and grassy banks where families enjoyed weekend picnics while watching planes take off and land, is now Charlotte International Airport, gateway to the Carolinas.

On the ground in Charlotte, you'll find a bustling downtown with an imposing skyline, sprawling urban and suburban areas, and world-class sports facilities including the Lowe's Motor Speedway, the Charlotte Coliseum and its Charlotte Hornets arena, and Ericsson Stadium, home of the Carolina Panthers. You'll also find a thriving symphony, museums, a major theme park, and carefully restored historic districts.

Named two centuries ago for the wife of King George III, Charlotte retained its name and its "Queen City" designation, even after the revolt that cut its ties to its namesake. When Lord Cornwallis occupied Charlotte in 1780, he was annoyed by the proliferation of patriot activities, and he described the town as a "hornet's nest," a name later incorporated into the city seal and still later chosen for its NBA team, the Charlotte Hornets.

With the Catawba River as a source of power, manufacturing plants and textile mills grew rapidly, and agriculture took a supplementary role in the economy. Today Charlotte has outstripped all other cities in the Carolinas in

CHARLOTTE

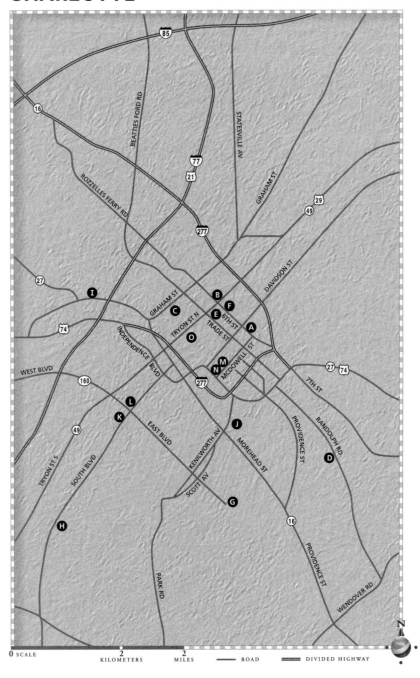

85

16

BEATTIES FORD RD

STATESVILLE AV

GRAHAM ST

77

21

ROZZELLES FERRY RD

277

29

49

DAVIDSON ST

27

I

GRAHAM ST

B

F

74

C

TRYON ST N

E 6TH ST

A

INDEPENDENCE BLVD

O

TRADE ST

MCDOWELL ST

WEST BLVD

M

N

277

27 74

7TH ST

160

L

K

EAST BLVD

J

PROVIDENCE ST

RANDOLPH RD

49

TRYON ST S

SOUTH BLVD

KENILWORTH AV

MOREHEAD ST

D

SCOTT AV

G

H

16

PROVIDENCE ST

PARK RD

WENDOVER RD

N

0 SCALE

2
KILOMETERS

2
MILES

ROAD

DIVIDED HIGHWAY

growth and development, emerging alongside Atlanta as a power in the New South.

A PERFECT DAY IN THE QUEEN CITY

The perfect time to visit Charlotte is in spring or fall, when temperatures are just right. In spring the city delights, with acres of azaleas and flowers throughout its parks and residential areas. In autumn the color palette changes but still delights. Depending on your mood, you can be alone or in a crowd. For the former, take an early morning walk in one of the many parks, visit the Mint Museum of Art, lunch at a neighborhood deli, drive to Belmont to view the beautiful Abbey, dine at a fine restaurant, and catch a performance at the Blumenthal Performing Arts Center. If you're more inclined toward crowds, visit Paramount's Carowinds, where you can take thrilling rides, hear music, eat hot dogs, and enjoy the water park. After a full day, if you still have the energy, visit the South End, where restaurants and nightlife beckon.

MORE CHARLOTTE HISTORY

Charlotteans have always been an independent lot. The Mecklenburg Declaration of Independence, which predated the national proclamation by more than a year, was signed in Charlotte on May 20, 1775. A plaque to that effect is embedded in the street at the intersection of Trade and Tryon, but don't stop to read it—city traffic waits for no one. A safer bet is a look at the Captain James Jack monument at 211 West Trade Street, a memorial to the man who carried the document on horseback to Philadelphia and the Continental Congress. Local legend has it that Thomas Jefferson modeled the national document after this one.

SIGHTS

- ⓐ Afro-American Cultural Center
- ⓑ Discovery Place
- ⓒ Ericsson Stadium
- ⓓ Mint Museum of Art
- ⓔ North Carolina Blumenthal Performing Arts Center
- ⓕ Spirit Square Center for Arts and Education

FOOD

- ⓖ Dilworth Diner
- ⓗ Greystone Restaurant
- ⓘ Open Kitchen
- ⓙ Pancho and Lefty's Border Café
- ⓚ Southend Brewery and Smokehouse
- ⓛ Vinnie's Rawbar

LODGING

- ⓜ Adam's Mark Hotel
- ⓝ Four Point Hotel by Sheraton
- ⓞ Hilton Charlotte

After gold was discovered at the Reed Gold Mine just north of Charlotte, the region became the nation's major gold producer until 1848, when the California Gold Rush began. A branch of the U.S. Mint was located here from 1837 to 1913, in a building that now forms part of the beautiful Mint Museum.

Although no major battles were fought here during the Civil War, Charlotte was the site of the last meeting of Confederate President Jefferson Davis's full cabinet. Following the war, the city set out to free itself from its dependency on agriculture and secured a position of industrial leadership in the South.

SIGHTSEEING HIGHLIGHTS

★★★★ **DISCOVERY PLACE**
301 N. Tryon St., 800/935-0553
www.discoveryplace.org.
Children and grownups alike flock to this downtown hands-on science and technology museum, which features an Omnimax Theatre, planetarium, tropical rain forest, aquariums, Science Circus, and Challenger Learning Center.
Details: Sept–May Mon–Fri 9–5, Sat 9–6, Sun 1–6. June–Aug Mon–Sat 9–6, Sun 1–6. Admission to Omnimax, planetarium, and exhibit halls: $6.50 adults, $5 ages 6 to 12 and over 60, $2.75 ages 3 to 5. $2 each additional area. (3–4 hours)

★★★★ **MINT MUSEUM OF ART**
2730 Randolph Rd., 704/337-2000
Originally the first branch of the United States Mint and subsequently North Carolina's first art museum, the Mint is one of the Southeast's leading museums. It has important collections of American and European paintings, furniture, and decorative arts; African, pre-Columbian, and Spanish Colonial art; an internationally acclaimed collection of porcelain and pottery; regional crafts; and historic costumes. The Mint is completely accessible for physically challenged visitors.
Details: Tue 10–10, Wed–Sat 10–5, Sun noon–5. $6 adults, $5 seniors, $4 students, under 12 free. (3–4 hours)

★★★★ **PARAMOUNT'S CAROWINDS**
14523 Carowinds Blvd., 800/888-4386 or 704/588-2606
www.carowinds.com
This member of the Paramount family of theme parks honors season

passes from its sister parks, the nearest of which is Paramount's Kings Dominion in Virginia. Although it shares some of the same attractions—Top Gun, a jet roller coaster inspired by the movie, for example—Carowinds has many unique features, including a paddle-wheel steamboat. On its 100 acres on the North Carolina–South Carolina state line, Carowinds has a water park, a kiddie land, an amphitheater where top musical acts perform, and a campground. Most of the park is wheelchair accessible.

Details: Late Mar–early Oct; hours of operation vary. $32 ages 7 and over, $20 ages 3 to 6 and over 55. (8–10 hours)

★★★ AFRO-AMERICAN CULTURAL CENTER
401 N. Myers St. Charlotte, 704/374-1565
www.aac-charlotte.org
African American heritage is preserved here through exhibitions, performances, workshops, and hands-on activities year-round.

Details: Tue–Sat 10–6, Sun 1–5. Free; fees charged for various programs. (2 hours)

★★★ CHARLOTTE MUSEUM OF HISTORY AND HEZEKIAH ALEXANDER HOMESITE
3500 Shamrock Dr., Charlotte, 704/568-1774
Built of stone quarried nearby, the Hezekiah Alexander Homesite is the oldest dwelling in Mecklenburg County. Adjacent to the main house are a reconstructed springhouse and log kitchen. Some of the site is wheelchair accessible.

Details: Tue–Fri 10–5, Sat and Sun 2–5. Call for tour times and fees. (2 hours)

★★★ CHARLOTTE NATURE MUSEUM
1658 Sterling Rd., Charlotte, 704/372-6261
Young children will delight in this museum, which emphasizes awareness and appreciation of nature. The site features a nature trail. The museum is wheelchair accessible, but the trail is not.

Details: Mon–Fri 9–5, Sat 10–5, Sun 1–5. $3. (2–3 hours)

★★★ JAMES K. POLK MEMORIAL
308 S. Polk St., Pineville, 704/889-7145
The 11th president of the United States was born in 1795 in Mecklenburg County. Today the birthplace is a state historic site and

offers guided tours through reconstructed typical nineteenth-century log buildings.

Details: Apr–Oct Mon–Sat 9–5, Sun 1–5; Nov–Mar Tue–Sat 10–4, Sun 1–4. Free. (2 hours)

★★★ KINGS MOUNTAIN NATIONAL BATTLEFIELD AND MILITARY PARK

S.C. 216, Kings Mountain, 864/936-7921

Just 30 minutes south of Charlotte is the site of the turning point of the American Revolution. The British were routed here in 1780, and British Colonel Patrick Ferguson lies buried in a grave piled high with stones. The visitor's center and the walking trails take you through the battle. Bring a picnic lunch to enjoy on the shaded grounds.

Details: Take I-85 south from Charlotte and follow the signs to the park. Labor Day–Memorial Day 9–5, Memorial Day–Labor Day 9–6. Free. (3 hours)

★★★ SPIRIT SQUARE CENTER FOR ARTS AND EDUCATION

345 N. College St., Charlotte, 704/372-1000

Throughout the year you'll find exceptional performers here, including the Actors Theatre of Charlotte and the Children's Theatre of Charlotte. Art galleries are on the premises; most areas are wheelchair accessible.

Details: Building tours Tue–Sat 10–6, Sun 1–6; performance times and admission fees vary. (1 hour tour)

★★ BACKING UP CLASSICS MEMORY LANE MOTOR CAR MUSEUM

4545 Hwy. 29, Harrisburg, 704/788-9494

Located next to Lowe's Motor Speedway, this car museum features rare cars, antiques, classics, 1950s and muscle cars, and memorabilia.

Details: Mon–Fri 9–5:30, Sat 9–5, Sun 10–5. $10 per family, $5 adults, $4 seniors and students. (2 hours)

★★ LOWE'S MOTOR SPEEDWAY

Concord Parkway, Harrisburg, 704/455-3200

More than 1 million spectators annually visit this facility, which hosts the NASCAR Coca-Cola 600 in May (drawing the third-largest crowd of any American sporting event) and the 500-mile Winston

NORTH CAROLINA TRANSPORTATION MUSEUM

Train buffs will enjoy a trip to the North Carolina Transportation Museum, 411 S. Salisbury Ave., Spencer, 704/636-2889. This 57-acre site, 45 miles north of Charlotte on I-85 to Exit 79 (follow the signs), offers train rides and highlights North Carolina's transportation history–from Indian canoes to the airplane. Admission is free.

Cup Stock Car Race in early October. The speedway (formerly Charlotte Motor Speedway) boasts condominiums, suites, sky boxes, and a lavish private club. Most facilities are wheelchair accessible.

Details: For information contact Lowe's Motor Speedway, P.O. Box 600, Concord, NC 28026. Admission varies with event; tours are available. (1 hour–full day)

★★ **NORTH CAROLINA BLUMENTHAL PERFORMING ARTS CENTER**
130 N. Tryon St., Charlotte, 704/372-1000
Home to the Carolinas Concert Association, Charlotte Symphony, Choral Society, Charlotte Repertory Theatre, Opera Carolina, and North Carolina Dance Theatre, the Performing Arts Center also presents national touring Broadway productions and special events. It's equipped with an infrared listening system for the hearing impaired and is wheelchair accessible.

Details: Prices vary. Call for a schedule of events. (3 hours)

★ **BELMONT ABBEY HISTORIC DISTRICT**
Hwy. 7 N., Belmont, 704/825-6700
A quick drive south of Charlotte on I-85 to Exit 26 will bring you to beautiful Belmont Abbey College, built in 1876 from Gaston County clay bricks made by monks. It is part of the Benedictine Monastery and the oldest private liberal-arts college in the Southeast. The church has seating for people in wheelchairs, and the bell tower and west entrance are ramped for visitors with disabilities.

Details: Daily 7–7:30. Free. (1 hour)

★ ERICSSON STADIUM
800 S. Mint St., 704/358-7407
Home of the Carolina Panthers, Ericsson is one of the newest stadiums in the National Football League. Games are usually sold out, but tickets can be had by canvassing the parking lot on game day.
Details: Tours Tue–Fri 9–3. $4 adults, $3 seniors, $2 ages 5 to 15. (1 hour)

FITNESS AND RECREATION
The fitness and recreation opportunities available in any large city are available here. You'll find all the big-name gyms and health clubs as well as facilities offered by the YMCA and many hotels. Charlotte's large parks, especially **Freedom** and **Independence**, offer fitness and walking trails. For the spectator, there are games played by the **Charlotte Hornets** (NBA), **Charlotte Sting** (WNBA), **Charlotte Checkers** (minor-league hockey), **Carolina Panthers** (NFL), and **Charlotte Knights** (AAA baseball).

FOOD
While Charlotte has all the fine dining establishments and the eclectic mix of cafés you would expect to find in any large city, the big story is the South End. Here, factories have been replaced with restaurants and nightspots, and an electric trolley is back in operation, running from uptown on Friday, Saturday, and Sunday. In this area you will find numerous dining establishments. **Greystone Restaurant**, 3061 South Blvd., 704/523-2822, is a Greek-style diner with a menu that includes items such as Andy's Heavyweight Sandwich (London Broil with cheese and onions on a hoagie). Most entrées are under $8; the restaurant is open for breakfast, lunch, and dinner. At the **Southend Brewery and Smokehouse**, 2100 South Blvd., 704/358-4677, you'll find a lively bar and dinner business as well as a microbrewery. This former warehouse features such smoked specialties as barbecued baby back ribs and chicken, plus fresh fish and steak from a wood-burning grill and pizza from a wood-burning oven. **Vinnie's Rawbar**, 1714 South Blvd., 704/332-0006, offers the relaxed charm of a neighborhood bar. You'll find all types of people in all types of attire enjoying seafood that includes fantastic steamed oysters and shrimp.

Open Kitchen, 1318 W. Morehead St., 704/375-7449, has been a favorite with Charlotte-area Italian-food lovers since 1952. Prices are extremely reasonable, and the ambiance is family casual. It's open Monday through Friday for lunch and dinner and Saturday and Sunday for dinner.

REED GOLD MINE

*Just 25 miles from Charlotte, at Georgeville, is the **Reed Gold Mine State Historic Site** (704/721-4653), where gold was first discovered in North America in 1799. Legend has it that a young boy found a 17-pound nugget here that was used as a doorstop until it was identified as gold. The site offers a museum, orientation film, guided underground tour, stamp mill, and walking trails; admission is free. An instructional gold-panning experience is available for a small fee on a seasonal basis. From Charlotte, take N.C. 24/27 E. (Albemarle Road).*

The 1950s-style **Dilworth Diner**, 1608 East Blvd., 704/333-0137, features all your old favorites. Of course, if fried bologna isn't your old favorite, you can check out the Blue Plate Special, order a cherry Coke, and listen to oldies on the jukebox. This very casual and inexpensive diner is open daily for lunch and dinner.

In business more than 30 years, **Hereford Barn**, Exit 40 on I-85 at Graham St., 704/596-0854, is a renovated barn that seats parties of two to eight in actual stalls. It's reputed to serve Charlotte's finest steaks (no argument here). All meals ($10–$35) include the Hereford's famous cheese-and-relish tray. Open Tuesday through Saturday for dinner.

Pancho and Lefty's Border Café, 601 S. Kings Dr., 704/375-2334, serves southwestern cuisine and frozen drink specialties. It's open for lunch and dinner Monday through Saturday and for dinner only on Sunday. Entrées are priced under $10. You can dine on the lakeside patio at **Providence Bistro and Bakery**, at the Village Center at University Place, next to the Hilton, 704/549-0050. Eclectic fare is accompanied by fresh-brewed cappuccino, fresh-baked bread, and specialty desserts. Open daily. Entrees are $10 to $15.

Silver Cricket, 4705 South Blvd., 704/525-0061, is a classic New Orleans–style restaurant specializing in French cuisine. Prices range from moderate to expensive; dinner for two could cost $50. The restaurant is open for dinner daily. **Sir Edmond Halley's Restaurant**, 4151-A Park Rd., 704/525-2555, serves traditional British fare and creative American cuisine in a main dining room or a cigar-friendly pub. It's open daily. Prices range from inexpensive to moderate. Also recommended is **Sonny's Real Pit Barbecue**, 704/333-3792, reputed to be Charlotte's best barbecue. You'll find

CHARLOTTE REGION

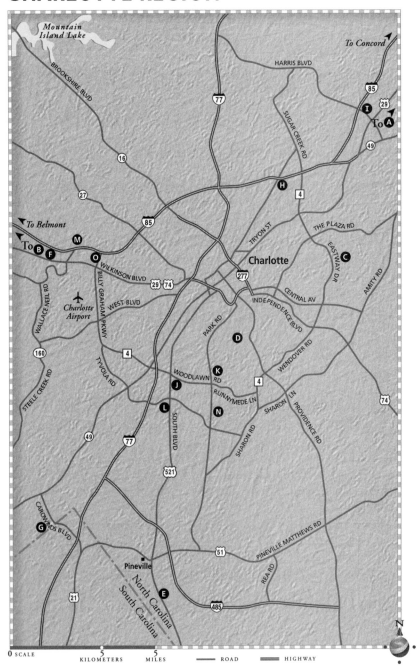

three locations: 4301 Monroe Road, 440 Tyvola Road, and 8332 Pineville-Matthews Road. The service is excellent, and prices are low.

LODGING

Charlotte is a major convention center for the Southeast and has the required accommodations, including such familiar names as Hilton, Doubletree, Holiday Inn, La Quinta, and Ramada. The following are recommended accommodations with a little something extra.

The **Adam's Mark Hotel**, 555 S. McDowell St., 704/372-4100 or 800/444-ADAM, is in Charlotte's business district, just four blocks from the Convention Center and surrounded by shopping and entertainment. Guest rooms are spacious, elegant suites are available, and a full-service health club is on the premises. For a different ambiance, try the friendly charm of **Country Inn & Suites by Carlson**, 2541 Little Rock Rd., 704/394-2000 or 800/456-4000, just a mile from the airport and six miles from town.

Four Points Hotel by Sheraton, 201 S. McDowell St., 704/372-7550 or 800/762-1995, offers 195 rooms, including facilities for the disabled, in uptown Charlotte, surrounded by cultural, dining, shopping, and entertainment opportunities. **Hyatt Charlotte at Southpark**, 5501 Carnegie Blvd., 704/554-1234, is just 10 minutes from town, across from SouthPark Mall and its 100-plus shops and General Cinema Theaters.

The **Morehead Inn**, 1122 E. Morehead St., Charlotte, 704/376-3357 or 888/MOREHEAD, was built in 1917. The inn is located in Dilworth, one of

SIGHTS

- Ⓐ Backing Up Classics Memory Lane Motor Car Museum
- Ⓑ Belmont Abbey Historic District
- Ⓒ Charlotte Museum of History and Hezekiah Alexander Homesite
- Ⓓ Charlotte Nature Museum
- Ⓔ James K. Polk Memorial

SIGHTS (continued)

- Ⓕ Kings Mountain National Battlefield and Military Park
- Ⓐ Lowe's Motor Speedway
- Ⓖ Paramount's Carowinds

FOOD

- Ⓗ Hereford Barn
- Ⓘ Providence Bistro and Bakery

FOOD (continued)

- Ⓙ Silver Cricket
- Ⓚ Sir Edmond Halley's Restaurant
- Ⓛ Sonny's Real Pit Barbecue

LODGING

- Ⓜ Country Inn & Suites by Carlson
- Ⓝ Hyatt Charlotte at Southpark
- Ⓞ Sheraton Airport Plaza

Note: Items with the same letter are located in the same area.

Charlotte's most distinctive historic districts. It was a private residence until the mid-1980s, when it was officially registered as a Charlotte Historic Landmark. Popular for weddings and business functions, it is also an elegant southern alternative to an uptown hotel, with four-poster, sleigh, and pencil-post beds, sitting rooms, a library, a tearoom and a solarium. Prices range from $135 to $185 per night, and the inn is conveniently located just minutes from uptown Charlotte.

Sheraton Airport Plaza, 3315 I-85 S. at Billy Graham Pkwy., 704/392-1200 or 800/325-3535, offers all you expect from a Sheraton facility, including a Jacuzzi, sauna, and exercise room. The **Hilton Charlotte**, 222 E. Third St., 704/377-1500 or 800/937-8461, also has upscale offerings, including more than 400 rooms and a jogging/nature trail.

NIGHTLIFE

Unlike many smaller southern cities, Charlotte does not roll up its streets and turn out the lights at eight o'clock. Nightlife booms in every part of town but especially at the following: **Bar Charlotte**, 300 N. College St., 704/342-2545, is a fun dance bar with atmosphere right in the center of uptown. Call for hours and dance night specials. **Lynn's Speakeasy**, 4819 S. Tryon St., 704/527-3064, is for older adults and features music from the swing era through the blues to early rock 'n' roll; open Tuesday through Saturday 5 p.m. to 1 a.m.

O'Hara's, 212 Woodlawn Rd., 704/525-8350, inside the Holiday Inn Woodlawn, is home to live beach music and Top-40 entertainment. Frequent performers include the Breeze Band, the Tams, and the Chairmen of the Board. The club is open nightly. **The Baha**, 4369 S. Tryon St., 704/525-3343, has one of the city's largest dance floors (10,000 square feet) and features retro and club dance music. It's open Thursday through Saturday 9 p.m. to 3 a.m.

Double Door Inn, 218 E. Independence Blvd., 704/376-1446, is Charlotte's "Home of the Blues" and the city's oldest live entertainment venue. Featuring live blues, rock, and zydeco, the club is open Monday through Friday 11 a.m. to 2 a.m.; Saturday and Sunday 8 p.m. to 2 a.m. If you're in the mood for low lighting, couches, and martinis, try **Tutto Mondo**, 1820 South Blvd., 704/332-5142. Sip a delicious Cosmopolitan martini and taste a $100 caviar sampler or sushi in the loft-style lounge. Open Monday through Thursday 5 p.m. to 12 a.m. and Friday and Saturday 5 p.m. to 2 a.m.

GOLFING

If you have connections in Charlotte, you may gain access to fantastic private golf courses (Quail Hollow and Carmel Country Clubs, for example), but the public courses are wonderful, too. Recommended are the **Eastwood Golf Club**, 4400 Plaza Rd., 704/537-7904; **Highland Creek Golf Club**, 7001 Highland Creek Pkwy., 704/948-0180; **Larkhaven Golf Club**, 4801 Camp Stewart Rd., 704/545-4653; **Oak Hill Golf Course**, 4008 Oak Dale Rd., 704/394-2834; **Pawtucket Golf Course**, 1 Pawtucket Rd., 704/394-5909; **Renaissance Park Golf Course**, 1525 Tyvola Rd., 704/357-3373; and **Sunset Hills Golf Course**, 800 Radio Rd., 704/399-0980.

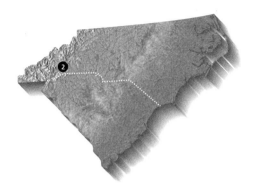

2
ASHEVILLE

When Thomas Wolfe said you can't go home again, he was talking about Asheville, where his mother ran the Dixieland boarding house made famous in *Look Homeward, Angel* and where his writing made residents so mad that . . . well, maybe that was why he couldn't go home again. All is forgiven now, however, and the Thomas Wolfe Memorial is a popular sight.

With more than 63,000 residents, Asheville is a sophisticated mountain city known for its arts, culture, and architecture. Downtown has the largest collection of art deco buildings in the Southeast outside of Miami, and the city has one of the nation's largest historic districts. Asheville also has a thriving economy and the largest airport in western North Carolina.

The city's development was profoundly affected by two wealthy men, George W. Vanderbilt and Dr. Edwin Wiley Grove. Vanderbilt was responsible for construction of the Biltmore Estate, which took 1,000 men six years to complete. When this 255-room European chateau opened on Christmas Eve 1895, it was hailed as the most spectacular private residence in America. It still is.

Grove built the Grove Park Inn in 1913 on 140 acres. The Grove Park Inn Resort, renovated in the past decade, is the grand old lady of resorts, famous throughout the South and justly so. This is where F. Scott Fitzgerald wrote and drank and brought his Zelda. This is where eight U.S. presidents, innumerable dignitaries, and at least one king—Elvis—have stayed. You will be welcome, too.

ASHEVILLE

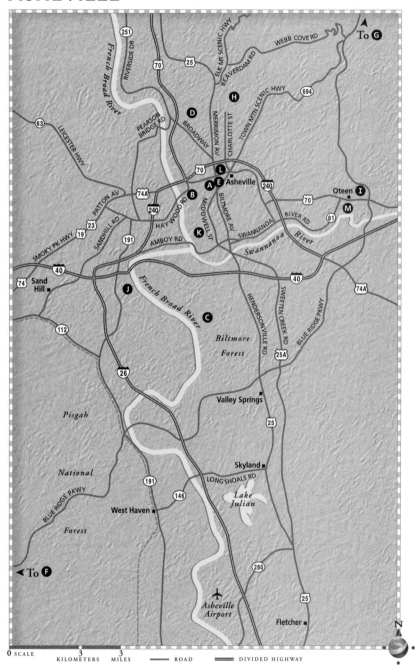

A PERFECT DAY IN ASHEVILLE

You cannot visit Asheville and not see Biltmore House and Gardens. The trouble is, you could easily spend the entire day touring the house and winery with taped guides and wandering the grounds at your leisure. But then, what better way to spend a day than amidst beauty? When you've had your fill of art and antiques, dining rooms that seat nearly 100, walls covered with ancient tapestries, an indoor pool and bowling alley, soaring atriums, and studied elegance, you can taste award-winning wines, marvel at the flower gardens, visit adjacent Biltmore Village (with restored English-style houses that were built for estate workers but now house shops and galleries), then sup at the estate's elegant Deerpark Restaurant. To top off the evening, return to your room at the Grove Park Inn, sit in a rocker on a terrace, and watch twilight slowly gather across the Blue Ridge.

SIGHTSEEING HIGHLIGHTS

★★★★ BILTMORE ESTATE
I N. Pack Square, 828/274-6333 or 800/543-2961
www.biltmore.com

Billed as "America's largest home," the 255-room Biltmore House was constructed with four acres of floor space by George Vanderbilt in 1895 on a 125,000-acre estate. The French Renaissance–style house, now on 8,000 acres, holds thousands of original artworks, furnishings, and antiques. It was also the setting for the Grace Kelly movie *The Swan*. Look for the desk drawer with the stains of Napoleon's heart, which was smuggled in the drawer into France for burial. The estate features landscaped gardens designed by Frederick

---

SIGHTS

- **A** Asheville Art Museum
- **B** Basilica of St. Lawrence
- **C** Biltmore Estate
- **D** Botanical Gardens
- **E** Colburn Gem and Mineral Museum
- **F** Cradle of Forestry
- **G** Craggy Gardens
- **H** Estes-Winn Automobile Museum
- **I** Folk Art Center
- **H** North Carolina Homespun Museum
- **A** Pack Place
- **J** Riverside Cemetery
- **K** Smith-McDowell House
- **L** Thomas Wolfe Memorial
- **M** Western North Carolina Nature Center

Note: Items with the same letter are located in the same area.

BILTMORE ESTATE

Law Olmsted, an award-winning winery, and three restaurants: the Deerpark Restaurant, the Stable Café, and the Bistro.

Details: *Daily 9–5. $30 adults, $22.50 ages 10 to 15, free for children 9 and younger with a parent. (4–6 hours)*

★★★★ **PACK PLACE**
2 S. Pack Square, 828/257-4500
This $14 million complex is western North Carolina's arts and science center and encompasses the Asheville Art Museum, Colburn Gem and Mineral Museum, Health Adventure, YMI (African American) Cultural Center, and Diana Wortham Theatre.

Details: *Tue–Sat 10–5. Admissions to attractions vary. (4–6 hours)*

★★★★ **THOMAS WOLFE MEMORIAL**
52 N. Market St., 828/253-8304
www.att.net/wolfememorial
The novelist's 29-room boyhood home is the Dixieland boarding house depicted in *Look Homeward, Angel*, a tale so frank that the book was banned for seven years from Asheville's public library.

Details: *Apr–Oct Mon–Sat 9–5, Sun 1–5. Nov–Mar Tue–Sat 10–4, Sun 1–4. $1 adults, 50 cents children. (30 minutes)*

★★★ ASHEVILLE ART MUSEUM
2 S. Pack Square, 828/253-3227
This museum specializes in twentieth-century American art and includes contemporary crafts, art related to the southeastern United States, and works by America's preeminent artists. The museum offers exhibits and programs for all ages.
Details: Tue–Sat 10–5. $3 adults, $2.50 senior citizens and children under 12. (2 hours)

★★★ COLBURN GEM AND MINERAL MUSEUM
2 S. Pack Square, 828/254-7162
In this heart of rock-hounding country, the Colburn facility features North Carolina gems and minerals as well as those from around the world. Many exhibits are hands-on and educational.
Details: Tue–Sat 10–5, summer Sun 1–5. $3 adults, $2.50 seniors and students with I.D., $2 ages 4 to 15. (30 minutes)

★★★ FOLK ART CENTER
Milepost 382, Blue Ridge Pkwy., 828/298-7928
Visitors won't want to miss the craft demonstrations and exhibits in the 100-year-old Allanstand Craft Shop, home of the Southern Highland Craft Guild.
Details: Daily 9–6. Free. (1–2 hours)

★★★ NORTH CAROLINA HOMESPUN MUSEUM
111 Grovewood Rd., 828/253-7651
Artifacts, storyboards, weaving demonstrations, and films illustrate the 1901–1980 history of Biltmore Industries, a handweaving operation.
Details: Daily 10–5. Free. (1 hour)

★★★ SMITH-McDOWELL HOUSE
283 Victoria Rd., 828/253-9231
Asheville's oldest residence is a circa-1840 restored brick Victorian home. Guided tours are available.
Details: Apr–Dec Tue–Sat 10–4, Sun 1–4. Jan–Mar Tue–Fri 10–4. Call for tour information and fees. (1 hour)

★★ BASILICA OF ST. LAWRENCE
97 Haywood St., 828/259-5836
This church, designed by Rafael Guastavino in 1909, boasts the

largest unsupported dome in North America and is on the National Register of Historic Places.

Details: *For visiting hours and information, call the Historic Resources Commission, 828/259-5836. (30 minutes)*

★★ BOTANICAL GARDENS
151 W.T. Weaver Blvd., 828/252-5190
This 10-acre area of native plants beckons lovers of flora and beauty.

Details: *Daily dawn to dusk. Free. (1–2 hours)*

★★ CRADLE OF FORESTRY
U.S. 276, Brevard, 828/877-3130
www.cradleofforestry.com
Of course it has forestry exhibits (from the early 1900s), but here you will also find restored and original historic buildings from the late 1800s, a restored steam locomotive, exhibits, guided tours, and a gift shop.

Details: *Four miles south of Milepost 412 on the Blue Ridge Parkway. Apr–late Oct daily 9–5. $4 adults, $2 ages 6 to 17. (2 hours)*

★★ CRAGGY GARDENS
Milepost 364, Blue Ridge Pkwy., 828/298-0398
www.nps.gov/blri
Rugged beauty awaits in the large Craggy Dome area, which offers hiking trails, picnic sites, and a visitors center.

Details: *25 miles north of Asheville. May–Oct dawn–dusk. Free. (2 hours)*

★★ WESTERN NORTH CAROLINA NATURE CENTER
75 Gashes Creek Rd., 828/298-5600
www.wncnaturecenter.org
You'll see flora and fauna in natural environments in this living museum that exhibits and interprets the plant and animal wildlife of the southern Appalachian Mountains. The center is a favorite of children.

Details: *Daily 10–5. $4 adults, $2 ages 3 to 14. (1–2 hours)*

★ ESTES-WINN AUTOMOBILE MUSEUM
111 Grovewood Rd., 828/253-7651
Like-new shines grace 20 vehicles from 1913 to 1957 and an antique fire engine displayed in the museum on the grounds adjacent to Grove Park Inn.

Details: Mon–Sat 10–5, Sun 1–5. Free. (30 minutes–1 hour)

★ RIVERSIDE CEMETERY
Birch St., 828/258-8480

Here are the graves of Thomas Wolfe, O. Henry, and thousands of others.

Details: Free. (30 minutes)

FITNESS AND RECREATION

You'll find the requisite national-franchise gyms and YMCA facilities here, but Asheville also offers more than 40 parks and play areas with a wide variety of recreational activities and facilities, including golf courses, swimming pools, tennis courts, and neighborhood recreation centers—all for your use, free. For information, call Asheville Parks, 828/259-5800.

Just a few miles south of Asheville on N.C. 280, you'll find fishing, boating, and recreational facilities in **Lake Julian District Park**, open year-round, 8 a.m. to dark, with some activities requiring fees. Asheville's resort areas also offer abundant fitness and recreational opportunities, from saunas to hang gliding. And there is always the **French Broad River**, with activities ranging from gentle tubing to fast and furious white-water rafting.

FOOD

Asheville has every type of restaurant imaginable, but three of the best are housed in the Grove Park Inn Resort (290 Macon Ave.). **Blue Ridge Dining Room** is an Asheville tradition for fixed-priced Sunday brunch, Friday-night seafood buffet, and all the meals in between. The elegant, gourmet **Horizons Restaurant** is open for dinner only, with prices up to $75. At the more casual (and less expensive) **Sunset Terrace**, you can enjoy bountiful breakfasts, light lunches, and delicious dinners outdoors, overlooking the mountains. All three restaurants can be reached at 828/252-2711.

If you don't recognize the name, you don't know your bluegrass, but you can always learn. **Mountain Smoke House**, 802 Fairview Rd., 828/298-8121 , is open for lunch and dinner daily. The specials here are beef, pork, and chicken barbecue–sandwiches, with plates priced less than $10 and foot-stompin' music after 8 p.m. You also can enjoy catfish, ham, turkey, corn on the cob, potato salad, hush puppies—what the natives call real southern mountain food.

ASHEVILLE

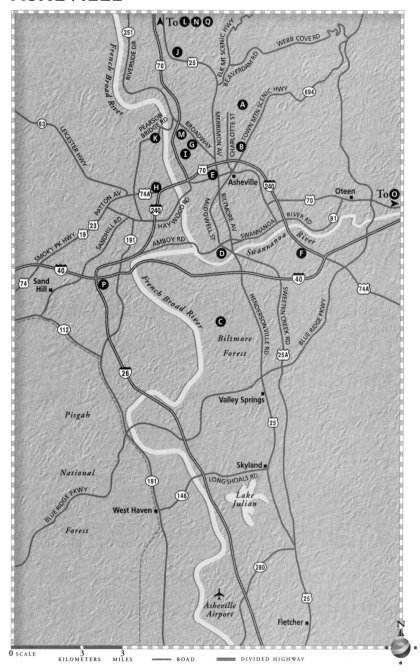

Deerpark Restaurant at the elegant Biltmore Estate (1 N. Pack Square, 800/543-2961) offers seasonal buffets. The restaurant is pricey, but the atmosphere is fine dining, and you can order the estate's award-winning wines. The **Market Place**, 20 Wall St., 828/252-4162, offers continental cuisine served in two areas, one lit by candles. The chef uses nothing but the freshest locally grown ingredients, and the pasta, pastries, and bread are made on the premises. Cost for dinner ranges from $25 to $30 per person.

Much less expensive is the **Depot Restaurant**, 30 Lodge St., 828/277-7651, where lunch costs less than $10 and dinner less than $15. Housed in an 1896 railway station, the restaurant offers a menu featuring chicken, seafood, pork, veal, and beef, but the house specialty is prime rib. **Charlotte Street Grill and Pub**, 157 Charlotte St., 828/253-5348, isn't much more expensive and features American continental favorites, steak, seafood, and pasta. It's open for lunch and dinner; closed holidays.

LODGING

Unique is not quite the word for **Southern Safari**, 800/454-7374, just outside Asheville—it's not descriptive enough. If you want to truly one-up your neighbors on vacation, book a luxury tent at this African-style camp. You also can enjoy a jogging/nature trail and gourmet open-air dining. An elegant base camp provides the perfect setting for adventure travelers. Southern Safari is located 25 miles north of Asheville in Weaverville.

If you want to splurge on luxury indoor accommodations ($140–$265) in Asheville, **Grove Park Inn Resort**, 290 Macon Ave., 828/252-2711 or

FOOD
- ❶ Blue Ridge Dining Room
- ❸ Charlotte Street Grill and Pub
- ❸ Deerpark Restaurant
- ❹ Depot Restaurant
- ❹ Horizons Restaurant
- ❺ Market Place
- ❻ Mountain Smoke House
- ❹ Sunset Terrace

LODGING
- ❻ Applewood Manor
- ❼ Great Smokies SunSpree Resort
- ❹ Grove Park Inn Resort
- ❽ The Lion and the Rose
- ❾ Old Reynolds Mansion
- ❿ Richmond Hill Inn
- ⓛ Southern Safari
- ⓜ Wright Inn and Carriage House

CAMPING
- ⓝ Appalachian Village Campground
- ⓞ Asheville Taps RV Park
- ⓟ Bear Creek RV Park & Club House
- ⓠ French Broad River Campground

Note: Items with the same letter are located in the same area.

QUALLA BOUNDARY

The route into Great Smoky Mountains National Park from the south, 50 miles west of Asheville on U.S. Highway 19, wends through the Qualla Boundary, the 56,000-acre reservation of the 12,000-member Eastern Band of the Cherokee. This area has been the heart of Cherokee Territory for thousands of years.

It was from here that the Cherokee were forced in 1838 onto the infamous Trail of Tears, in an attempt by whites to resettle all eastern tribes into the West. Many Indians hid out in the Great Smokies, refusing to leave their homeland. Later, William H. Thomas, an Indian agent for the U.S. government, bought part of the land that is now the reservation and gave it to the Indians who had managed to stay. Still later, the U.S. government deeded 50,000 acres to the tribe.

In the town of Cherokee on the reservation, you'll find **Oconaluftee Indian Village** on U.S. 441 N., where you will be treated to an intimate view of how the Cherokee lived in the 1750s. Guides in native costumes will lead you through the seven-sided Council House, where the history of the Cherokee is revealed and where rituals are preserved and handed down from generation to generation. You'll also see primitive cabins and rustic arbors where Cherokee women string colorful beads and mold ropes of clay into pots, make baskets, practice the ancient art of finger weaving, and pound Indian corn into meal. You will see Cherokee men chipping flint into arrowheads, making dugout canoes, and carving wooden spoons, combs, and bowls, as well as hunting with blowguns—yes, blowguns.

Cherokee also offers miles of trails to hike, rivers to tube and raft, and trout streams rated by experts as among the nation's best. You'll also find the **Museum of the Cherokee Indian** and **Qualla Arts & Crafts Mutual** alongside more commercial ventures such as the **Harrah's Cherokee Casino** (it never closes), **Cherokee Fun Park**, **Cherokee Bear Zoo**, and outfits offering to "take your picture with a real Cherokee in full regalia."

To end the day, attend a performance of Unto These Hills, an outdoor drama that tells the story of the Cherokee struggle from the mid-1500s to 1838. Shows are nightly except Sunday from mid-June to late August. For information about all events and activities in Cherokee, call 800/438-1601 or write to the Cherokee Visitors Center, P.O. Box 460-27, Cherokee, NC 28719.

800/438-5800, is the place. One of the South's oldest and most famous resorts, Grove Park is an engineering marvel, built of massive granite boulders in 1913 on 140 acres overlooking the city. F. Scott Fitzgerald wrote here, and the register of other famous guests is long. The European-style accommodations, gourmet restaurants, and views explain why.

Still expensive but much smaller (10 rooms as opposed to more than 500 for the Grove Park) is the **Wright Inn and Carriage House**, 235 Pearson Dr., 828/251-0789 or 800/552-5724, with a meal plan available. Another upscale bed-and-breakfast with a meal plan is **The Lion and the Rose**, with five rooms (some have Jacuzzis) at 276 Montford Avenue in the Montford Historic District; 828/255-7673 or 800/546-6988.

More moderately priced but also beautiful is the **Old Reynolds Mansion**, 100 Reynolds Heights, 828/254-0496. Also in the city is **Richmond Hill Inn**, 87 Richmond Hill Dr., a National Historic Register, Queen Anne–style 1890s mansion with guest cottages. It's pricey, but the accommodations are topnotch, and breakfast from a gourmet kitchen is included. The inn also has a library with a fine collection of books, including many first editions by western North Carolina authors. The inn is open seasonally, so call ahead, 828/252-7313 or 800/545-9238.

If resort quarters beckon, try the **Great Smokies SunSpree Resort**, 1 Holiday Inn Dr., 828/254-3211 or 800/733-3211. This 270-room facility has it all—restaurant, swimming pool, lounge, playground, golf and tennis privileges, jogging/nature trail, and more. Rates range from $85 to $150 per night.

Also recommended is **Applewood Manor**, 62 Cumberland Circle, 828/254-2244 or 800/442-2197, in the historic Montford District. Room rates range from $95 to $120, and the environment is smoke free in this turn-of-the-century colonial-style home on 1.5 acres. Here guests awaken to homemade muffins and breads and specially blended coffee or tea, are within strolling distance of the Botanical Gardens, and are provided with bicycles to pedal through the historic neighborhood. Afternoon refreshments are complimentary, and badminton and croquet are always available.

CAMPING

Camping, from primitive campsites to full-service trailer/RV parks, is available in abundance. Highly recommended is the **Appalachian Village Campground**, 828/645-5847, five minutes north of Asheville on the Old Marshall Highway and within a 10-mile radius of more than 25 attractions. It has more than 60 mountaintop campsites with water, electricity, a village store, and a modern bath house. **Bear Creek RV Park and Club House**, off I-40 at Exit 47, 800/833-0798 or 828/253-0798, is in view of the Biltmore Estate and has 90 full-hookup sites. **Asheville Taps RV Park**, 1327 Tunnel Rd., 828/299-8277 or 800/831-4385, has trailer and tent sites, shaded sites, pull-throughs, hot showers, a playground, fishing, and recreational facilities and is open all year. Also open all year and with similar amenities is the **French Broad River Campground**, 1030 Old Marshall Hwy., Asheville, 828/658-0772.

GOLFING
Golfing in the mountains is entirely different from golfing in the lowcountry. The hazards, the humidity, and the lay of the land—not to mention the scenery—differ greatly. Among the numerous Asheville courses recommended are the private **Biltmore Forest Country Club**, 31 Stuyvesant Rd., 828/274-1261; **Great Smokies SunSpree Resort**, 1 Holiday Inn Dr., 828/253-5874; the public **Buncombe County Municipal Golf Club**, 226 Fairway Dr., 828/298-1867; and the **Grove Park Inn and Country Club**, 290 Macon Ave., 828/252-2711. This the oldest operating course in North Carolina—built in 1899 and redesigned in 1924 by Donald Ross.

3
WESTERN
NORTH CAROLINA

Tourism is one of western North Carolina's leading industries; crafts follow closely. The "Handmade in America" campaign, launched here in 1993, is expected to put Western North Carolina on the map as the largest center of contemporary and traditional crafts in the nation. Western North Carolina is also home to the Southern Highland Handicraft Guild and High Country Crafters. The Folk Art Center on the Blue Ridge Parkway (see Chapter 2) near Asheville is a retail center for artisans who belong to the craft guilds.

But breathtaking scenery was the original and is still the primary reason people come to the mountains of western North Carolina. Here you will find cascading waterfalls, gentle streams, and mighty rivers that nourish fertile valleys carved eons ago by Ice Age glaciers. You will see wilderness areas and wildlife preserves with more varieties of plants and animals than just about anywhere else on earth. You will enjoy quaint villages and fun-filled towns.

You'll find a gentle climate that produces four distinct seasons. In spring, come for the mountain laurel and rhododendron; in fall, for the riotous colors; the rest of the year, for beauty unparalleled and all kinds of fun, from tubing and trout fishing to horseback riding, white-water rafting, and snow skiing. And when mountain folk wave from their front porches as you whiz past in your car, wave back—it's the friendly thing to do.

WESTERN NORTH CAROLINA

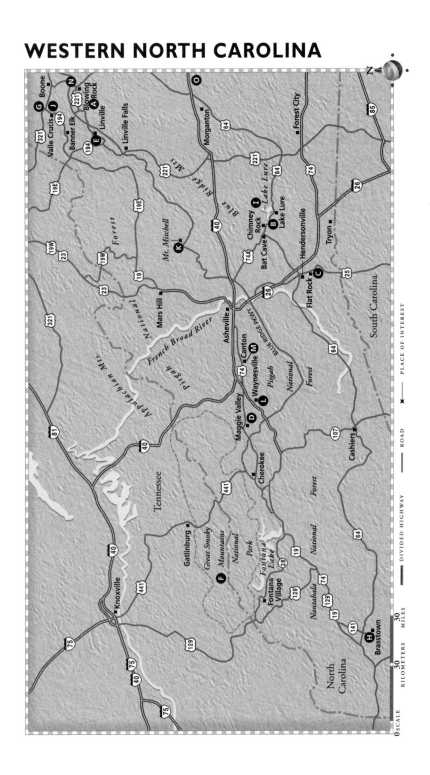

N

Boone
N
G J
Valle Crucis
Banner Elk
194
Blowing
A Rock
Linville
E
194
321
321
Linville Falls

O
Morganton
64
Forest City
85

19E
221
Blue Ridge Mts
221
64
Lake Lure
64
74
26

19W
23
19W
19E
Mt. Mitchell
K
40
T
Chimney
Rock
B
Lake Lure
Bat Cave
74A
Hendersonville
Tryon
25

321
23
19
National
Forest
Mars Hill
French Broad River
Asheville
26
Flat Rock
C
South Carolina

81
Appalachian Mts
Pisgah
Canton
M
74
Waynesville
L
D
Maggie Valley
Pisgah
National
Forest
64

40
Cherokee
107
Cashiers

Tennessee
441
National
Forest
64

40
Gatlinburg
Great Smoky
Mountains
National
Park
F
Fontana
Lake
Fontana
Village
28
19
Nantahala
129
74
129
19
141
H
Brasstown

Knoxville
441

75
40
75
129
75

North
Carolina

PLACE OF INTEREST

ROAD

DIVIDED HIGHWAY

30
MILES
30
KILOMETERS
0 SCALE

A PERFECT DAY IN WESTERN NORTH CAROLINA

An early morning drive along U.S. 321/221 with the windows rolled down—the average summer temperature is 68 degrees—leads to Tweetsie Railroad at Blowing Rock. OK, it's mostly for the kids, but adults will enjoy the trip by chairlift to the western theme park, and all will enjoy a ride on Tweetsie, the 100-plus-year-old Engine No. 12 of the Eastern Tennessee and Western North Carolina Railroad. The train travels a three-mile track, crossing a 255-foot-high trestle, and is attacked by Indians and train robbers along the way. After returning safely to the station, you can pan for gold, visit a petting zoo, catch a performance of the Tweetsie Clogging Jamboree, enjoy a treat from an old-fashioned ice cream parlor, and visit the county fair.

If you haven't had enough of the good old days after leaving the park, head to Valle Crucis and Mast General Store on Highway 194, where you will find a delightful mix of antiques and reproductions in an original, rambling emporium from the turn of the century. Modern shopping is available at a factory-outlet mall on the route back from Blowing Rock to Boone, which should be your destination for an unforgettable, family-style dinner at the Daniel Boone Inn.

SIGHTSEEING HIGHLIGHTS

★★★★ **CHIMNEY ROCK PARK**
U.S. 74 and 64, Chimney Rock
704/625-9611 or 800/277-9611
A 26-story elevator carries you through solid granite to Inspiration Point for a 75-mile view of the Blue Ridge, which provided much of

SIGHTS

- **A** Blowing Rock
- **B** Chimney Rock Park
- **C** Connemara, Carl Sandburg Home
- **B** Flat Rock Playhouse
- **D** Ghost Town in the Sky
- **E** Grandfather Mountain
- **F** Great Smoky Mountains National Park
- **G** Horn in the West
- **H** John C. Campbell Folk School
- **I** Lake Lure
- **E** Linville Caverns
- **D** Maggie Valley
- **J** Mast General Store
- **K** Mount Mitchell
- **L** Museum of North Carolina Handicrafts
- **M** Old Pressley Sapphire Mine
- **N** Tweetsie Railroad
- **O** Waldensian Museum

Note: Items with the same letter are located in the same area.

the scenery for the movie *Last of the Mohicans*, filmed here in the early 1990s. Scenic nature trails lead to Hickory Nut Falls.

Details: Daily 8:30–6 (to 7 during Daylight Saving Time). $9.95 adults, $5 ages 6 to 15. (2 hours)

★★★★ **GHOST TOWN IN THE SKY**
Ghost Mountain, Maggie Valley
828/926-1140 or 800/446-7886
Atop Ghost Mountain is a large recreational facility for the entire family, with rides and mile-high entertainment including daily western-style gunfights. You can ride the chairlift or take the incline railway to the top.

Details: U.S. 19 between Lake Junaluska and Cherokee. May–mid June 9:30–6, mid-June–Aug 9–7, Sept and Oct 9:30–6. $19 ages 10 and up, $14 ages 3 to 9. (6–8 hours)

★★★★ **GRANDFATHER MOUNTAIN**
U.S. 221 and the Blue Ridge Pkwy., Linville
828/733-2013 or 800/468-7325, www.grandfather.com
This highest peak in the Blue Ridge has the Mile High Swinging Bridge, six environmental habitats displaying native wildlife, a dozen miles of hiking trails, picnic areas, a nature museum, and a theater showing award-winning movies. Call about special events, including "Singing on the Mountain," held the fourth Sunday in June, and the Highland Games and Gathering of the Scottish Clans, held the second weekend in July.

Details: Winter 8–5 (weather permitting), spring and fall 8–6, summer 8–7:30. $10 adults, $5 ages 4 to 12. (2–3 hours)

★★★★ **GREAT SMOKY MOUNTAINS NATIONAL PARK**
U.S. 441 N., 423/436-1200
The country's most popular national park extends about 70 miles along the North Carolina–Tennessee border and contains more than a half million acres of protected forest and a resident population of nearly 600 black bears.

Details: The North Carolina entrance to the park is through the Cherokee Indian Reservation on U.S. 441 N. Open year-round. Free. (2–4 hours)

★★★★ **HORN IN THE WEST**
591 Horn in the West Dr., Boone, 828/264-2120
www.boonenc.org/saha.

This outdoor historical drama, performed at the Daniel Boone Theater, tells the story of Daniel Boone and settlers' struggle for freedom from British rule during the American Revolution. Also on the site, with the same address and phone number, is the **Hickory Ridge Homestead**, a living-history museum containing authentic cabins. *Details: Performances mid-June–mid-Aug Tue–Sun 8:30 p.m. $12 ages 12 and up, $6 ages 11 and under. (2–3 hours)*

★★★ **CONNEMARA, CARL SANDBURG HOME**
1928 Little River Rd., Flat Rock, 828/693-4178
www.nps.gov.carl
Built in 1838 by Christopher Gustavus Memminger, secretary of the Confederate treasury, this 264-acre farm was purchased in 1945 by the famous poet and Lincoln biographer. Sandburg spent his last 22 years here with his wife, who raised prize-winning goats on the grounds. The house, reached by shuttle or a steep winding path, is open for guided tours. *Details: Daily 9–5. $3 ages 17 to 61, free for others. (3 hours)*

★★★ **LAKE LURE**
Hwy. 64/74, Lake Lure, 828/625-2725
This gorgeous lake is 27 miles long and provides a beautiful setting for boating, swimming, or just lazing on the shore—bring a picnic. This is where much of the Patrick Swayze movie *Dirty Dancing* was filmed, though it supposedly took place in upstate New York. *Details: Open year-round. Free. (4–6 hours)*

★★★ **LINVILLE CAVERNS**
U.S. 221, Marion, 828/756-4171, www.linvillecaverns.com
This brightly lit limestone cavern extends deep into the mountainside, features many interesting stalactites and stalagmites, and is home to blind trout. *Details: Four miles south of the Blue Ridge Parkway. Mar–Nov daily 9–6. Dec–Feb weekends only. Admission varies, call for more information. (30-minute guided tour)*

★★★ **MAGGIE VALLEY**
Hwy. 19, Haywood County, www.smokeymountains.net
Yes, there was a real Maggie, the daughter of "Uncle Jack" Setzer, who lived here at the turn of the century. The local post office officially

became Maggie Post Office in 1904, and the name stuck. Maggie isn't just a place; it's a treasure trove of attractions, including mountain music halls, craft shops, museums, a western-style theme park (Ghost Town in the Sky), world-famous ski areas, trout fishing, golf, and more. You could spend your entire vacation in Maggie Valley or use it as a base of operations to explore all of Western North Carolina.

Details: *For a free area vacation guide, call 800/334-9036. (8 hours)*

★★★ MUSEUM OF NORTH CAROLINA HANDICRAFTS
307 Shelton St., Waynesville, 828/452-1551

The 1875 Shelton House is the site of a comprehensive exhibit of heritage crafts, including wood carvings, quilts, pottery, handpainted china, handcrafted jewelry, period furniture, and Cherokee and Navajo artifacts.

Details: *Tue–Fri 10–4. $4. (1–2 hours)*

★★★ TWEETSIE RAILROAD
U.S. 321 S., between Boone and Blowing Rock
828/264-9061 or 800/526-5740
www.tweetsie-railroad.com

A steam train takes you on a three-mile, forested mountain journey, replete with Old West train robbers. Here also are crafts, amusement rides, live entertainment, and shops.

Details: *Mid-May–Oct daily 9–6, Sept and Oct weekends 9–6. $18 adults, $14 seniors and ages 3 to 12. (If you enter the park after 3, the next day's admission is free.) (4–6 hours)*

★★ BLOWING ROCK
U.S. 321 S., Blowing Rock, 828/295-7111
www.theblowingrock.com

An Indian brave who leaped from this high rock was magically returned to the arms of a maiden who prayed to the Great Spirit for his life. Thus says the legend of the Blowing Rock. Actually, light objects do return when cast over the void of the Johns River Gorge. The phenomenon is caused by the gorge's rocky walls, through which the wind sweeps with such force that some items prove undroppable. This is also the only place in the world where snow falls upside down.

Details: *Apr and May daily 9–6, June–Oct daily 8–8, Nov–Mar daily 8–6 (as weather permits). $4 adults, $1 ages 6 to 11. (1 hour)*

MILE HIGH SWINGING BRIDGE AT GRANDFATHER MOUNTAIN

NC Travel & Tourism

★★ FLAT ROCK PLAYHOUSE
U.S. 25 S., Flat Rock, 828/693-0731

The 50-year-old State Theatre of North Carolina presents professionally produced hit plays and musicals here from late May to late October.

Details: *Performances Wed–Sat 8:15, matinees Thu, Sat, and Sun 2:15. Admission varies. (2–3 hours)*

★★ MAST GENERAL STORE
Hwy. 194, Mission Crossing Scenic Byway, Valle Crucis, 828/963-6511, www.mastgeneralstore.com

This 116-year-old landmark, in the heart of the state's first rural historic district, is listed on the National Historic Register as one of the best examples of an old country store. While some of its displays are only for viewing, most goods are for sale. A special treat is the "candy by the pound" area.

Details: *Daily 9–6. Free. (1–2 hours)*

★★ MOUNT MITCHELL
Hwy. 128, Burnsville, 828/675-4611

This highest peak (6,684 feet) east of the Mississippi River is located in a state park. It offers nature trails, a lookout tower (the climb up the stairs isn't difficult, and the view from the top is fantastic), museum, restaurant, picnic area, and nine primitive tent sites.

Details: Exit Blue Ridge Parkway at Milepost 355. Open year-round, weather permitting. Free. (2 hours)

★★ OLD PRESSLEY SAPPHIRE MINE
I-40 Exit 33, Canton, 828/648-6320

The world's largest blue sapphires were discovered here, and you can search for gems of your own.

Details: Daily 9–6. $5, plus 50 cents for each bucket of ore you wash at the flume. (2 hours)

★★ WALDENSIAN MUSEUM
152 E. Main St., Valdese, 828/874-1893

The museum covers the history of the Waldensians, who immigrated to Valdese from northern Italy over a century ago. The **Trail of Faith** is a tour of 14 building replicas and monuments, and *From This Day Forward* is a drama that shows the history of the persecution and faith of the Waldensians.

Details: Daily 8:30–5:30. Free. (3 hours)

★ JOHN C. CAMPBELL FOLK SCHOOL
Rt. I off U.S. 64 E., Brasstown, 800/365-5724

You can visit the acres of campus and watch folk artists at work or you can enroll in a class in traditional crafts, music, or dance (call for list of class offerings and costs). The school has been operating since 1925.

Details: Open year-round. Free. (2 hours)

FITNESS AND RECREATION

Outdoor enthusiasts will be closer to heaven in western North Carolina than almost anywhere else on earth. Activities include hiking on the **Appalachian Trail**, white-water rafting in the **Nantahala River Gorge** or on the **Pigeon** and **French Broad Rivers**, hiking in **Moses H. Cone Memorial Park**, and rock climbing in Boone. You can even go llama trekking in Clyde (contact Winddancers Llama Treks, 1966 Martins Creek Rd., 828/627-6986). You can ski on world-class slopes at **Appalachian**

Ski Mountain in Blowing Rock, **Cataloochee Ski Area** in Maggie Valley, **Wolf Laurel Resort** in Mars Hill, and **Ski Beech, Hawksnest,** and **Sugar Mountain** in Banner Elk.

FOOD

Maggie Valley alone boasts more than 40 dining establishments, so you'll find no reason to go hungry in "them thar hills." In Maggie, you'll want to try **Saratoga's Café**, 735 Soco Rd., 828/926-1516, featuring whatever you want from the grill along with a variety of entertainment and no cover charge. Also in Maggie is the **Springhouse Steakhouse and Saloon**, Soco Rd., 828/926-2710. In addition to the usual fare, the Springhouse has a two-level country and western dance club. **Backdoor Grill & Bar**, open daily year-round in Maggie, advertises the best burgers in town, but the entire menu—ranging from steaks to chicken—is unbeatable. You can dine on the patio, in the bar, or upstairs. After dinner, enjoy music and dancing in Club 611. The Backdoor is located at 611 Soco Road, 828/926-2229.

    Lomo Grill, offering Italian Mediterranean cuisine, a wood-burning brick oven, and an Argentine grill, also features live entertainment. It's a unique gathering place at 44 Church Street in downtown Waynesville, 828/452-5222. Also in Waynesville at 109 Dolan Road, 828/456-3333, is the intimate dining room at **Old Stone Inn**. It provides more European than down-home food, but your palate will welcome the change. **Caro-Mi Dining Room** at 1433 Highway 176 North in Tryon, 828/859-5200, distributes a business card that proclaims simply "The Ham What Am." That card refers to the most popular entrée in the family-style restaurant. Prices are reasonable, but lines can be long.

    The food is so delicious you'll forget your diet at the **Daniel Boone Inn**, 130 Hardin St., Boone, 828/264-8657. Lunch and dinner are served family style with soup, salad, a choice of three meats and five vegetables, homemade biscuits, dessert, and beverage. Refills of all dishes except the country ham biscuits are unlimited. The cost is $12 per person and $4 to $6 for children. Breakfast, served Saturday and Sunday, is $7. Lines tend to get long early, so be prepared to wait. Reservations are not accepted.

LODGING

Ninety-five miles west of Asheville at Fontana Dam is the year-round **Fontana Village Resort**, N.C. Hwy. 28, 828/498-2211, the largest and most complete resort—featuring an inn, cottages, hostel, and campsites—in the Great

WESTERN NORTH CAROLINA

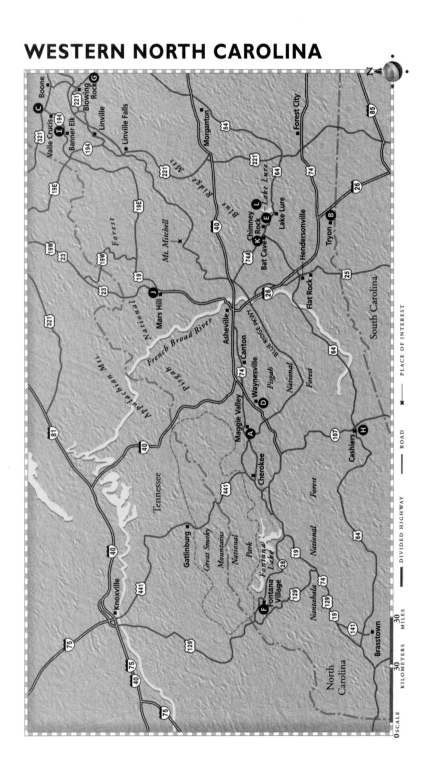

Boone · Blowing Rock **G** · **C** · Valle Crucis · **I** 194 · Banner Elk · Linville · Linville Falls · 221 · 221 · 194 · Morganton · 64 · Forest City · 85

19E · 221 · Blue Ridge Mts · 221 · Lake Lure · 74 · 74 · 26

19E · 40 · Lake Lure · **L** · Lake Lure · Hendersonville · **B** Tryon · 26

19W · 23 · 19W · Mt. Mitchell · **K** Chimney Rock · **E** · 74A · Bat Cave · 25

19W · 23 · 19 · National · **J** Mars Hill · 26 · Flat Rock · South Carolina

321 · Forest · French Broad River · Asheville · Canton · 64 · PLACE OF INTEREST

Appalachian Mts · Pisgah · Waynesville 74 · Pisgah · National · Forest · ROAD

81 · 40 · Maggie Valley · **A** · **D** · **H** Cashiers · 107 · DIVIDED HIGHWAY

Tennessee · Cherokee · 441 · National · Forest · 64

Gatlinburg · Great Smoky Mountains National Park · Fontana Lake · 19 · 28 · 74 · 64 · MILES · KILOMETERS

Knoxville · 441 · **F** Fontana Village · 129 · 143 · 19 · 141 · 30 · 30

75 · 129 · Brasstown · North Carolina

40 · 75 · 75 · SCALE

Smokies. The Jodie Foster movie *Nell* was shot here amid gorgeous scenery. Amenities include a variety of restaurants, indoor and outdoor pools, a lake, water slide, miniature golf, and a fitness center.

If you take U.S. 23 north from Asheville and follow the signs, you'll come to **Wolf Laurel Resort** with its villas, condos, private homes, and log cabins in Mars Hill. The private resort, which borders the Appalachian Trail, offers access to a golf course nearby and is convenient to many area attractions. Make reservations in advance by calling 800/541-1738. **Old Stone Inn**, 30 minutes from Asheville and Cherokee at 109 Dolan Rd., Waynesville, 828/456-3333 or 800/432-8499, is an authentic mountain lodge. After you dine on regional cuisine served fireside in the intimate dining room, you can relax in a rocker on your private porch. At Maggie Valley near Cherokee, you will love the mile-high **Cataloochee Ranch**, a 1,000-acre spread bordering Great Smoky Mountains National Park. For reservations or information, call 828/926-1401 or 800/868-1401.

High Hampton Inn & Country Club, 1525 Hwy. 107 S., Cashiers, 800/334-2551 or 828/743-2411, is justly famous for its scenic beauty, hospitality, and complete family vacation facilities. Features include an 18-hole golf course; golf schools and tournaments; tennis courts; a 40-acre lake for fishing, boating, and swimming; hiking trails; and children's programs. At 3,600 feet in the Blue Ridge Mountains, the inn is set amid landscaped lawns, flower gardens, and tall hemlocks on a 1,400-acre estate.

Also recommended are the **Pine Crest Inn** in Tryon, 800/633-3001, **Sugar Ski & Country Club** in Banner Elk, 800/634-1320, **Green Park Inn** in Blowing Rock, 828/295-3141 or 800/852-2462, and **Dogwood Inn**,

FOOD

- **A** Backdoor Grill & Bar
- **B** Caro-Mi Dining Room
- **C** Daniel Boone Inn
- **D** Lomo Grill
- **D** Old Stone Inn
- **A** Saratoga's Café
- **A** Springhouse Steakhouse and Saloon

LODGING

- **A** Cataloochee Ranch
- **E** Dogwood Inn
- **F** Fontana Village Resort
- **G** Green Park Inn
- **H** High Hampton Inn & Country Club
- **D** Old Stone Inn
- **B** Pine Crest Inn
- **I** Sugar Ski & Country Club
- **J** Wolf Laurel Resort

CAMPING

- **G** Buffalo Camp RV Park
- **K** Creekside Mountain Camping Resort
- **E** Dogwood Travel Park
- **E** Hickory Nut Falls Family Campground
- **L** Lake Lure Campground

Note: Items with the same letter are located in the same area.

originally a stagecoach stop between Asheville and Charlotte in Chimney Rock, 828/625-4403 or 800/992-5557. Reservations for bed-and-breakfasts, country inns, resorts, and cabins in the Asheville and western North Carolina area can be simplified by calling one number toll free, 800/770-9055.

CAMPING

Buffalo Camp RV Park, 151 Harding Dr., Blowing Rock, 828/295-7518, is open April through November and has all the amenities. **Hickory Nut Falls Family Campground** on Highway 74, one-quarter mile west of Chimney Rock, 828/625-4014, is open April through October and also has trailer and tent sites and amenities including fishing, playgrounds, and church services. **Dogwood Travel Park**, one-half mile west of Chimney Rock on Highway 74, is open year-round. It offers season leases, a camp store, a playground, and river swimming. Call 828/625-2400 for information or reservations. **Creekside Mountain Camping Resort**, U.S. 74A, less than three miles west of Bat Cave, 828/625-4257 or 800/248-8118, has it all, including 100 year-round sites, a camp store, pool, recreation center, and AAA discounts. **Lake Lure RV Park and Campground,** on Boy's Camp Road off Highway 64/74 between Chimney Rock and Lake Lure, 828/625-9160, is open April through October with 70 sites (full hookups and pull-throughs) as well as pool swimming, canoes, and paddle boats.

NIGHTLIFE

If you want to sit on a front porch and rock till the sun goes down, you can do it here. But if your idea of nightlife includes more than going to bed with the chickens, you have options. Maggie Valley is the undisputed nightlife center of western North Carolina. The **Stompin' Ground** in Maggie Valley, 828/926-1288, billed as "the Clogging Capital of the World," features some of the area's best mountain clog teams. If you don't know what clogging is, you're in for a foot-stompin' treat.

Here also is the **Maggie Valley Opry House**, 828/926-9336, starring Raymond Fairchild, five-time World Banjo Pickin' Champion, with music and dancing nightly. Also in Maggie, **Shephard's Thunder Ridge**, 828/926-9470, houses a restaurant and huge dance floor and hosts local and national bands year-round. Among a host of other nightspots scattered throughout western North Carolina is the **Full Circle Café**, 136 N. Main St. in Waynesville, 828/456-3050, open nightly, with jazz, folk, and bluegrass music on Friday and Saturday.

GOLFING

You won't work up a sweat when you golf in the mountains of North Carolina, where summer temperatures average in the high 60s to low 70s, but your attention could possibly be distracted by the views. Among numerous recommended courses are **Beech Mountain Golf Club**, 30 Club House Rd., Banner Elk, 828/387-4717, the semi-private **High Hampton Inn and Country Club** in Cashiers, 828/743-2411, **Waynesville Country Club**, 176 Country Club Dr., 828/452-4617, and **Maggie Valley Resort and Country Club**, 1819 Country Club Dr., 828/926-6013.

Blue Ridge Parkway

The Blue Ridge Parkway intersects Asheville at Highways 25, 70, and 74, offering spectacular views heading north or south from the city. The parkway winds 469 miles along the highest ridges, from the Shenandoah National Park in Virginia to the Great Smoky Mountains National Park in North Carolina and Tennessee. The toll-free road is open year-round, except during heavy snowfall. There are plenty of scenic pullouts and picnic areas. Although it has only recently opened to visitors, the **Linn Cove Viaduct**, which winds 1,243 feet around the side of Grandfather Mountain and provides spectacular views of the valleys below, has become one of the parkway's most popular attractions.

Information about the parkway, including peak fall foliage color dates, is available by calling 828/298-0398. The free **Blue Ridge Parkway Accommodations Guide** is available by writing to the Blue Ridge Parkway Association, P.O. Box 2136, Asheville, NC 28802. The parkway may be entered and exited anywhere along its path, so allow a few hours up to a full day.

Other nearby scenic tours include the **Forest Heritage Scenic Bypass**. Get on this scenic loop at Highway 276 in Waynesville and explore the **Pisgah National Forest**, **Looking Glass Falls**, and other beautiful places. Highway

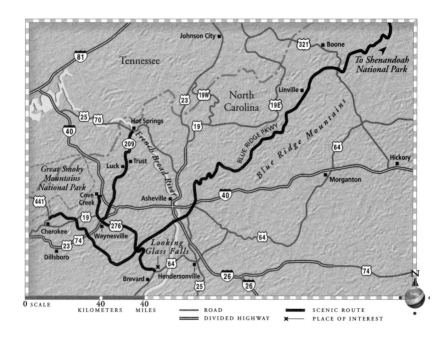

209 takes you past old country stores, unique shops, restaurants, and a turn-of-the-century church and offers spectacular views from elevations up to 5,000 feet. The **Great Smoky Mountain Railway** *in Dillsboro offers a variety of rail trips, including a four-hour excursion in an open-air or air-conditioned car through scenic passes and gorges from March through December. For information, call 800/872-4681.*

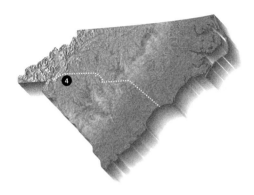

4
UPCOUNTRY

The Greenville-Spartanburg area was the land of the Cherokee when the first European traders and settlers made their way upcountry from Charleston. In 1776, Richard Paris established a trading post at the falls of the Reedy River in what is now downtown Greenville. Treaties with the Indians soon brought more settlers, many of whom planted cotton. By the late 1800s, the local Indians had been destroyed by disease and warfare, and the only reminders of the Lower Cherokee Nation left here were river and place names.

Two of the Revolution's most important battles, Cowpens and Kings Mountain, were fought here, and historical markers recalling Revolutionary days are everywhere. Spartanburg took its name from the Spartan Regiment, which marched to battle from the town.

With the advent of the cotton gin, Greenville and Spartanburg grew from agricultural to textile communities, with mills spinning a lucrative path to the future. Textiles remain a force, but over the past 30 years, industrial diversification has brought new life to the area's economy. Today you will find BMW, Michelin, Hoechst Celanese, Union Camp, R. R. Donnelley & Sons, and other domestic and foreign businesses here.

Upcountry boasts everything found in large cities—opera, theater, fine restaurants. But you'll also find small-town values and famed southern hospitality. Here also are the Peachoid, the most photographed water tank in the United States—with its own exit on I-85 in Gaffney—and the annual "Mighty

UPCOUNTRY

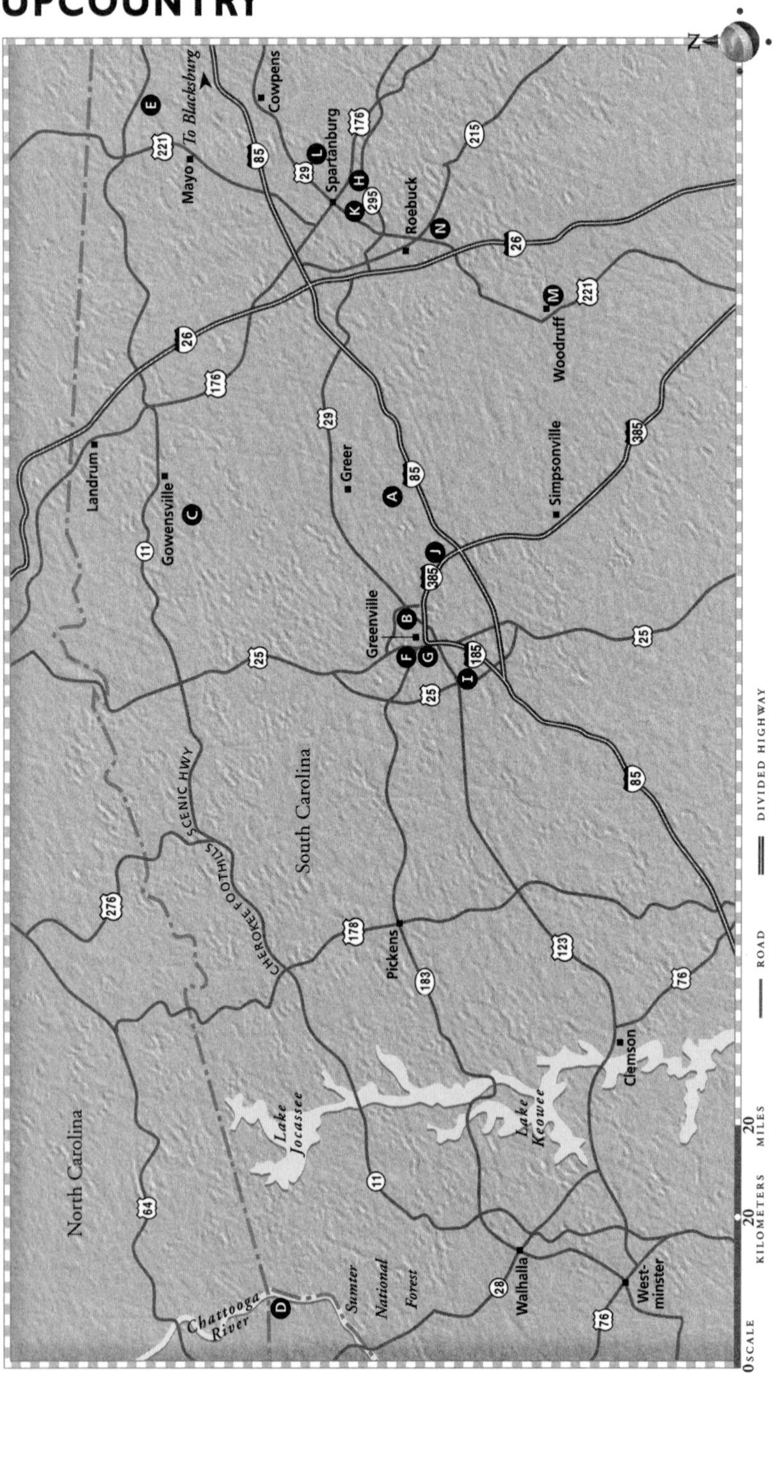

N

To Blacksburg

221
Mayo
Cowpens
Spartanburg
85
29
J
176
215
K H
295
Roebuck
N
26
26
M
176
221
Woodruff
Landrum
29
385
26
C
Greer
A
85
Gowensville
Simpsonville
11
J
385
Greenville
B
F G
185
25
25
I
85
SCENIC HWY
25
South Carolina
276
178
Pickens
183
123
76
CHEROKEE FOOTHILLS
Lake
Jocassee
Lake
Keowee
Clemson
North Carolina
64
11
Sumter
National
Forest
Walhalla
28
West-
minster
Chattooga
River
D
76

SCALE
0   20
KILOMETERS
0   20
MILES

ROAD   DIVIDED HIGHWAY

Moo" Festival in Cowpens. These attractions tend to bring visitors back down to earth just a little.

A PERFECT DAY IN THE UPCOUNTRY

Few sights are as beautiful as upcountry in early spring, when peach trees bloom in glorious shades of pink in orchard after orchard, as far as the eye can see. Spartanburg County is the world's largest peach exporter, but peaches aren't the only fruits that grow here. The Greenville-Spartanburg area boasts numerous pick-your-own operations, offering everything from strawberries in spring to apples and pumpkins in fall.

A perfect day might start with an outing to an orchard or a farm, perhaps near Chesnee. Then take your share of nature's bounty along the Cherokee Foothills Scenic Highway to Cowpens National Battlefield, where you can retrace the past before celebrating today with a picnic. The vistas will restore your soul. But if the bucolic becomes overbearing, head back to Greenville for dinner and dancing.

SIGHTSEEING HIGHLIGHTS

★★★★ **BOB JONES UNIVERSITY MUSEUM AND GALLERY, INC.**
1700 Wade Hampton Blvd., Greenville, 864/242-5100
www.bju.edu/art_gallery
Whether or not you agree with the Reverend Bob Jones's fundamentalist philosophy, you will be attracted to one of the world's most extraordinary collections of religious art and biblical antiquities, including works by Rembrandt, Rubens, and Van Dyck.

SIGHTS

- Ⓐ BMW Zentrum
- Ⓑ Bob Jones University Museum and Gallery
- Ⓒ Campbell's Covered Bridge
- Ⓓ Chattooga National Wild and Scenic River
- Ⓔ Cowpens National Battlefield
- Ⓕ Greenville County Museum of Art
- Ⓖ Greenville Zoo
- Ⓗ Hatcher Gardens
- Ⓘ Nippon Center and Yagoto Restaurant
- Ⓙ Roper Mountain Science Center
- Ⓚ Seay House
- Ⓛ Spartanburg County Regional Museum
- Ⓜ Thomas Price House
- Ⓝ Walnut Grove

Details: Tue–Sun 2–5. Free; children under 6 not admitted. (2-3 hours)

★★★★ **COWPENS NATIONAL BATTLEFIELD**
Hwy. 11, Chesnee, 864/461-2828, www.nps.gov/cowp
General Daniel Morgan's troops stood firm against Colonel Banastre Tarleton at the Battle of the Cowpens and defeated the British on January 17, 1781, as the tide began to turn in the colonists' favor during the American Revolution. When the battle was over, the British regulars had suffered 110 men killed, 200 wounded, and 550 taken prisoner; Morgan lost 12 men and had only 60 wounded. The visitors center and walking trail remind you of how soldiers from North Carolina got the name Tarheels, by standing to fight as though their heels were stuck in tar.
Details: From Spartanburg, take 221 north to Highway 11, from Greenville, take Highway 11 through Chesnee. Daily 9–5. Wheelchair accessible. Free. (2-3 hours)

★★★★ **GREENVILLE COUNTY MUSEUM OF ART**
420 College St., Greenville, 864/271-7570
You won't want to miss the large collection of southern art, featuring works by Jasper Johns and Georgia O'Keeffe.
Details: Tue–Sat 10–5, Sun 1–5. Free. (2 hours)

★★★★ **GREENVILLE ZOO**
E. Washington St., Greenville, 864/467-4300
www.greenvillezoo.org
It's not as large as many zoos, but it's family-friendly. Several hundred animals from around the world live here, and that's not counting the residents of the reptile house. A playground and picnic area add to the casual ambiance.
Details: Daily 10–4:30. $4 adults, $2 ages 3 to 15. (2-3 hours)

★★★ **CHATTOOGA NATIONAL WILD AND SCENIC RIVER**
803/561-4000 (National Forest Service)
www.fs.fed.us/rh/fms
A star of the movie *Deliverance*, the Chattooga serves as a 40-mile border between South Carolina and Georgia and offers rafting, canoeing, and kayaking.
Details: For information about white-water rafting, call Wildwater

Ltd., 800/451-9972, or Nantahala Outdoor Center, 800/232-7238. For additional information, contact the National Forest Service. (4 hours)

★★★ **SPARTANBURG COUNTY REGIONAL MUSEUM**
Main St., Spartanburg, 864/596-3501
The history of the area is explored in memorabilia and exhibits, including a doll collection.
Details: Tue–Sat; call for times. $2 adults, 50 cents students, under 12 free. (1 hour)

★★★ **WALNUT GROVE PLANTATION**
1200 Otts Shoal Rd., Roebuck, 864/576-6546
The circa-1765 plantation home of Kate Moore Barry, who became a scout for General Daniel Morgan at the Battle of Cowpens, is fully restored and furnished and has a separate kitchen filled with early cookery items. The grounds include an herb garden, the Moore family cemetery, and a nature trail.
Details: Off U.S. 221 North (take Exit 28 off I-26), nine miles south of Spartanburg. Apr–Oct Tue–Sat 11–5, year-round Sun 2–5. $4.50 adults, $2 students. (2 hours)

★★ **BMW ZENTRUM**
Hwy. 101 S., Greer, 888/868-7269, www.bmwzentrum.com
The BMW Roadster driven by Pierce Brosnan's James Bond in *Goldeneye* is displayed here where it was made, at BMW's only North American automobile manufacturing plant. The visitor's center and museum show the influence of BMW engineering in the automotive, motorcycle, and aviation industries. Plant tours are by reservation only, but the readily available virtual tour is the next best thing.
Details: Exit 60 off I-85. Tue–Sat 9:30–5:30. Call for admission fees. (1 hour)

★★ **HATCHER GARDENS**
820 Reidville Rd., Spartanburg, 864/582-2776
Friends of the 90-plus-year-old Harold Hatcher know how delighted he always was by the groups of schoolchildren and other visitors viewing the world that was just outside his door. Hatcher and his wife donated these gardens to the city of Spartanburg as a haven for birds and wildlife, featuring more than 10,000 plants, plus ponds, dams, and trails.
Details: Daily dawn to dusk. Free. (1 hour)

★★ NIPPON CENTER AND YAGOTO RESTAURANT
500 Congaree Rd., Greenville, 864/242-6700
Nowhere else in South Carolina can you participate in a genuine Japanese tea ceremony. Cultural programs are offered at this fifteenth-century-style Japanese mansion with its cherry trees, rock garden, five-star restaurant, and pond of lotus flowers.

Details: Tours and tea ceremony by appointment only. Guided tour $3, tea ceremony $7. (1-2 hours)

★★ ROPER MOUNTAIN SCIENCE CENTER
Roper Mountain Rd. off U.S. 385, Greenville, 864/281-1188
Schoolchildren use it as a resource, teachers use it as a training center, and everybody else finds it a fun place to visit. Here are the nation's eighth-largest refractor telescope, a living history farm, Discovery Room, Sealife Room, observatory, health education center, chemistry/physics shows, and a planetarium.

Details: Educational center open second Sat of each month 9–1; $4 adults, $2 students. Planetarium shows Fri 7:30; $3. Nature trails open weekdays 8:30–5. Admission to the grounds is free. (2-3 hours)

★★ SEAY HOUSE
106 Darby Rd., Spartanburg, 864/596-3501
Built of hand-hewn logs and fieldstone in 1790 by a Revolutionary War soldier, this is the oldest standing dwelling in Spartanburg and among the oldest in the state.

Details: Open by appointment. Free. (1 hour)

★★ THOMAS PRICE HOUSE
1200 Oak View Farms Rd., Woodruff, 864/576-6546
This Flemish bond house, built in 1795 from bricks made on the premises, has a Dutch gambrel roof and other unusual architecture. Built by a gentleman farmer, it once was licensed as a "house of entertainment" for stagecoach travelers. Furnishings are authentic to the period.

Details: Off I-26 at Exit 35. Apr–Oct Sat 11–5, year-round Sun 2–5. $3.50 adults, $1.50 students. (1 hour)

★ CAMPBELL'S COVERED BRIDGE
South Carolina's only remaining covered bridge was built in 1909 in the Gowensville community near Greenville. Walk-through fences

provide visitors with a close view, but traffic on the bridge itself is prohibited.

Details: *Off S.C. 14, southwest of Gowensville (15 minutes)*

FITNESS AND RECREATION

Gold's Gym, the Spartanburg Swim Center, and the Spartanburg Athletic Club are just three of the many gyms and sports facilities in the upcountry. Outdoor activities range from white-water rafting on the Chattooga River and lazy tubing or fishing in the Broad River to hiking the battlefield trail at Cowpens and Kings Mountain State Parks or the 100-mile Foothills Trail from Table Rock State Park to Oconee State Park. Premier golf courses abound, and you can even ice-skate at the Greenville Pavilion Ice Rink, 864/322-7529, the upcountry's only public indoor ice rink.

FOOD

Seven Oaks, 104 Broadus Ave., 864/232-1895, is the nicest place to go in Greenville for a special evening out. Diners enjoy a traditional southern menu in a white clapboard mansion with a grand verandah and outside table service. Better yet, Seven Oaks is affordable—dinner for two runs about $45. It's open Monday through Saturday for dinner, and reservations are recommended.

Addy's Dutch Café and Restaurant, 17 E. Coffee St., Greenville, 864/232-ADDY, provides a European atmosphere along with more than 40 beer labels and a variety of cheeses. The cuisine is continental, and reservations are recommended. Addy's is open Monday through Friday 4:30 p.m. to 2 a.m. and Saturday 4:30 to midnight. You can hear live jazz on Tuesday and Friday. Remember, blue laws are in effect in most South Carolina cities, meaning no alcohol is served on Sunday. Main courses cost $9 to $16.

Omega Diner/Stax's Bakery, 72 Orchard Park Dr., Greenville, 864/297-6639, is a great place to eat after hours. The cuisine is best described as eclectic American, and the bakery is fantastic. Dinner for two rarely exceeds $30.

It's called the **World-Famous Beacon Drive-In** and with good reason. The Spartanburg restaurant (255 Reidville Rd., 864/585-9387) not only offers curb service but also has a fast-moving line inside, where workers have been known to take an order for 10 people without writing down anything and delivering it correctly with just a few seconds' wait. Everybody is greeted with a smile. Try the "Plenty" plates and the humongous onion rings,

UPCOUNTRY

accompanied by iced tea and, if you have room left, a "Pig's Dinner," the biggest banana split you'll ever see.

Fish camps, found few other places in the country, are popular here. These are basically fish restaurants, serving catfish, perch, flounder, oysters, and a variety of other entrées, sometimes crossing into beef and chicken. But fish—salt-and-pepper, deep-fried, baked, broiled, Cajun, calabash—is the star. Surroundings are usually rustic, and servings may be family-style. Two recommended spots are **Tall Tales Fish Camp**, at 160 Springdale Lane off Highway 221 in Mayo, 864/461-5200, where small plates start at $5.95, and **Bailey's Fish Camp**, 606 N. Shelby, Blacksburg, 864/839-6023, where you will find an authentic fish camp that offers not only very reasonable meal prices and but also a great selection of food.

For steaks and atmosphere, you can't beat elegant **Le Baron**, 2600 E. Main St., Spartanburg, 864/579-3111. For delicious family-style cooking with an emphasis on vegetables, try **Wade's Restaurant**, 1000 N. Pine St., Spartanburg, 864/582-3800, a Spartanburg tradition for a half-century, open for lunch and dinner (closed Sunday for dinner). Two can dine here for less than $20, and kids' plates cost even less.

Kelly's Steak House, 30 minutes north of Spartanburg on Highway 29, Blacksburg, 864/839-4494, attracts regular customers from both Carolinas. Founded 40 years ago, the restaurant is noted for cut-to-order, cooked-to-order steaks. A family operation, the restaurant offers sophisticated dining in a town of just 2,000. But you'd never guess the numbers from the always-crowded parking lot. Reservations are accepted for groups of five or more. Open for dinner Monday through Saturday.

FOOD

- Ⓐ Addy's Dutch Café and Restaurant
- Ⓑ Bailey's Fish Camp
- Ⓒ Kelly's Steak House
- Ⓓ Le Baron
- Ⓐ Omega Diner/Stax's Bakery
- Ⓐ Seven Oaks
- Ⓔ Tall Tales Fish Camp
- Ⓕ Wade's Restaurant
- Ⓖ World Famous Beacon Drive-In

LODGING

- Ⓗ Greenville Hilton and Towers
- Ⓐ Hyatt Regency Greenville
- Ⓘ Nicholls-Crook Plantation House Bed and Breakfast
- Ⓐ Pettigru Place
- Ⓙ The Phoenix
- Ⓚ Ramada Inn
- Ⓛ Red Horse Inn
- Ⓜ Wilson World Hotel

CAMPING

- Ⓝ Croft State Park
- Ⓞ Cunningham RV Park
- Ⓟ Dogwood RV Park
- Ⓠ Paris Mountain State Park
- Ⓡ Pine Ridge Campground
- Ⓢ Southern Pioneer Campgrounds

Note: Items with the same letter are located in the same area.

LODGING

Greenville has more big city–type lodgings than Spartanburg and the surrounding area, but many familiar names are found in both locations. **Greenville Hilton and Towers**, 45 W. Orchard Park Dr., Greenville, 864/232-4747, provides luxury accommodations, including rooms equipped for the disabled. Similar accommodations are found at the **Hyatt Regency Greenville**, 220 N. Main St., 864/235-1234, with a lobby that is actually designated a city park. For bed-and-breakfast lodgings, try **Pettigru Place**, with its five gracious units at 302 Pettigru St., Greenville, 864/242-4529. **The Phoenix**, 246 N. Pleasantburg Dr., 864/233-4651 or 800/257-3529, has rooms for the disabled.

Spartanburg has Best Western, Comfort Inn, Econo Lodge, Ramada, and others that can be located through their nationwide 800 numbers. Recommended are the **Ramada Inn**, I-85 and I-26, 864/576-5220 or 800/972-7511, with an indoor pool just off the lobby, and **Wilson World Hotel**, 9027 Fairforest Rd., Spartanburg, 864/574-2111 or 800/945-7667. It has 200 units, with facilities for the disabled available.

Small but delightful is the three-unit **Nicholls-Crook Plantation House Bed and Breakfast**, 120 Plantation Dr., Woodruff, between Greenville and Spartanburg, 864/476-8820, a Georgian-style plantation home built around 1793. To the west of Spartanburg, in the shadow of Hogback Mountain, is the **Red Horse Inn**, 310 N. Campbell Rd., Landrum, 864/895-4968, with Victorian cottages and beautiful mountain views.

CAMPING

Campgrounds are plentiful and rarely require advance reservations. These are recommended: **Cunningham RV Park**, 600 Campground Rd., Spartanburg, 864/576-1973, with 69 sites, and **Pine Ridge Campground**, 199 Pine Ridge Campground Rd., Roebuck, 864/576-0302, with 57 sites on wooded grounds, along with a pool, recreation room, and playground. **Croft State Park**, once home to the U.S. Army base known as Camp Croft, now offers 50 campsites at 450 Croft State Park Road, Spartanburg, 864/585-1283.

In Greenville you'll find 50 sites at **Paris Mountain State Park**, 2401 State Park Rd., 864/244-5565. **Southern Pioneer Campgrounds**, 1430 Donaldson Rd., 864/277-0615, has 28 sites. **Dogwood RV Park**, with owners on the premises, has 42 year-round sites with full hookups. The park is located 17 miles north of Greenville on Highway 25 North, just two miles south of S.C. 11, 864/834-8150.

Cherokee Foothills and Savannah River Scenic Highways

Highway 11—the Cherokee Foothills Scenic Highway—follows an ancient Cherokee path, often right at the foot of the mountains. The well-maintained two-lane road leaves I-85 at Gaffney and runs 130 miles through peach orchards, past several state parks, and over Lake Keowee, finally rejoining I-85 at the Georgia line.

Detours from the highway will take you to the 1909 **Campbell's Bridge**, *the state's only covered bridge; the thousand-foot sheer rock face of* **Glassy Mountain**; **Raven Cliff Falls**; *and* **Sassafras Mountain**, *the state's highest peak at 3,548 feet. From there you can view four states: Tennessee, North and South Carolina, and Georgia. The drive is a nice change from the interstate during any season, but it's spectacularly beautiful in spring and fall.*

If you're up for more adventure, leave Highway 11 at its junction with Highway 24 in Oconee County and travel the 100 miles of the **Savannah River Scenic Highway**, *along three major lakes in four counties that form the Old 96 District of South Carolina.*

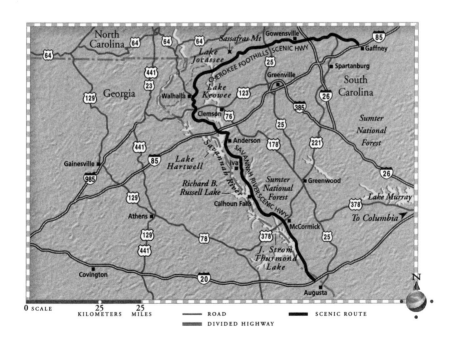

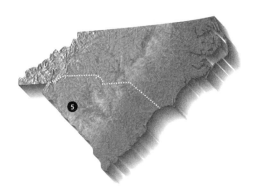

5
OLD 96 DISTRICT

Greenwood and Abbeville are in the Old 96 District, named after an early British fort located 96 miles south of the Lower Cherokee capital, Keowee. Old 96 is not very imaginatively named, but neither is the town of Ninety Six, within the district.

The town of Greenwood received its name in 1823 from a bridegroom's gift. Judge John McGeehee's young wife, Charlotte, decided to call the log house he built for her on a 600-acre plantation Green Wood. The village that grew up around the home came to share the name.

Old 96 today encompasses friendly small towns, deep woodlands, and wide water. It's frequently referred to by locals as a gardener's inspiration and a sportsman's paradise. Greenwood is home to 23,000 people, also hosting Monsanto, Greenwood Mills, Sara Lee Knit Products, and Fuji Photo Film. Abbeville has a population of less than 6,000.

The South Carolina Festival of Flowers has been held in Greenwood the third weekend in June for more than three decades. The festival celebrates the beginning of summer with Park Seed Company's trial gardens tours; concerts offering beach, country, jazz, and bluegrass music; sports tournaments; and a flotilla on Lake Greenwood.

Abbeville's historic district includes the old central business district built around the restored town square. Every May the square becomes a festive marketplace filled with arts and crafts, hosting an antique and collectors' car show, a parade, and entertainment. Antiques shops and restaurants surround the square.

A PERFECT DAY IN OLD 96

Take a drive along the "freshwater coast" of the Savannah River, which is impounded in a series of lakes and forms the state's and Old 96's western boundary. If you're an angler, you'll find paradise. If you're an angler's spouse, take a book—unless, of course, you can lose yourself for hours in sheer scenic beauty. An afternoon tour of the Revolutionary War battlefield at Ninety Six should round off the day. Campers will enjoy frying their freshly caught fish over a campfire or camp stove—there's nothing like the great outdoors for enhancing the appetite. Turn in early. Tomorrow you'll want to take in the Abbeville historic district.

MORE OLD 96 HISTORY

Old 96 has witnessed its share of American history. South Carolina's first Revolutionary battle took place here at the British fort. Abbeville was the site of the birth and death of the Confederacy—South Carolina's secession papers were read here, and the Confederate armies were disbanded here at war's end.

The district has also yielded its share of leaders. It was birthplace to General Andrew Pickens, a strategist of the Revolution, as well as Vice President John C. Calhoun (1782–1850). Edgefield County alone has produced 10 state governors, including the indomitable Strom Thurmond, who ran for president as a "Dixiecrat" and, in 1997, became the longest-serving U.S. senator.

SIGHTSEEING HIGHLIGHTS

★★★★ **ABBEVILLE COUNTY MUSEUM**
Poplar and Cherry Sts., Abbeville, 864/459-4600
Adjacent to the historic Creswell Log Cabin and an educational garden, the 1859 jail houses memorabilia from early Abbeville.
Details: *Wed and Sun 3–5; other times by appointment. Free.* (2 hours)

★★★★ **GARDENS OF PARK SEED COMPANY**
S.C. Hwy. 254, Greenwood, 864/223-8555
Flower lovers won't want to pass up the opportunity to visit the trial

OLD 96 DISTRICT

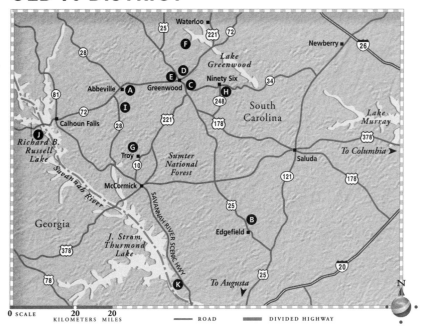

SIGHTS

- **Ⓐ** Abbeville County Museum
- **Ⓐ** Abbeville Opera House
- **Ⓐ** Burt-Stark House
- **Ⓑ** Cedar Grove Plantation
- **Ⓒ** Emerald Farm
- **Ⓓ** Gardens of Park Seed Company
- **Ⓔ** Greenwood Museum

- **Ⓕ** Lake Greenwood State Park
- **Ⓖ** Long Cane Indian Massacre Site
- **Ⓗ** Ninety Six National Historic Site
- **Ⓘ** Parsons Mountain Park
- **Ⓙ** Richard B. Russell Dam and Lake
- **Ⓚ** Thurmond Lake Visitor's Center
- **Ⓐ** Trinity Episcopal Church

Note: Items with the same letter are located in the same area.

gardens of this venerable seed supplier, whose catalogs and products are world famous. The gardens are most brilliant May through July but worth visiting anytime.

Details: *Seven miles north of Greenwood. Gardens open daily during daylight hours; garden center open Mon–Sat 9–5. Free. (2 hours)*

★★★ ABBEVILLE OPERA HOUSE
Town Square, Abbeville, 864/459-2157
This opulent opera house, now exquisitely restored, featured Fanny Brice, Jimmy Durante, and Groucho Marx on its stage during the era of traveling road shows. Today live theater is offered regularly.

Details: Free tours daily except during rehearsals. (30 minutes)

★★★ BURT-STARK HOUSE
N. Main St., Abbeville, 864/459-4297
The first reading of the secession papers took place here. Four long hard years later, on May 2, 1865, the War Council of the Confederate forces met here with President Jefferson Davis and formally disbanded the armies.

Details: Winter Fri and Sat 1–5, and by appointment. Summer Tue–Sat 1–5. $4. (1 hour)

★★★ CEDAR GROVE PLANTATION
1365 Hwy. 25 N., Edgefield, 803/637-3056
Cedar Grove, circa 1790, is one of the oldest plantations in the area and features hand-carved moldings and mantels and hand-painted French wallpaper. The original kitchen and slave quarters remain.

Details: Five miles north of Edgefield. Open by appointment only; $3; group tours only. No children allowed on tour (1–2 hours)

★★★ GREENWOOD MUSEUM
106 Main St., Greenwood, 864/229-7093
The museum displays an entire village street, including an old-time general store, a drugstore, and a one-room schoolhouse, as well as other turn-of-the-century relics, Indian artifacts, and natural history exhibits.

Details: Wed–Fri 10–5, Sat and Sun 2–5. $2 adults, $1 children under 12. (2 hours)

★★★ NINETY SIX NATIONAL HISTORIC SITE
S.C. Hwy. 248, 864/543-4068, www.nps.gov/nisi
The National Park Service operates this frontier settlement and Revolutionary War battle site and historic fort. You can retrace the steps of the early colonial antagonists at a visitor's center, along an interpretive trail, and through archaeological digs and restorations.

Details: Two miles south of Ninety Six. Daily 8–5. Free. (2 hours)

★★ EMERALD FARM
Greenwood, 864/223-9747
This real working farm has a variety of animals and a soap factory, and it sells handmade goat's milk products.
Details: *Off E. Cambridge Ave., east of Greenwood. Daily 9–5. Free. (1 hour)*

★ LAKE GREENWOOD STATE PARK
864/543-3535
Boating, fishing, hiking, mountain biking, camping, and picnicking are available at the park, a project of the Depression era's Civilian Conservation Corps. The park spreads over five peninsulas in Lake Greenwood.
Details: *Take S.C. 34 to Highway 702. Apr–Dec. $2. (2 hours)*

★ LONG CANE INDIAN MASSACRE SITE
S.C. Hwy. 117, Troy
864/984-2233 (Old 96 District Tourism Commission)
Only two large rough stones mark the common gravesite of South Carolina statesman John C. Calhoun's grandmother and 22 others killed by the Cherokee Indians in 1760. A reenactment of the Battle of Long Cane is held adjacent to the site every October.
Details: *(30 minutes)*

★ PARSONS MOUNTAIN PARK
S.C. Hwy. 28, Abbeville, 803/561-4000 (Forest Service)
www.fsfed.us/r8/fms
This recreation area in the Sumter National Forest offers a 24-mile motorcycle trail and a 26-mile horse trail, as well as hiking trails, swimming, camping, fishing, and picnic areas.
Details: *Seven miles south of Abbeville. Open daily early spring to late fall; closed in winter. Fee depends on activity. (2–4 hours)*

★ RICHARD B. RUSSELL DAM AND LAKE
S.C. Hwy. 81 south of Calhoun Falls, 864/984-2233
(Old 96 District Tourism Commission), www.old96.org
This 26,650-acre impound on the Savannah River overlooks the dam and the lake. It's a perfect place for all types of water sports.
Details: *Open daily. Free. (1–4 hours)*

★ **THURMOND LAKE VISITOR'S CENTER**
U.S. 221 at Thurmond Dam, McCormick County
864/333-1100, www.sas.usace.army.mil
Hands-on exhibits and an aquarium offer an introduction to South
Carolina lake country at this massive impoundment with a 1,200-mile
shoreline.
*Details: Open year-round. Fee for swimming, boating, and camping;
free power plant tours Apr–Dec Sat at 10. (1 hour)*

★ **TRINITY EPISCOPAL CHURCH**
Church St., Abbeville, 864/459-4600 (Greater Abbeville
Chamber of Commerce)
A historical and spiritual landmark for over 130 years, this church has
a stained-glass chancel window that was made in England and deliv-
ered to Trinity—through a Charleston blockade—during the Civil
War. The cemetery, with graves dating from 1850, is at the rear of
the church.
Details: Daily 9–5. Free. (1 hour)

FITNESS AND RECREATION

Anything you can do on water is a pastime here. From canoeing and pleasure boating to swimming and fishing, South Carolina lake country offers
water sports of all kinds. Miles of hiking and biking trails allow you to work
completely different sets of muscles. Wildlife enthusiasts and hunters will
enjoy a visit to the **Wild Turkey Center** on U.S. 25. Assembled by the
National Wild Turkey Federation, this array of wild turkey artifacts teaches
about wildlife conservation and appreciation of the game bird that, if Ben
Franklin had had his way, might have become the national symbol instead of
the bald eagle.

FOOD

The chains are here, but the locally owned and operated restaurants are a
better bet. In Abbeville, **Yoder's**, Hwy. 72 E., 864/459-5556, offers delicious
Pennsylvania Dutch dishes, including vegetarian entrées. Rotisserie chicken is a
specialty at the **Village Grill**, 114 Trinity St., 864/459-2500, but you also can
order gourmet burgers and sandwiches. The restaurant is open for lunch and
dinner Tuesday through Saturday and offers a full bar. For upscale southern
cuisine, visit the **Belmont Inn** on the Court Square 864/459-9625. Next

OLD 96 DISTRICT

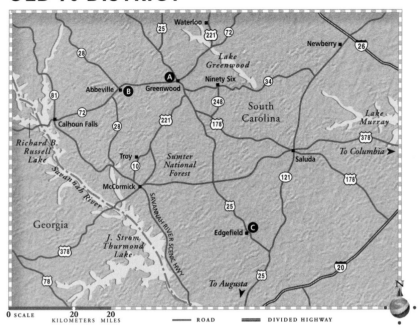

FOOD
- **A** Angelo's
- **B** Belmont Inn
- **A** Blazer's
- **A** Inn on the Square
- **A** Montague's
- **A** Ranch House
- **B** Veranda Café
- **B** Village Grill
- **B** Yoder's

LODGING
- **B** Abbewood Bed and Breakfast
- **B** Belmont Inn
- **A** Cross Creek Inn
- **A** Grace Place Bed and Breakfast
- **A** Inn on the Square
- **A** Villager Lodge
- **B** Vintage Inn

CAMPING
- **B** Hickory Knob State Resort Park
- **C** Parsons Mountain Recreation Area

Note: Items with the same letter are located in the same area.

door to the historic Abbeville Opera House, this restaurant offers a menu and service that would be the envy of any Atlanta eatery. For lunch, join the soup, salad, and sandwich crowd at the **Veranda Café**, 102 Trinity St., Abbeville, 864/459-2224.

In Greenwood, **Inn on the Square** offers an English-style pub at 104 Court Street, 864/223-4488. **Angelo's**, 2315 Montague Ave. Extension (Hwy. 25), 864/229-7222, serves prime rib, pasta, steak, and a fantastic Sunday buffet. **Blazer's** on Lake Greenwood, 4714 Hwy. 72 E., 864/223-1917, is home of "the original shrimp dip" and has an enviable reputation for serving fresh fish, seafood, and steak. **Montague's**, 115 Hampton Place Shopping Center, 864/223-1149, won "Best Restaurant" and "Best Bartender" honors in a vote by Greenwood residents. The **Ranch House**, 1213 Hwy. 72 Bypass E., 864/223-5909, specializes in steaks and seafood. The Great Flounder is recommended for dinner.

LODGING

You won't find a lot of the major hotel/motel chains here, although Greenwood has a Comfort Inn and an Econo Lodge. So exercise your adventurous spirit and look to local operations for accommodations. In Greenwood, you'll find the **Cross Creek Inn**, 1216 Montague Ave., 864/229-0642. **Inn on the Square** has 46 units at 104 Court Street, 864/223-4488 or 800/231-9109. The inn combines turn-of-the-century architecture with modern conveniences: a three-story skylit atrium, an English-style pub, and a Charleston-style courtyard with pool. **Villager Lodge**, 230 Birchtree Dr., Greenwood, 864/223-1818 or 800/328-7829, has 62 units. Greenwood also hosts **Grace Place Bed and Breakfast**, 115 Grace St., 864/229-0053, with two units.

In Abbeville, your best bets are bed-and-breakfasts and historic inns. Try the **Vintage Inn**, 909 N. Main St., 864/459-4784 or 800/890-7312, an elegantly restored, professionally decorated 1870s Victorian home with three rooms. The master suite has a Jacuzzi for two. The **Belmont Inn**, Abbeville Court Square, 864/459-9625, is on the restored town square, with its original brick streets and turn-of-the-century aura. Charming guest rooms are decorated in traditional nineteenth-century style.

Abbewood Bed and Breakfast, 605 N. Main St., Abbeville, 864/459-5822, is a circa-1860s restored home featuring leaded glass in the entranceway and a wraparound verandah with rocking chairs. Guests can stroll to the town square along a tree-lined street and talk or read in the B & B's cozy upstairs parlor.

CAMPING

Hickory Knob State Resort Park, off U.S. 378 in McCormick, 800/491-1764, offers luxury when "camping out." At the center is a modern, 80-room lodge surrounded by lakefront cottages and campsites. You can also rent the restored, 200-year-old French Huguenot Guillebeau House on the premises. Your top-of-the-line outdoor experience is embellished with a restaurant, conference center, nature trail, 18-hole championship golf course, pro shop, tennis courts, pool, skeet and archery ranges, boat slips and ramps, tackle shop, and nearby bird dog field-trial area. It's all on Thurmond Lake, which boasts incomparable bass, crappie, and catfish fishing.

Parsons Mountain Recreation Area, located on S.C. Hwy. 28 south of Abbeville, 803/561-4000, has primitive campsites and excellent trails for hiking, horses, biking, and motorcycles. Part of the Sumter National Forest, it's open April through December.

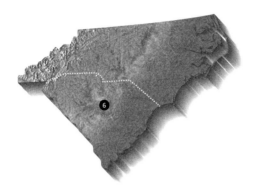

6
COLUMBIA

The capital of South Carolina is centrally located within the state in an area called, appropriately, the Midlands. It's also midway between New York and Miami, at the intersection of three major interstate highways (I-26, I-20, and I-77), and near I-85 and I-95.

The city was developed in 1786 as a compromise capital to satisfy upcountry and lowcountry political factions (although many state citizens continued to consider Charleston the center of all things cultural, even to this day). The South Carolina General Assembly held its first meeting in the new State House in January 1790, and the city was visited a year later by George Washington.

Today the city is home to nine colleges, including the University of South Carolina on its Historic Horseshoe. Here also is Fort Jackson, the United States Army's largest and most active basic training post—responsible for training about half the army's recruits each year.

Just a short drive west is the 50,000-acre impoundment of Lake Murray, ringed by marinas, campgrounds, and outdoor recreation sites on its 510 miles of shoreline. On a clear day, while crossing what was once the world's largest earthen dam, you can see the Columbia skyline in the distance. Some of the finest fishing in the world is available here, and temperatures remain moderate. January's average low is in the 40s, while the average high in July ranges in the 80s.

COLUMBIA

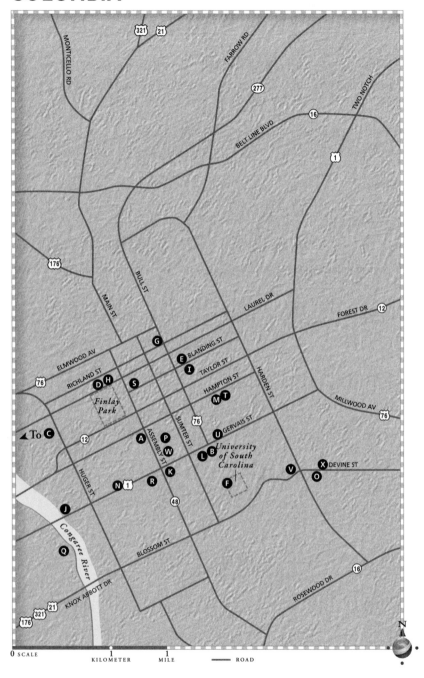

A PERFECT DAY IN COLUMBIA

Dedicated shoppers will find paradise in the malls here. But if you're on vacation with the family in tow, go first to Riverbanks Zoo, where the chatter of the monkeys will delight the children, and the shaded walkways and benches will allow you to rest as they run from habitat to habitat. This zoo is, after all, the top-ranked travel attraction in the Southeast. Plan ahead and bring fresh bread, sandwich meats or cheeses, fruit, and maybe a few pastries for a picnic lunch on the grounds. In the afternoon, visit Finlay Park, a free 14-acre downtown sight that boasts a lake, waterfall, and playground. Top off the day at Villa Tronco, Columbia's oldest Italian restaurant, which first introduced pizza to city residents. If you're still not ready for bed, ask around about nightspots.

MORE COLUMBIA HISTORY

The first Secession Convention was held in the First Baptist Church here on December 17, 1860, a year after the church was built. Ironically, the Ordinance of Secession in the Southern States had to be carried to Charleston and signed there because of a smallpox epidemic in Columbia. The historic church, which escaped the fires set by General William Tecumseh Sherman's Union forces on February 17, 1865, retains its pulpit furnishings, slave gallery, and brick-pillared portico at 1306 Hampton Street. The capitol was one of the few structures to survive when an 84-block area containing nearly 1,400 buildings was burned.

SIGHTS

- Ⓐ The Big Apple
- Ⓑ Columbia Museum of Art
- Ⓒ Columbia Riverfront Park and Historic Canal
- Ⓓ Governor's Mansion
- Ⓔ Hampton-Preston Mansion
- Ⓕ McKissick Museum
- Ⓖ Mann-Simons Cottage
- Ⓗ Palmetto Armory
- Ⓘ Robert Mills House and Park
- Ⓙ South Carolina State Museum

SIGHTS (continued)

- Ⓚ State House
- Ⓛ Trinity Episcopal Cathedral
- Ⓜ Woodrow Wilson Boyhood Home

FOOD

- Ⓝ Blue Marlin
- Ⓞ Dianne's on Devine
- Ⓟ Finlay's
- Ⓠ Joe's Crab Shack
- Ⓡ Motor Supply Company Bistro
- Ⓢ Villa Tronco

LODGING

- Ⓠ Adam's Mark Hotel
- Ⓣ Chestnut Cottage Bed and Breakfast
- Ⓤ Clarion Town House Hotel
- Ⓥ Claussen's Inn at Five Points
- Ⓦ Governor's House Hotel
- Ⓧ Whitney Hotel

Note: Items with the same letter are located in the same area.

SIGHTSEEING HIGHLIGHTS

★★★★ **RIVERBANKS ZOO AND BOTANICAL GARDEN**
500 Wildlife Pkwy., 803/779-8717, www.riverbanks.org
Ranked among the top 10 zoos in the nation and named the top travel attraction in the Southeast, Riverbanks offers natural habitats for its 2,000 animals, including sea lions, snakes, tropical birds, penguins, and even Carolina milk cows. The zoo is divided into sections, including a rain forest, desert, undersea kingdom, and down-home southern farm. The 70-acre botanical garden features formal gardens and woodland trails.

Details: Off I-126 at the Greystone Boulevard exit. Daily 9–5. $6.25 adults, $3.75 ages 3 to 12. (4 hours)

★★★★ **SOUTH CAROLINA STATE MUSEUM**
301 Gervais St., 803/898-4921, www.museum.state.sc.us
Four floors of the renovated 1894 Columbia Mill, the first totally electric textile mill in the world, house hands-on exhibits as well as art, artifacts, and natural history, science, and technology displays. The museum is fully wheelchair accessible.

Details: Mon–Sat 10–5, Sun 1–5. $4 adults, $3.50 seniors, military, and college students, $1.50 ages 6 to 17; unaccompanied children under age 13 not admitted. (3–4 hours)

★★★★ **STATE HOUSE**
Main and Gervais Sts., 803/734-2430
The South Carolina State House and grounds reopened in 1998 after a three-year, $48-million renovation. This historic capitol was constructed, beginning in 1855, of granite from a nearby quarry. It survived the shelling by Sherman's troops, although bronze stars set into the outer walls mark the strikes of Yankee cannonballs. The building was not completed until 1907. The lobby features a sweeping double staircase and art and artifacts galore. Upstairs are the two chambers, where viewers are allowed to tour the galleries. Outside, the grounds offer plenty of statuary and benches, inviting strollers and impromptu picnickers.

Details: Mon–Fri 9–5. Free. (1 hour)

★★★ **COLUMBIA MUSEUM OF ART**
Main and Hampton Sts., 803/799-2810
www.colmusart.org

SOUTH CAROLINA STATE CAPITOL BUILDING

These eclectic galleries hold masterworks of the Baroque and Renaissance periods (the famed Samuel H. Kress Collection), as well as the work of native South Carolinians and a children's gallery.

Details: Tue–Sat 10–5, Sun 1–5. $4 adults, $2 students and seniors. (3 hours)

★★★ CONGAREE SWAMP NATIONAL MONUMENT
200 Caroline Sims Rd., Hopkins, 803/776-4396
www.nps.gov/cosw

Just 20 miles southeast of Columbia is a 22,000-acre nature preserve known for its biological diversity and record-size trees—some with trunks more than 20 feet in circumference. Self-guided canoe trails, a 2.3-mile boardwalk loop for the disabled, and 18 miles of hiking trails are available.

Details: Daily dawn till dusk; call for information on guided nature walks. Free. (2 hours)

★★★ FORT JACKSON MUSEUM
Jackson Blvd., Fort Jackson, 803/751-7419

The history of the training of the American soldier from 1917 to the present is here, in this fort named for President Andrew Jackson.

Details: Tue–Fri 10–4, Sat 1–4. Closed the last two weeks in December. Free. (2 hours)

★★★ GOVERNOR'S MANSION
800 Richland St., 803/737-1710

Built in 1855 to house officers of the Arsenal Academy, this building was destroyed by Sherman's troops during the Civil War. After its reconstruction, in 1868, the house became home to the state's governors.

Details: Major renovations to be completed in 2000. Tue–Thu; tours by appointment only. Free. (1 hour)

★★★ HAMPTON-PRESTON MANSION
1615 Blanding St., 803/252-1770

Restored to its antebellum grandeur, this 1818 house was the family home of General Wade Hampton, a Confederate leader who became one of the state's most popular governors. It was spared destruction during the burning of Columbia in 1865 because it was occupied by Union officers. The house is furnished with Hampton and Preston family pieces.

Details: Tue–Sat 10:15–3:15, Sun 1:15–4:15. $4 adults, $3.50 AAA members, $2.50 students. Tickets available at the Robert Mills House gift shop, 1616 Blanding St. (1 hour)

★★★ MANN-SIMONS COTTAGE: MUSEUM OF AFRICAN-AMERICAN CULTURE
1403 Richland St., 803/252-1770

In the early 1800s, Celia Mann bought her freedom in Charleston, walked to Columbia, purchased this white frame cottage, and became a widely respected midwife. The house remained in her family for over 100 years.

Details: Tue–Sat 10:15–3:15, Sun 1:15–4:15. $4 adults, $3.50 ages 6 to 21; tickets available at Robert Mills House gift shop, 1616 Blanding St. (1 hour)

★★★ McKISSICK MUSEUM OF THE UNIVERSITY OF SOUTH CAROLINA AND THE SOUTH CAROLINIANA LIBRARY
Sumter St., 803/777-7251 (museum), 03/777-3131 (library)

A collection of museums houses art, geology, and gemstones, silver collected by Bernard Baruch, and the archives of the University of

South Carolina. The library, which dates from 1840, was the first separate college library building in the nation. The college itself was established in 1801. The center of the 218-acre campus is the Historic Horseshoe, where you'll find the McKissick.

Details: Museum open Mon–Fri 9–4, weekends 1–5. Library open Mon, Wed, Fri 8:30–5, Tue–Thu 8:30–8, Sat 9–1 in summer, until 5 remainder of year. Free. (3 hours)

★★★ ROBERT MILLS HOUSE AND PARK
1616 Blanding St., 803/252-1770

Robert Mills, one of the country's most celebrated architects and the designer of the Washington Monument, planned this mansion, built in 1823 for a prominent Columbia merchant. The house was the subsequent site of the Columbia Theological Seminary, Winthrop College (now in Rock Hill), and Columbia Bible College. One of the few extant private residences designed by Mills, the house is furnished with a fine collection of early-nineteenth-century English Regency, French Empire, and American Federal furniture. The grounds contain a maze of boxwood hedges in a finely manicured park.

Details: Tue–Sat 10:15–3:15, Sun 1:15–4:15. $4 adults, $3.50 AAA members, $2.50 students. (1½ hours)

★★ SOUTH CAROLINA CRIMINAL JUSTICE HALL OF FAME
5400 Broad River Rd., 803/896-8199

The history of law enforcement is detailed in this institution, created in honor of law enforcers who died in the line of duty. Here you will find the Melvin Purvis gun display (Purvis was the FBI agent who caught John Dillinger).

Details: Mon–Fri 8:30–5. Free. (1 hour)

★★ TRINITY EPISCOPAL CATHEDRAL
1100 Sumter St., 803/771-7300

Built in 1846, this church, a replica of England's Yorkminster Cathedral, is listed on the National Register of Historic Places. Six former governors are buried in Trinity's graveyard.

Details: (1 hour)

★★ WOODROW WILSON BOYHOOD HOME
1705 Hampton St., 803/252-1770

Thomas Woodrow Wilson lived here for four years as a teenager while his father taught at Columbia Theological Seminary and preached at First Presbyterian Church. The house is the only home Wilson's parents ever owned and includes some of the family's original furnishings, such as the bed in which the future president was born.

Details: Tue–Sat 10:15–3:15, Sun 1:15–4:15. $4 adults, $3.50 AAA members, $2.50 students; tickets available at the Robert Mills House gift shop, 1616 Blanding St. (1 hour)

★ THE BIG APPLE
1000 Hampton St., 803/252-7742
The story is that a national dance craze had its origin here in the 1930s, when young blacks danced and white children could watch for a quarter. It is also purported that the state's official dance, the shag, later originated here. Today the club, built as a synagogue in 1916, is listed on the National Register of Historic Places. It can be rented for special occasions.

Details: (15 minutes)

★ COLUMBIA RIVERFRONT PARK AND HISTORIC CANAL
Laurel St., 803/733-8331
Trails for walking, jogging, and cycling rim the Congaree River near the city's original 1906 waterworks and first hydroelectric plant.

Details: Mar–Thanksgiving daily 10–6. Free. (2 hours)

★ LEXINGTON'S OLD MILL
Hwy. 1, Lexington, 803/951-2100
Built in 1891, the mill produced mattress ticking until it closed during the Great Depression. Reclaimed as a festive marketplace offering family-oriented restaurants, shopping, and entertainment, it is home also to the Patchwork Players, a nationally known children's theater group that performs throughout the year.

Details: (2 hours)

★ PALMETTO ARMORY
1802 Lincoln St., Columbia, 803/252-7742
The armory once produced arms issued to Confederate troops during the Civil War. Muskets, rifles, and pistols bore the palmetto tree insignia.

Details: (1 hour)

FITNESS AND RECREATION

Parks with hiking and jogging trails and tennis, golf, and racquetball facilities abound. Water sports enthusiasts will automatically head for **Lake Murray**. But if you want to stay in town, go to **Frankie's Fun Park**, 140 Parkridge Dr., 803/781-2342, a 14-acre family entertainment center that includes three 18-hole Island Golf courses, a batting cage, three go-cart tracks for both rookies and experts, bumper boats, a huge arcade, and a snack bar. It's open Monday through Saturday 10 to midnight and Sunday 11 to midnight.

FOOD

A University of South Carolina graduate founded the first **Blue Marlin** here, 1200 Lincoln St., 803/799-3838, and took it to other southern cities, including Charlotte, Greensboro, and Richmond. This 1940s-style "dinner house" offers lowcountry-inspired dishes as well as fresh fish, pasta, and char-grilled steaks. It's open for lunch Monday through Friday and dinner daily. Dress is casual. Reservations are not accepted.

Dianne's on Devine, 2400 Devine St., 803/254-3535, features unique continental and Italian dishes in the place in Columbia to dine and be seen. Dianne's is open Monday though Saturday for lunch and dinner and Sunday for lunch only. Grownups and children alike will enjoy **Joe's Crab Shack**, 701 Alexander Rd., West Columbia, 803/926-8173, where you can eat in a crabshack party atmosphere on the banks of the Congaree River. It's a good-food, casual-dress, inexpensive kind of place that's open for lunch and dinner every day.

Finlay's, 1200 Hampton St., 803/771-7000, in the Adam's Mark Hotel, serves three meals daily with a brunch buffet on Sunday. The menu is traditional American with regional specialties. **California Dreaming** at 401 South Main Street, 803/254-6767, located in the city's 100-year-old Union Railroad Station, has it all, from seafood platters to prime rib. Children's dishes are priced around $4. Open for lunch and dinner daily.

You simply can't visit Columbia and not eat at **Lizard's Thicket**. Begun in a renovated house in 1978, the restaurant now has 11 locations and continually wins Best Country Cooking, Best Family Restaurant, and Best Fried Chicken honors from *The State* newspaper readers. If you hunger for a taste of the South, the place will satisfy, with hot biscuits, macaroni and cheese, fried okra, fried chicken or country ham, and sweet iced tea. To find the location nearest you, call 803/779-6407. Open daily for breakfast, lunch, and dinner.

There is barbecue, and then there is barbecue. In North Carolina, the sauce

COLUMBIA REGION

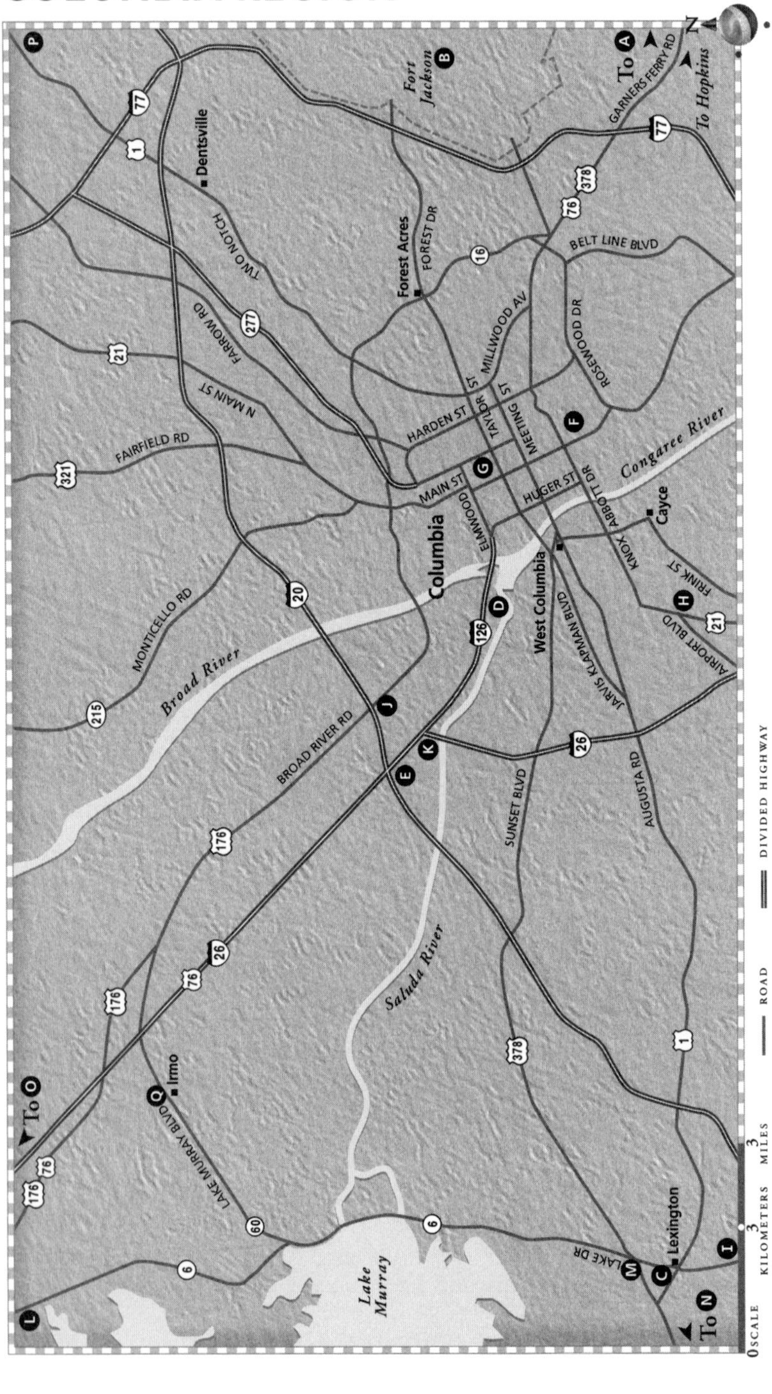

To A
To Hopkins
GARNERS FERRY RD
N

P

77
1
Dentsville
TWO NOTCH
FARROW RD
277
N MAIN ST
21
FAIRFIELD RD
321

Fort Jackson
B

Forest Acres
FOREST DR
16
BELT LINE BLVD
76
378
77

MILLWOOD AV
HARDEN ST
TAYLOR ST
MEETING ST
ROSEWOOD DR
F

Columbia
MAIN ST
G
ELMWOOD
HUGER ST
KNOX ABBOTT DR
Congaree River
Cayce
FRINK ST
H
21
AIRPORT BLVD

MONTICELLO RD
Broad River
20
126
D
West Columbia
JARVIS KLEMAN BLVD

215
BROAD RIVER RD
J
K
E
SUNSET BLVD
26
AUGUSTA RD

176
176
26
76
Saluda River
378
1

To O
176 75
Irmo
Q
LAKE MURRAY BLVD
60
6

Lake Murray
L
6
LAKE DR
M
C
Lexington
I
To N

SCALE
0
KILOMETERS   MILES
3
3

ROAD   DIVIDED HIGHWAY

is red; at **Maurice's Piggy Park** (main location at 1600 Charleston Hwy., West Columbia, 803/791-5887), it's golden. Pork and chicken barbecue are offered at nine locations throughout the area, and Maurice's famous sauce is sold in grocery stores. Open for lunch and dinner.

Motor Supply Company Bistro, 920 Gervais St., 803/256-6687, was once an actual motor supply company. Today this trendy restaurant in an 1890s Historic Register building offers a daily-changing menu featuring regional cuisine (such as grilled quail and pink-peppercorn salmon). It's open for brunch Sunday, lunch Monday through Saturday, and dinner Tuesday through Sunday.

At the **Restaurant at Cinnamon Hill**, 808 South Lake Drive off I-20 West in Lexington, 803/957-8297, you'll find quite the impressive Sunday buffet. Dine on the outside terrace, while children roam the grounds of the 1890s Victorian house, listed on the National Historic Register. Open Tuesday through Sunday for lunch, Thursday through Saturday for dinner, and Sunday for brunch. Expect Carolina crab cakes, seafood bisque, Cajun scallops, grilled tuna, and much, much more.

Saving the best for last, try **Villa Tronco**, 1213 Blanding St., 803/256-7677, in the last remaining volunteer firehouse in Columbia. Home of the Palmetto Fire Engine Company from the 1870s to 1921, the building now houses the first Italian restaurant in Columbia. Started when a local couple began cooking spaghetti and meatballs for soldiers of Italian descent at Fort Jackson during World War II, the restaurant offers traditional Italian lunch and dinner favorites, homemade pastas and breads, fresh seafood specialties, and Tronco's famous cheesecake.

SIGHTS

- Ⓐ Congaree Swamp National Monument
- Ⓑ Fort Jackson Museum
- Ⓒ Lexington's Old Mill
- Ⓓ Riverbanks Zoo and Botanical Garden
- Ⓔ South Carolina Criminal Justice Hall of Fame

FOOD

- Ⓕ California Dreaming
- Ⓖ Lizard's Thicket (11 locations)
- Ⓗ Maurice's Piggy Park
- Ⓘ Restaurant at Cinnamon Hill

LODGING

- Ⓙ Royal Inn
- Ⓚ Sheraton Hotel and Conference Center
- Ⓛ Stewart House Inn and Meeting Place

CAMPING

- Ⓜ Barnyard RV Park
- Ⓝ Cedar Pond Campground
- Ⓞ Dreher Island State Park
- Ⓟ Sesquicentennial State Park
- Ⓠ Woodsmoke Campground

LODGING

Adam's Mark Hotel, 1200 Hampton St., 803/771-7000, is Columbia's largest hotel and its only uptown luxury hotel. It offers full service to 300 units, is wheelchair accessible, and has a health club. In case yours is a working vacation, secretarial services are available. **Governor's House Hotel**, 1301 Main St., 803/779-7790, is one-third the size of the Adam's Mark and is conveniently located uptown near the University of South Carolina, state capitol, and federal courthouse. Also uptown, at 1615 Gervais St., 803/771-8711 or 800/277-8711, is the **Clarion Town House Hotel**, Columbia's most historic hotel. The all-suite **Whitney Hotel**, southeast of the town center at 700 Woodrow Street, 803/252-0845 or 800/637-4008, costs about $120 per night. Suites have complete kitchens as well as washers, dryers, and balconies.

Claussen's Inn at Five Points, 2003 Greene St., 803/765-0440 or 800/622-3382, is Columbia's landmark 29-unit bed-and-breakfast inn near USC and the Capitol. A continental breakfast is delivered to your room, and complimentary wine, sherry, and brandy are served in the lobby. Even smaller is the **Chestnut Cottage Bed and Breakfast**, 1718 Hampton St., 803/256-1718, with just five rooms. Turn-down service and a delightful breakfast are included at this 1850 Federal-style cottage.

Among the newest of Columbia's motels is the **Royal Inn**, 1323 Garner Lane, 803/750-5060. **Sheraton Hotel and Conference Center**, 2100 Bush River Rd., 803/731-0300 or 800/325-3535, is what you'd expect of a Sheraton, including 40 whirlpool suites, indoor/outdoor pools, and a tropical atrium bar. Anticipate lots of conferences in session, since the hotel is easily accessible to interstate highways and the airport. Located on Lake Murray, the **Stewart House Inn and Meeting Place**, 500 Club Pointe, Prosperity, 803/364-0558, offers a change from the usual uptown hostelries.

CAMPING

Numerous camping opportunities are available in the Columbia-Lake Murray area. These include 97 sites at **Barnyard RV Park**, 201 Oak Dr., Lexington, 803/957-1238; 25 sites at **Cedar Pond Campground**, 4721 Fairview Rd., Leesville, 803/657-5993; and 43 sites at **Woodsmoke Campground**, 11302 Broad River Rd., Irmo, 803/781-3451.

You will find upscale lakeside villas and 112 campsites, complete with a boat ramp and nature trails, at **Dreher Island State Park** on Lake Murray. It's located at 3677 State Park Rd. (Exit 91 off I-26 in Newberry County), Prosperity, 803/364-4152. At **Sesquicentennial State Park**, 9564 Two

Notch Rd., 13 miles northeast of Columbia on U.S. 1, 803/788-2706, you'll find 87 camping sites, plus picnic shelters, swimming, exercise and nature trails, pedal boats, and lake fishing. Of special interest is a log house on the grounds dating to 1756 and believed to be the oldest building in Richland County.

NIGHTLIFE

This is a college town, so expect nightspots with a lot of loud music and flashing lights. But Columbia is the center of the state's business and government, so you'll also find many low-key, laid-back entertainment venues. From among the variety, these offer something different: **Jillian's Billiards and Games**, 800 Gervais St., 803/779-7789, is a playground for grownups, with virtual simulator games, billiards, a cigar lounge, and video games galore. It's open nightly. **Remingtons**, in the Sheraton Lounge, 2100 Bush River Rd., 803/731-0300, opens at 4:30 Monday through Saturday. On Thursday, people from all over the Carolinas arrive to shag with Roger Daley. Don't know how to shag? Watch—you'll learn. End your day or evening at **Tiffany Rose Lounge** at the Adam's Mark Hotel, 1200 Hampton St., 803/771-7000, in an elegant hotel setting.

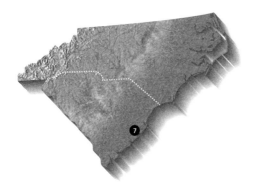

7
SANTEE COOPER

This five-county area experienced the lingering effects of the Great Depression before the U.S. Army Corps of Engineers dammed the Santee River and created the Santee Cooper lakes, Marion and Moultrie. When the New Deal brought electricity to rural South Carolina in 1942, the economy began to rebound. Today the Santee Cooper lakes generate both electric and tourism power, attracting 1.5 million tourists annually.

Fishing is king here, and much of community life revolves around that activity. Covering more than 171,000 acres, the Santee Cooper lakes are ringed with fish camps, marinas, campgrounds, and modern motels. The lakes boast world- and state-record catches of striped, largemouth, hybrid, and white bass and catfish (an Arkansas blue catfish weighed in at just under 110 pounds).

Careful attention has been paid to preservation. Santee Cooper provides a haven for nature lovers with state parks, refuges, and gardens. These include the Santee National Wildlife Refuge, Woods Bay State Park, the Dennis Wildlife Center, and the Pocotaligo Conservatory Area Park. The Edisto River, running through more than 200 miles of swamp forests, is the longest black-water river in the world.

The town of Santee, population about 700, started life as an intersection but now boasts three golf courses and a recently constructed Greek Revival town hall. The largest area city is Sumter, population 42,000, settled about 1740 and named for General Thomas Sumter, the Revolutionary War hero nicknamed

SANTEE COOPER

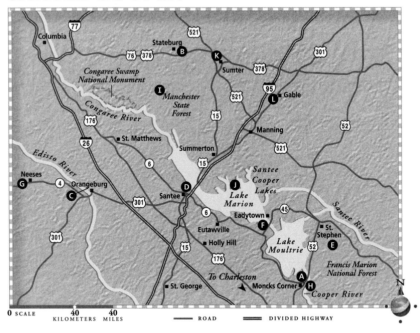

SIGHTS

- **A** Berkeley Museum
- **B** Church of the Holy Cross
- **C** Edisto Memorial Gardens and Horne Wetlands Park
- **D** Fort Watson
- **E** Francis Marion National Forest
- **F** Francis Marion Tomb
- **G** I.P. Stanback Museum and Planetarium
- **A** Mepkin Abbey
- **G** Neeses Farm Museum
- **H** Old Santee Canal State Park
- **I** Poinsett State Park
- **J** Santee National Wildlife Refuge
- **K** Sumter County Museum and Archives
- **L** Swan Lake – Iris Gardens
- **B** Thomas Sumter Tomb

Note: Items with the same letter are located in the same area.

"the Fighting Gamecock." Now you know where the University of South Carolina got its mascot.

A PERFECT DAY IN SANTEE COOPER

If you visit Santee Cooper country, there's a 99 percent chance it's because you are a fishing aficionado. So arise before daybreak, pack a lunch, take your fishing gear to the pier where you've already booked a boat, put on your life jacket, and cast off. Every place is a good place to fish here, so don't waste time hunting for the spot a local told you is the best. Fish and snooze the morning, or most of the day, away. When you've caught all you want, head for shore and the camp stove or campfire to cook your catch. Go to bed early so you can get up at dawn again tomorrow. The fish are calling. Or is that a whippoorwill?

SIGHTSEEING HIGHLIGHTS

★★★★ EDISTO MEMORIAL GARDENS AND HORNE WETLANDS PARK
U.S. 301, Orangeburg, 803/536-4074

Sheer beauty is the attraction of this 110-acre city park, located on the banks of the North Edisto River in Orangeburg. The park features moss-draped oaks, camellias, azaleas, flowering crab apples, day lilies, dogwoods, and nearly 10,000 rose bushes—it's a testing ground for the All American Rose selection process. It also has tennis courts and picnic areas.

Details: Daily 8 to dusk. Free. (2 hours)

★★★★ SWAN LAKE-IRIS GARDENS
Sumter, 800/688-4748, www.sumter.sc.us

Eight species of swan—the royal white mute, whistling, bewick, black necked, coscoroba, whooper, black Australian, and trumpeter—glide over a dark-water lake ringed by Dutch and Japanese irises and dotted with water lilies. The 150 acres of irises peak in early summer, but the gardens—including azaleas, dogwoods, yellow jessamines, wisterias, day lilies, southern magnolias, gardenias, crape myrtles, annuals, camellias, hollies, and evergreens—schedule their blooms to guarantee a year-round show.

Details: East of I-95 above Lakes Marion and Moultrie, Sumter. Free. (1–2 hours)

★★★ BERKELEY MUSEUM
Moncks Corner, 843/899-5101
This museum inside the entrance to Old Santee Canal State Park houses historical exhibits and interpretive displays about the region. *Details: Off U.S. 52 Bypass. Mon–Sat 9–5, Sun 1–5. $2, plus parking fee. (1 hour)*

★★★ I. P. STANBACK MUSEUM AND PLANETARIUM
300 College St. NE, Orangeburg, 803/536-7174
www.draco.scsu.edu
On the grounds of South Carolina State University in Orangeburg, the museum is a treasure trove of African and African American work. *Details: Sept–May weekdays 9–4:30. Planetarium shows Oct–Apr second Sun 3, 4, and by appointment. Admission varies. (2 hours)*

★★★ SANTEE NATIONAL WILDLIFE REFUGE
803/478-2217
This sanctuary, frequented by migrating waterfowl, has a foot trail, an observation tower, and a visitor's center with interpretive exhibits. *Details: Off U.S. 301-15, seven miles south of Summerton. Weekdays 8–4. Free. (2–3 hours)*

★★ MEPKIN ABBEY
1098 Mepkin Abbey Rd., 843/761-8509
www.mepkinabbey.org
Once the home of patriot Henry Laurens, who was imprisoned in the Tower of London, and later of Henry and Clare Boothe Luce (who are buried on the grounds), this plantation is now a monastery noted for its church and gardens. *Details: 13 miles southeast of Moncks Corner off S.C. 402. Daily 9–4:30. Free. (1–2 hours)*

★★ NEESES FARM MUSEUM
U.S. 321, Neeses, 803/247-5811
Antique farm and domestic implements are displayed here. *Details: Open by appointment only. Admission by donation. (1 hour)*

★★ SUMTER COUNTY MUSEUM AND ARCHIVES
122 N. Washington St., Sumter, 803/775-0908

The Williams-Brice House, built in 1845, is filled with Victorian furnishings, historical objects, and an archives. The grounds feature formal gardens.

Details: *Museum open Tue–Sat 10–5, Sun 2–5. Archives open Tue–Sat 10–5. Admission by donation. (2 hours)*

★★ CHURCH OF THE HOLY CROSS
S.C. 261, Stateburg, 803/854-2131
(Santee Cooper Counties Promotion Commission),
www.santeecoopercountry.org

It's a beautiful Gothic revival church, with a circa-1850 sanctuary built of packed earth blocks, but its prime attraction at Christmas is the poinsettia-bedecked grave of Joel Poinsett, who was buried here in 1851. Poinsett is the South Carolina statesman who brought the flower from Mexico to the United States, where it became synonymous with Christmas.

Details: *(30 minutes)*

★ FORT WATSON
803/854-2131 or 800/227-8510
www.santeecoopercountry.org

The fort was originally an Indian mound (a prehistoric ceremonial center and burial site), the largest of its kind discovered on the Atlantic coastal plain. It later became the site of an intensive Revolutionary War battle (the Americans won). The fort allows a panoramic view of Santee Cooper and the countryside.

Details: *Three miles north of Santee on U.S. 301 and 15. Free. (30 minutes)*

★ FRANCIS MARION NATIONAL FOREST
803/561-4000, www.fs/fed.us/r8/fms

This wildlife-rich, 250,000-acre forest welcomes campers, hikers, and picnickers to the site of the battle between the forces of British colonel Banastre Tarleton and Revolutionary general Francis Marion, "the Swamp Fox."

Details: *Off U.S. 17 north of Charleston. (2 hours)*

★ FRANCIS MARION TOMB
803/854-2131, www.santeecoopercountry.org

The Revolutionary War hero of French Huguenot descent, dubbed

SCDPRT

"the Swamp Fox," is buried here on land that was once his family's plantation, Belle Isle. The city of Marion and Francis Marion University are named for him.

Details: Off S.C.45 between S.C. 6 and Eadytown. (30 minutes)

★ OLD SANTEE CANAL STATE PARK
Moncks Corner, 843/899-5200
This park features the southern end of the Santee Canal, which opened in 1800 and operated for 50 years. Canoe rentals, trails, boardwalks, picnicking, and an interpretive center are offered.

Details: Off U.S. 52 Bypass. Daily 9–5. Parking $3. (2 hours)

★ POINSETT STATE PARK
803/494-8177
This 1,000-acre park, named for U.S. statesman Joel Roberts Poinsett, is noted for its live oaks and rhododendron, a curious blend of upcountry and lowcountry flora. The park provides rental cabins and boats, camping facilities, and a variety of nature programs.

Details: Off S.C. 261, 18 miles southwest of Sumter. Daily 9–6. Parking $2. (2 hours)

★ THOMAS SUMTER TOMB

"The Fighting Gamecock," Thomas Sumter, was a Revolutionary War hero who gave his name to a county and a city in South Carolina and his nickname to the University of South Carolina athletic teams.
Details: *Near Statebrug; follow signs from intersection of U.S. 76-328 and S.C. 261. (30 minutes)*

FITNESS AND RECREATION

A toll-free hotline in South Carolina provides an up-to-date fishing report for the state's major lakes and coastal reports on inshore, offshore, and pier fishing. You can find out about fishing regulations, licenses, boat launches, and disabled access to camping and fishing sites by calling 800/ASK-FISH.

FOOD

If it's fish you want, check out **Bell's Marina Restaurant** at 12907 Old Highway 6 in Eutawville, 803/492-7924, where catfish is a specialty. You can also choose country homestyle cooking, including steak and seafood. Open for breakfast and lunch daily. If you have a hankering for lowcountry cuisine, visit **The Dock** on Trailrace Canal, Moncks Corner, 843/761-8080. It's famous for hushpuppies as well as ribs and steak. Motor your boat right up to the dock and eat enjoying the view. Open for lunch and dinner Tuesday through Sunday. Eutawville offers a more upscale menu built around great steak at **Chef's Choice Steakhouse**, Hwy. 6, 803/492-3410. It's open for lunch and dinner every day.

House of Pizza is located at 910 Calhoun Dr. (U.S. 301), Orangeburg, 803/531-4000. Although the menu offers pizza, sandwiches, burgers, and salads, the specialty is Greek cooking, including moussaka and baklava. Prices are moderate, and you can get a picnic to go. Open daily for lunch and dinner.

Jake's Steak and Ribs, Hwy. 6, Santee, 803/854-3999, is a restaurant and lounge specializing in—what else?—steak and barbecued ribs. There's live entertainment, too. Open from 5 p.m. to 2 a.m. daily. Also in Santee is the **Verandah Seafood Restaurant**, Hwy. 6, I-95 Exit 98, 803/854-4695, where seafood is the specialty, but the steaks are delicious. Open daily for dinner. In Holly Hill, you'll find that the **Smoak House Family Restaurant** on Old State Road, 803/496-3717, is just what it claims to be, with country cooking and sandwiches. Open for breakfast and lunch Monday through Saturday.

Finally, eat-in or take-out barbecue—pork, chicken, and all the fixings—is a treat from **Sweatman's Barbecue**, Hwy. 453, Eutawville. Every room in this

SANTEE COOPER

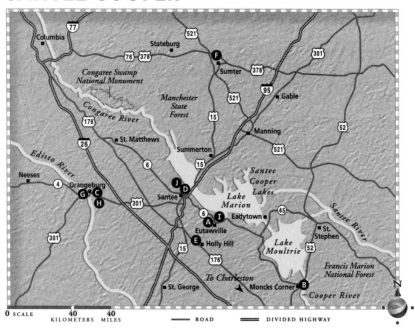

FOOD

- **A** Bell's Marina Restaurant
- **A** Chef's Choice Steakhouse
- **B** The Dock
- **C** House of Pizza
- **D** Jake's Steak and Ribs
- **E** Smoak House Family Restaurant
- **A** Sweatman's Barbecue
- **D** Verandah Seafood Restaurant

LODGING

- **D** Ashley Inn/Tara Inn
- **F** Bed and Breakfast of Sumter
- **G** Magnolia House
- **G** Orangeburg Motor Inn
- **D** Ramada Inn
- **D** Randolph's Landing Motel and Restaurant
- **H** Sun Inn

CAMPING

- **I** Rocks Pond Campground and Marina
- **J** Santee Resort State Park

Note: Items with the same letter are located in the same area.

old country home is a dining area, and the eatery was once featured in *Southern Living* magazine. Open for lunch and dinner Friday and Saturday only.

LODGING

As Santee Cooper's largest city, Sumter has the most hotel/motel accommodations, including Best Western, Economy, Hampton, Holiday, and Ramada. But also consider the **Bed and Breakfast of Sumter**, 6 Park Ave., 803/773-2903, in the historic district, a charming 1896 home with a large front porch complete with a swing and rocking chairs. Rates run $60 to $70 and include a gourmet breakfast. No children younger than 12 are allowed. Also in Sumter, and with slightly higher rates, is **Magnolia House**, 230 Church St., 803/775-6694, a Greek Revival home in the historic area. Its host (his name is Buck Rogers, but don't tease) does allow children. A full southern breakfast is served, and the walled English garden is a feast for the eyes.

Randolph's Landing Motel and Restaurant, at the end of Route 260 south of Manning, 803/478-2152, is the home of the annual national and state championship catfishing tournament on Lake Marion. It has everything you need, including a fishing pier, guide service, boat ramps, a tackle shop, and live bait.

Ashley Inn/Tara Inn, 9112 Old Hwy. 6, Santee, 803/854-3870 or 800/ 827-4539, has nothing to do with *Gone With the Wind* but is an extremely reasonable place to stay. A double room costs less than $40 per night, and golf packages are available. Also recommended are **Orangeburg Motor Inn**, 2805 Bamberg Rd., Orangeburg, 803/534-7180; **Ramada Inn**, 123 Mall St., Santee, 803/854-2191 (rates $50 to $60, with a putting green on the premises); and the **Sun Inn**, 610 Calhoun Dr., Orangeburg, 803/531-1921.

CAMPING

Campgrounds abound in Santee, and the following are highly recommended. At **Rocks Pond Campground and Marina**, 235 Rocks Pond Rd., Eutawville, 803/492-7711, rates range from $14 to $26 per night. This favorite camping spot offers boat, pontoon, and camper rentals, as well as camper and tent sites, guide service, hunting and fishing, a beach, and more.

Santee Resort State Park, off Highway 6, three miles northwest of Santee, 803/854-2408, is the site of numerous major fishing tournaments. Located in the heart of Santee Cooper, the park offers 30 cabins and 150 campsites in two family camping areas. It provides boat rentals, swimming, fishing, nature trails, and interpretive programs.

8
HILTON HEAD AND
THE LOWCOUNTRY

Hilton Head, one of South Carolina's Sea Islands, first hit the newspapers when its discoverer, William Hilton, advertised for settlers in seventeenth-century London. He cited the island's "pleasant ayr" as an attraction. Today Hilton Head attracts people who can afford to vacation anywhere. Millionaires shop in the island's villages, sun themselves on the incomparable beaches, and golf on its links.

The Sea Islands and surrounding lowcountry were explored and settled in the early sixteenth century, when indigo and rice were the region's primary crops. Later, Sea Island cotton made many planters rich.

The Gullahs, or Sea Island blacks, developed a language and way of life almost foreign to the rest of the state and nation. The Gullah language is heard here even today. The movie *Glory* was filmed in this area, primarily because five Gullah regiments served beside the Massachusetts 54th, the famed black regiment depicted in the film. One of them, the First South Carolina Volunteers, was the earliest regiment of freed Southern slaves to join the Union service.

Today, the major crop here is tourists—or, you might argue, golfers. Hilton Head has more than 20 championship golf courses, as well as 300 tennis courts. Mild temperatures, averaging in the 50s in winter and the high 80s in summer, encourage outdoor activities year-round. You might never want to go home.

HILTON HEAD AND
THE LOWCOUNTRTY

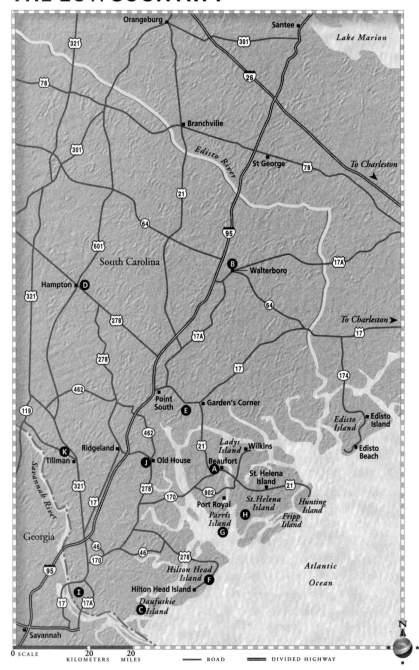

Orangeburg

Santee

Lake Marion

321

301

26

78

Branchville

Edisto River

St George

78

To Charleston

301

21

64

95

601

South Carolina

B

Walterboro

17A

Hampton ■ D

321

278

64

To Charleston ➤

17A

17

278

17

174

462

Point
South

Garden's Corner

*Edisto
Island*

■ Edisto
Island

119

E

■ Edisto
Beach

462

*Ladys
Island*

Wilkins

K

Ridgeland ■

21

Tillman ■

J

■ Old House

Beaufort
A

St. Helena
Island

21

*St.Helena
Island*

*Hunting
Island*

Savannah River

321

278

170

802

17

Port Royal ■

H

*Fripp
Island*

*Parris
Island*

G

Georgia

46

46

278

Atlantic

95

170

*Hilton Head
Island*
F

Ocean

17

I

Hilton Head Island ■

17A

Daufuskie
C *Island*

Savannah

N

0 SCALE   20   20
KILOMETERS   MILES   ━━━ ROAD   ══════ DIVIDED HIGHWAY

A PERFECT DAY IN HILTON HEAD AND THE LOWCOUNTRY

Golf. Golf. Golf. The name Hilton Head is synonymous with golf, with people from northern climes flocking here for balmy golf weather year-round. The annual MCI Classic—the Heritage of Golf on Pete Dye's Harbour Town Golf Links at Sea Pines Plantation—is held here. And Hilton Head and the surrounding islands of Fripp, Cat, and Callawassie, as well as the lowcountry city of Beaufort, have 40 resort courses. You won't get your fill of golf here in a day. It will take more than a week of perfect days, on courses designed by Robert Trent Jones, George Fazio, Arthur Hills, Bob Cupp, Jack Nicklaus, and Clyde Johnston, before you will be willing to settle at the nineteenth hole. Then you'll want to get to bed early, anticipating a dawn tee time.

SIGHTSEEING HIGHLIGHTS

★★★★ BEAUFORT MUSEUM
713 Craven St., Beaufort, 843/525-7077

Once an arsenal, this building was constructed in 1798 of brick and tabby (a cement first made here by the Spanish, who burned oyster shells to extract lime, then mixed it with sand and shells). The museum exhibits relics of war and early industry in Beaufort. It once housed the Beaufort Volunteer Artillery, a pre–Civil War, African American unit that included Robert Smalls, famous for escaping slavery by piloting a Confederate ship past rebel forces and delivering it into Union hands in Beaufort. Smalls later became the first African American in the U.S. Congress.

Details: Mon–Tue, Thu–Sat 10–5. $2 adults, 50 cents students. (2 hours)

SIGHTS

- Ⓐ Beaufort Museum
- Ⓑ Colleton County Court House
- Ⓑ Colleton Museum
- Ⓒ Daufuskie Island
- Ⓓ Hampton County Museum
- Ⓔ Old Sheldon Church
- Ⓕ Old Zion Cemetery
- Ⓖ Parris Island Museum
- Ⓗ Penn Center
- Ⓐ St. Helena's Episcopal Church
- Ⓘ Savannah National Wildlife Refuge
- Ⓙ Thomas Heyward Jr. Tomb
- Ⓚ Tillman Sand Ridge Heritage Preserve

Note: Items with the same letter are located in the same area.

★★★★ COLLETON MUSEUM
239 N. Jefferies Blvd., Walterboro, 843/549-2303
A restored 1855 jail holds a collection of artifacts and information about the cultural heritage of Colleton County (named for its lord proprietor, Sir John Colleton), once a major center of rice production.
Details: Tue–Fri 10–5. Free. (2 hours)

★★★★ PARRIS ISLAND MUSEUM
Marine Corps Recruit Depot, Parris Island, 843/525-2951
The museum presents the history of the island from 1564 and features U.S. Marine Corps uniforms and weapons. In addition to the Iron Mike monument, there are monuments to 1564 Huguenot pioneer Jean Ribaut and to the flag-raising on Iwo Jima.
Details: Daily 10–4:30, Thu 10–7, Fri 8–4:30. Free. (2–3 hours)

★★★ HAMPTON COUNTY MUSEUM
702 First St. W., Hampton, 803/943-5484
Located in a 115-year-old jail, the museum features a military room, genealogical research room, country store, and artifacts of local and natural history.
Details: Thu 10–noon and 4–7, Sun 3–5. Free. (2 hours)

★★★ PENN CENTER
Martin Luther King Dr., St. Helena Island, 843/838-2432
The first school for freed slaves in the South was established here during the Civil War, and the center's York W. Bailey Museum offers exhibits on the history of African Americans of the Sea Islands.
Details: Mon–Fri 11–4. $4 adults, $2 children. (2 hours)

★★ COLLETON COUNTY COURT HOUSE
Hampton St., Walterboro, 843/549-5791
This is where Robert Barnwell Rhett (is this where Margaret Mitchell found her hero's name?) called for the immediate secession of the state legislature at South Carolina's first nullifaction meeting in 1828. Completed in 1822, the building has outside walls three bricks (28 inches) thick.
Details: Mon–Fri 8:30–5. (1 hour)

★★ DAUFUSKIE ISLAND
This remote rural island, accessible by boat, has hosted former slaves

and their descendants, who made a living from the land and the sea. Today, part of the island is under resort development. It was the setting for South Carolina novelist Pat Conroy's *The Water is Wide*, which was translated into the movie *Conrack*. Several Hilton Head marinas offer tours.

Details: (2–3 hours)

★★ OLD ZION CEMETERY
U.S. 278, Hilton Head Island
The cemetery's gravesites include those of families from prominent Lowcountry Sea Island cotton plantations, most predating 1860. This is also the site of the Zion Chapel of Ease, part of the Anglican St. Luke's Parish, established in 1767.

Details: (1 hour)

★★ ST. HELENA'S EPISCOPAL CHURCH
505 Church St., Beaufort, 843/522-1712
Built in 1724, the church served as a hospital during the Civil War for the Union army, when its flat tombstones were used as operating tables.

Details: Church closed for renovations until the year 2000, but the churchyard is open. Free. (1 hour)

★ OLD SHELDON CHURCH
Junction of Hwys. 21 and 235
843/726-8126 (Jasper County Chamber of Commerce)
All that remains are ruins of the graceful church that was built in 1753, burned by the British in 1779, rebuilt, then burned again by Sherman's Union forces in 1865.

Details: (30 minutes)

★ SAVANNAH NATIONAL WILDLIFE REFUGE
U.S. 17, Jasper County, 912/652-4415
Once a community of rice plantations, the refuge now offers a nature drive winding through 26,295 acres. They provide sanctuary for migratory birds and innumerable species of wildlife.

Details: Daily dawn–dusk. Free. (3 hours)

★ THOMAS HEYWARD JR. TOMB
Hwys. 28 and 462, Jasper County

HILTON HEAD
AND THE LOWCOUNTRY

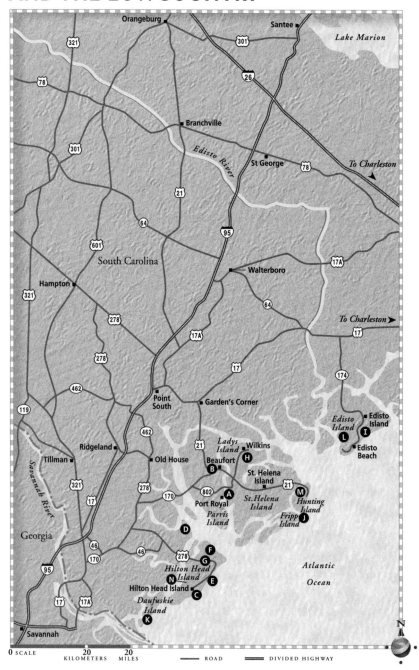

Heyward, a signer of the Declaration of Independence, is entombed at Old House Plantation.

Details: *Open daily. Free. (30 minutes)*

★ **TILLMAN SAND RIDGE HERITAGE PRESERVE**
Hwy. S-17-119, Jasper County, 803/625-3569
This 952-acre tract protects the endangered gopher tortoise and has trails for hiking.

Details: *Five miles west of Tillman. Hiking by permit only. (2 hours)*

FOOD

No matter what your taste, you can satisfy your cravings in the lowcountry. Everybody here knows about **Aunt Chilada's Easy Street Café**, 69 Pope Ave., Hilton Head, 843/785-7700, which serves Mexican and Italian specialties, plus great steaks and seafood. Open daily, Sunday for brunch only. Another favorite is the **Old Oyster Factory**, Marshland Rd., Hilton Head, 843/681-6040, a family restaurant built on the site of one of the island's original oyster canneries. The seafood and steaks are great, and only moderately expensive.

Hilton Head Brewing Company, 7-C Greenwood Dr., Hilton Head, 843/785-BREW, open daily at Hilton Head Plaza, is the state's first brewpub and restaurant. The menu offers baby back ribs, steak, seafood, chicken, bratwurst, and pizza. An added attraction is a children's menu. Also on Hilton

FOOD
- **A** 11th Street Dockside Restaurant
- **B** Anchorage House
- **C** Aunt Chilada's Easy Street Café
- **D** Crazy Crab
- **E** Fitzgerald's Restaurant
- **F** Hilton Head Brewing Company
- **G** Old Oyster Factory
- **H** Plantation Inn Restaurant
- **I** Steamer's Restaurant
- **I** Sunset Grill

LODGING
- **D** Crowne Plaza Resort
- **D** Disney's Hilton Head Island Resort
- **J** Fripp Island Resort
- **D** Hilton Head Island Beach and Tennis Resorts
- **H** Main Street Inn
- **G** Plantation Inn
- **K** South Beach Marina Village

CAMPING
- **L** Edisto Beach State Park
- **M** Hunting Island State Park
- **N** Outdoor Resorts Motor Coach Resort
- **N** Outdoor Resorts RV Resort and Yacht Club

Note: Items with the same letter are located in the same area.

Head is **Fitzgerald's Restaurant**, on the ocean at South Forest Beach Drive, 843/785-5151. It's open for dinner daily and serves live Maine lobster, prime rib, and fresh shrimp, with entrées priced from $10.95. A complete children's menu and take-out are also available.

Among other highly recommended lowcountry restaurants is **11th Street Dockside Restaurant**, 1699 11th St. W., Port Royal, 843/524-7433, which has moderate prices. **Anchorage House**, 1103 Bay St., Beaufort, 843/524-9392, is expensive but worth it. **Sunset Grill** on Edisto Beach, 843/869-1010, is moderately priced, while the **Crazy Crab**, Harbour Town Yacht Basin, 843/363-2722, is famous for its fresh seafood. It's open daily for lunch and dinner. On Lady's Island, **Plantation Inn Restaurant**, White Hall Dr., 843/521-1700, and **Steamer's Restaurant**, Hwy. 21, 843/522-0210, are both expensive, but the food is fantastic.

LODGING

Upscale accommodations are available here in record numbers, from all the names you like to be pampered by: Westin, Players Club, Hyatt, Radisson, Hilton. You aren't likely to be dissatisfied with any of these choices, but others exist, including plenty of weekly or monthly vacation rentals.

Crowne Plaza Resort, 130 Shipyard Dr., Shipyard Plantation, Hilton Head Island, 843/842-2400 or 800/334-1881, offers more than 340 rooms. Included are Camp Castaway for Kids, a complete fitness center, indoor and outdoor pools, golf and racquet clubs, and 12 miles of white-sand beach. The much, much smaller but luxurious and more romantic **Main Street Inn**, 2200 Main St., Hilton Head, 843/681-3001 or 800/471-3001, features Charlestonian gardens and a European spa.

You know what you can expect from Disney, and you get it at **Disney's Hilton Head Island Resort**, 22 Harborside Lane, 843/341-4100 or 800/453-4911. This is no Mickey Mouse operation. The resort combines luxury with modern conveniences. Its one- to three-bedroom lowcountry-style villas start at $99.

Also on Hilton Head is **South Beach Marina Village**, 232 S. Sea Pines Dr., 800/367-3909, a quiet New England–style fishing village full of restaurants, shops, and services. Located at the head of the island, the **Plantation Inn**, 200 Museum St., 843/681-3655 or 800/995-3928, is a reasonably priced option. Hilton Head Island Beach and Tennis Resorts, 800/445-8664, offers information on a number of area resorts.

Fripp Island Resort, 1 Tarpon Blvd., Fripp Island, 800/845-4100, offers golf, tennis, beaches, a marina, restaurants, and accommodations ranging from old-style beach bungalows to modern resort villas. This is a controlled-access resort island, once the ancient hunting ground of the Yemassee Indians, where bicycles, golf carts, and foot traffic outnumber cars.

CAMPING

Believe it or not, you can still find some camping in this place, where the word *primitive* means only an art form. Check out the **Outdoor Resorts Motor Coach Resort** and **Outdoor Resorts RV Resort and Yacht Club**, both in Hilton Head. The former has 400 sites at 133 Arrow Rd., 843/785-7699 or 800/722-2365. The latter has 200 sites at 43 Jenkins Rd., 843/681-3256 or 800/845-9560.

Hunting Island State Park, U.S. 21, 16 miles east of Beaufort, 843/838-2011, offers 200 family campsites and 15 completely supplied cabins on 5,000 acres. A boardwalk provides access to a wonderland of beaches, forest trails, and marshes, plus an abandoned 140-foot (181 stair-step) lighthouse.

Edisto Beach State Park, 8377 State Cabin Rd., Edisto Island, 843/869-2756, has 103 sites (cabins and camping) for rent by the night or the week. The beachfront park includes salt marshes and some of the tallest palmetto trees in the state.

NIGHTLIFE

When you have had your fill of pristine beachfront and halcyon days, a lively mix of nightspots across Hilton Head may draw your interest. Venues for comedy, cabaret, and family entertainment with music and dancing dot the island. Try these: **Buoy Bar** at the Hilton Resort, 843/842-8000; **Callahan's Sports Bar**, 49 New Orleans Rd., 843/686-POOL; **Signals Lounge** at the Crowne Plaza Resort, 843/842-2400; **Hemingway's Lounge** at the Hyatt Regency, 843/785-1234; and **Monkey Business** at Park Plaza, 843/686-3545.

GOLFING

Hilton Head National, Hwy. 278, 843/842-5900, has a Gary Player–designed course. **Island West Golf Club**, Hwy. 278, 843/689-6660, has a course designed by Fuzzy Zoeller and Clyde Johnston that is a favorite of golfers of all levels. **Golden Bear Golf Club at Indigo Run**, 72 Golden Bear Way, 843/689-2200, has the Golden Bear Golf Club, with a design by— guess who—Jack Nicklaus.

Ocean Course at Sea Pines Resort, 100 N. Sea Pines Dr., 843/842-8484 or 800/925-GOLF, was Hilton Head's first course. Designed by George Cobb and redesigned and rebuilt in 1995 by Mark McCumber, it is still a favorite. It features one of the most photographed holes on the island: the dramatic beachfront fifteenth. **Palmetto Dunes Resort**, 7 Trent Jones Way, 843/785-1138, offers courses by George Fazio, Arthur Hill, and Robert Trent Jones. **Port Royal Plantation**, 10-A Grass Lawn Ave., 843/689-GOLF or 800/2-FIND-18, is the site of the Barony Course, designed by George Cobb and Willard Byard, and houses the Hilton Head Island School of Golf, featuring Ron Cerrudo. For more information on golf on Hilton Head and in the Lowcountry, call 800/682-5553 for a free *South Carolina Golf Guide*.

9
CHARLESTON

If you claim to have been to the "holy city," southerners will want to know when you visited Charleston. While some consider the city the font of all things cultural, others revere it for the historic houses of worship. Here are the Circular Congregation Church, from which Meeting Street took its name; Congregation Beth Elohim, the second oldest synagogue in the country and the oldest in continuous use; Emanuel African Methodist Episcopal Church, arising from the Free African Society formed in 1791; First (Scots) Presbyterian Church, circa 1814, whose bells were donated to the Confederacy and never replaced; the French Protestant (Huguenot) Church, built in 1844; and more. But churches don't tell the whole story.

Charleston is probably best known for the site where the first shot of the Civil War was fired on Fort Sumter, but the city predates that event by almost 200 years. Though it has withstood great fires, earthquakes, pirates, civil war, and hurricanes, much of it remains unchanged since its founding in 1670.

Charleston is home of the famous Battery, from which you can view Charleston Harbor seaward, and landward see pastel-painted houses with almost filigreed ironwork. You can take a horsedrawn carriage through brick-laid streets, tour historic homes and museums, and enjoy walled gardens and shaded verandas. Charlestonians delight in their heritage and enjoy sharing it with visitors.

CHARLESTON

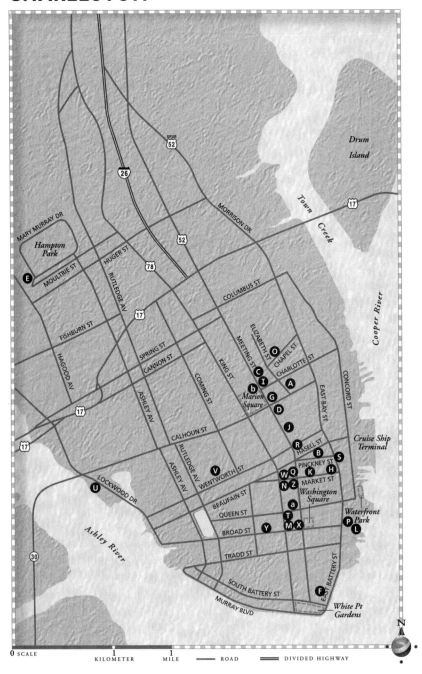

A PERFECT DAY IN CHARLESTON

A perfect week in Charleston would be more to the point, but a perfect day would begin with a leisurely breakfast on a veranda in one of the city's historic inns. Next, spend the morning shopping in the Old City Market and touring one of the historic homes of Charleston Place. Buy the makings of a picnic lunch and take them to Charleston Waterfront Park along Concord Street, with its public green, miles of walkway, and 400-foot fishing pier. For dinner, visit one of the city's famous restaurants to sample lowcountry cuisine. Or, you could take in a Charleston Stage Company show, then head to a late-night eatery or raw bar.

SIGHTSEEING HIGHLIGHTS

★★★★ AIKEN-RHETT HOUSE
48 Elizabeth St., 843/723-1159

Antebellum life is completely documented in one of Charleston's most palatial residences, and the intact work yard is one of the nation's best examples of African American urban life. Built in 1817, restored and reopened in 1996, the house has Charleston's best-preserved nineteenth-century domestic interiors.

Details: Mon–Sat 10–5, Sun 2–5. $12 admission includes Russell House. (2 hours)

SIGHTS
- Ⓐ Aiken-Rhett House
- Ⓑ American Military Museum
- Ⓒ Charleston Museum
- Ⓓ Circular Congregation Church
- Ⓔ The Citadel
- Ⓕ Edmondston-Alston House
- Ⓖ Gibbes Museum of Art
- Ⓗ Heyward-Washington House
- Ⓘ Joseph Manigault House
- Ⓙ Nathaniel Russell House

SIGHTS *(continued)*
- Ⓚ Old City Market
- Ⓛ Old Exchange and Provost Dungeon

FOOD
- Ⓜ 82 Queen
- Ⓝ Alice's Fine Foods and Southern Cooking
- Ⓞ Arizona Bar and Grill
- Ⓟ Carolina's
- Ⓠ Charleston Grill
- Ⓡ Hyman's Seafood Company
- Ⓢ Kaminsky's Most Excellent Café

FOOD *(continued)*
- Ⓣ Poogan's Porch
- Ⓤ Pusser's Landing

LODGING
- Ⓥ 1837 Bed and Breakfast
- Ⓦ Charleston Place
- Ⓧ Historic Charleston Bed & Breakfast
- Ⓨ John Rutledge House Inn
- Ⓩ Meeting Street Inn
- ⓐ Mills House Hotel
- ⓑ Westin Francis Marion Hotel

★★★★ AMERICAN MILITARY MUSEUM
40 Pinckney St., 843/723-9620

Dedicated to members of the United States armed forces, this museum displays artifacts covering Vietnam, Korea, World Wars I and II, the Spanish-American War, Indian Wars, the Civil War, and the wars with Britain.

Details: Mon–Sat 10–6, Sun 1–6. $5 adults, $1 ages 12 and under; free to military. (3 hours)

★★★★ BOONE HALL PLANTATION
Hwy. 17, 843/884-4371

When you think of moss-draped live oaks lining an avenue to a southern plantation, this is the one that comes to mind. The half-mile avenue was planted by Captain Thomas Boone in 1743 on a 730-acre cotton plantation. Today visitors receive a guided tour of the first floor of the mansion. Original buildings include eighteenth-century slave cabins and the Gin House, used to process cotton.

Details: Eight miles north of Charleston, east of the Cooper River. Spring and summer Mon–Sat 8:30–6:30, Sun 1–5; fall and winter Mon–Sat 9–5, Sun 1–4. $12.50 adults, $10 age 60 and older, $6 ages 6 to 12. (3 hours)

★★★★ CHARLESTON MUSEUM
360 Meeting St., 843/722-2996
www.charlestonmuseum.com

Founded in 1773, this is the oldest museum in the United States. It features a full-scale replica of the Confederate submarine *Hunley* and a depiction of Charleston's history told in clothing, furniture, silver, games, vehicles, photographs, and more. Children will enjoy the "Discover Me" room. The site is easily accessible to those in wheelchairs.

Details: Mon–Sat 9–5, Sun 1–5. $7 adults, $4 ages 3 to 12. (3 hours)

★★★★ CHARLES TOWNE LANDING
Hwy. 171, 843/852-4200

What would later become the city of Charleston was settled in a beautiful wilderness in April 1670. Modern visitors can walk, bicycle, or take a tram tour through 80 acres of landscaped gardens with freshwater lagoons, great oaks, and more than 50 plant varieties providing year-round color. A full-scale replica of a seventeenth-century

SCDPRT

ship is moored in Old Towne Creek. Settlers Life Area, a re-creation of an early South Carolina village, invites visitor participation. The Animal Forest features animals native to South Carolina in 1670— bison, pumas, bears, wolves, alligators, bobcats, and birds—that roam in natural environments.

Details: Sept–May daily 9–5, June–Aug daily 9–6. $5 adults, $2.50 ages 6 to 14 and seniors, disabled free. (4–5 hours)

★★★★ **DRAYTON HALL**

3380 Ashley River Rd., 843/766-0188, www.draytonhall.org
The only Ashley River plantation to survive the Civil War intact, the house is preserved in almost original condition after 250 years. This National Historic Landmark is one of the oldest and best examples of Georgian Palladian architecture in the nation. Drayton Hall reportedly avoided destruction by Union forces in 1865 when the mistress met the Yankee commander on the front porch and told him the family had smallpox. Dreading a scourge that could decimate his forces, the officer ordered his men to move on.

Details: Mar–Oct 10–4, Nov–Feb 10–3. $8 adults, $6 ages 12 to 18, $4 ages 6 to 11. Price includes guided tour. (3 hours)

★★★★ GIBBES MUSEUM OF ART
135 Meeting St., 843/722-2706, www.gibbes.com
One of the finest collections of American art in the Southeast is housed here. There are views of Charleston, portraits of notable South Carolinians, and paintings, prints, and drawings from the eighteenth century to the present day.
Details: Tue–Sat 10–5, Sun 1–5. $6 adults, $5 ages 6 to 18. (2–3 hours)

★★★★ MAGNOLIA PLANTATION AND GARDENS
Hwy. 61, 843/571-1266, www.magnoliaplantation.com
Established in 1680, America's oldest garden blooms year-round. The accompanying house, built in 1865, has served as the Drayton family residence for 10 generations (the original house was built in the 1670s). The plantation has something for everyone: nature train tour, petting zoo, wildlife observation tower, canoe and bike rentals, theater, art gallery, horticultural maze, Biblical garden, herb garden, Barbados tropical garden, and antebellum cabin. Reservations are required for a Saturday guided bird walk.
Details: 10 miles northwest of Charleston. Daily 8:30–4:30. Admission to grounds and gardens: $10 adults, $9 teens, $5 ages 6 to 12. House tour: $6 all ages; children under 6 not admitted. Nature train: $5 adults, $4 teens, $3 ages 6 to 12. Audubon Swamp tour: $5 adults, $4 teens, $3 ages 6 to 12. (3–4 hours)

★★★★ MIDDLETON PLACE AND MIDDLETON PLACE HOUSE MUSEUM
Ashley River Rd. (Hwy. 61), 843/556-6020 or 800/782-3608
These landscaped gardens beautify a carefully preserved eighteenth-century plantation. The Middleton family story, from colonial days to the Civil War, is exhibited in a fully furnished wing. Built in 1755 as a gentlemen's guest wing, it became the family residence when the plantation was burned after the Civil War. The story of the plantation's African American community is explored at the stableyards and Eliza's House. The grounds and gardens are gorgeous, and the old rice mill shows how buildings were shored up following the great earthquake of the late nineteenth century.
Details: 14 miles northwest of Charleston. Daily 9–5. Admission to grounds and gardens: $14 adults, $7 ages 6 to 12. House tour: $7 per person. (3 hours)

★★★★ PATRIOTS POINT NAVAL AND MARITIME MUSEUM
Charleston Harbor, Mt. Pleasant, 843/884-2727
The Medal of Honor Museum resides on the hangar deck of the USS *Yorktown*, World War II's famous "Fighting Lady." Among the memorials and exhibits are the destroyer *Laffey*, the submarine *Clamagore*, the Coast Guard cutter *Ingham*, 25 vintage military aircraft, and the Vietnam Naval Support Base. Most of the site is wheelchair accessible.
Details: Daily 9–6:30. $10 adults, $5 ages 6 to 11. (4 hours)

★★★ THE POWDER MAGAZINE
79 Cumberland St., 843/805-6730
The Powder, built in the early 1700s, is the oldest public building still standing in Charleston and was used during the Revolutionary War to store munitions. It now serves as a museum with armor, costumes, and furniture from eighteenth-century Charleston.
Details: Mon–Sat 10–5, Sun 2–5. Free. Donations are accepted. (1 hour)

★★★ HEYWARD-WASHINGTON HOUSE
87 Church St., 843/722-0354
Part of the Charleston Museum, this 1772 house was the home of a prominent rice planter and his son, Thomas Heyward, a signer of the Declaration of Independence. George Washington was a guest here in 1791. Many furnishings are by eighteenth-century Charleston artisans. The original kitchen building is the only one in the area open to the public.
Details: Mon–Sat 10–5, Sun 1–5. $7 adults, $4 ages 3 to 12. (1 hour)

★★★ JOSEPH MANIGAULT HOUSE
350 Meeting St., 843/723-2926
One of the country's most beautiful examples of neo-classical architecture, the house was built in 1803 and recently restored. It's furnished with Charleston, English, and French period pieces.
Details: Mon–Sat 10–5, Sun 1–5. $7 adults, $4 ages 3 to 12. (1 hour)

★★★ NATHANIEL RUSSELL HOUSE
51 Meeting St., 843/724-8481

This example of Adam architecture was built about 1809 and has a flying staircase—spiraling unsupported from floor to floor. Full of fine period furniture and decorative arts, the house headquarters some offices of the Historic Charleston Foundation.

Details: *Mon–Sat 10–5, Sun 2–5. $7 guided tour; $14 combination ticket that includes the Aiken-Rhett House. (1 hour)*

★★★ **OLD CITY MARKET**
Meeting and Market Sts.
This area was a public fish, meat, and vegetable market throughout the nineteenth century. The Center Market, between Church and Meeting Streets, contains specialty shops and boutiques. The Rainbow Market, at the foot of State Street, is a complex of small shops capturing the essence of Old Charleston. And in the Open Air Market, between Church and East Bay Streets, are stalls leased by local artisans and international importers. Here you can watch craftspeople weave lowcountry sweetgrass baskets and hear vegetable vendors ply their wares in Gullah, a West African patois unique to this area. The 1841 Old Market building, on the corner of Meeting and Market Streets, has withstood two tornados, a major earthquake and fire, the Civil War, and the much more recent Hurricane Hugo.

Details: *(2 hours)*

★★★ **OLD EXCHANGE AND PROVOST DUNGEON**
122 E. Bay St., 843/727-2165, www.oldexchange.com
The Old Exchange, one of America's most historic colonial buildings, was built by the British as an exchange and customs house for the port of Charles Towne. The British imprisoned American patriots in its dungeon before sending them to St. Augustine. Also here is the original seawall of Charles Towne, which was frequented by pirates in the early 1700s. George Washington was entertained in the building's great hall, and the U.S. Constitution was ratified by South Carolina here.

Details: *Daily 9–5. $6 adults, $3.50 ages 7 to 12. (2 hours)*

★★ **CIRCULAR CONGREGATION CHURCH**
150 Meeting St., 843/577-6400
Organized in 1681, this congregation became the Independent Church of Charles Towne and the meeting house for which Meeting

Street is named. It is also home of the first Sunday school in the state. In 1804 Robert Mills designed the circular building, which was burned in 1861. Thirty years later the fourth and present church was constructed, incorporating brick from the building burned during the 1886 earthquake.

Details: Open only when tour guides are available; call first. (1 hour)

★★ **THE CITADEL**
Ashley River near Hampton Park, 843/953-6726
www.citadel.edu
Shannon Faulkner brought the Citadel into the international spotlight, and headlines, when she stormed the gates in 1995 for entrance as a cadet to the previously (since 1842) all-male Military College of South Carolina. She was admitted under court order but later withdrew. Four more young women picked up her banner and enrolled at the school in 1996. Two of them quit at the end of their first semester, charging sexual harrassment and hazing by male cadets. Despite the controversy, visitors might want to tour the gracious campus with its impressive buildings. The Carolinas have a strong military tradition, and it is evident here. Dress Parade is held at 3:45 Fridays during the academic year. Exhibits feature photographs, uniforms, and archival documents.

Details: Daily 8–6. Museum House open Sun–Fri 2–5, Sat noon–5. Free. For information on events call 800/868-DAWGS. (2–3 hours)

★★ **EDMONDSTON-ALSTON HOUSE**
21 E. Battery St., 843/722-7171, www.middletonplace.org
Built in the early nineteenth century, with a commanding view of Charleston Harbor, this Federal-style house was redecorated in 1838 in Greek Revival style. It contains documents, portraits, engravings, a library, furniture, silver, china, and family furnishings. The piazzas offer views of Charleston Harbor; it was from one of them that General P.G.T. Beauregard watched the bombardment of Fort Sumter. General Robert E. Lee later slept here, when a fire threatened his hotel.

Details: Tue–Sat 10–4:30, Sun and Mon 1:30–4:30. $7 for guided tour. (1 hour)

★★ **FORT MOULTRIE**
W. Middle St., Sullivan's Island, 843/883-3123
Originally a palmetto-log fort erected in 1776, the third fort on this

site—the one you see today—was built in 1809. This was the location for one of the first decisive patriot victories in the Revolutionary War.

Details: 10 miles east of Charleston. Daily 9–5. $2 adults, $1 ages 6 to 15. (1–2 hours)

★★ FORT SUMTER
843/881-BOAT
Its construction, which began in 1829, was unfinished when the first shot of the Civil War was fired on the Union-occupied fort on April 12, 1861. After a 34-hour bombardment, Union forces surrendered, and the fort became a symbol of Southern resistance—it was besieged from 1863 to 1865.

Details: Fort Sumter Tour Boats leave from City Marina and Patriots Point. Limited wheelchair access at City Marina. $10.50 adults, $5.50 ages 6 to 11. (2½ hours)

★★ OLD ST. ANDREWS PARISH
2604 Ashley River Rd., 843/766-1541
Founded and built in 1706, this is the oldest surviving church in the Carolinas. Its churchyard holds numerous historic tombs.

Details: (1 hour)

FOOD

Food is integral to the city's history, and Charleston has a vast number of three- and four-star restaurants. But if your taste is simpler and your purse not bulging, you can still be satisfied. For some of the finest cuisine in the South, with entrées ranging from $13 to $22, visit **82 Queen**, 82 Queen St., 843/723-7591, serving specialties such as Charleston She Crab Soup in a turn-of-the-century garden courtyard and restored eighteenth-century dining rooms. Lunch or dinner reservations are suggested. **Carolina's**, 10 Exchange St., 843/724-3800, is where Charlestonians go for regional cuisine including pea cakes, shrimp and crab wontons, and crayfish tasso pasta. Open daily for dinner.

Hyman's Seafood Company, 215 Meeting St., 843/723-6000, is in a historic warehouse next to Charleston Place. It's casual, fun, and affordable, with entrées averaging $10 to $15. As many as 25 different fish are featured for lunch and dinner daily. **Kaminsky's Most Excellent Café**, 78 N. Market St., 843/853-8270, is a late-night institution serving wines, cocktails, specialty coffees, and homemade desserts. It opens daily at noon.

Charleston Grill, 224 King St., 843/577-4522, has entrées priced at over $20, but Chef Bob Waggoner's regional foods draw rave reviews and a four-star rating. You'll hear jazz nightly from seven o'clock, and the restaurant is wheelchair accessible. Truly a unique experience is **Middleton Place Restaurant**, Ashley River Rd., 843/556-6020. The restaurant serves lunch daily (diners must pay gate admission—see Sightseeing Highlights—to the plantation grounds) and candlelit dinners Tuesday through Saturday (no gate admission). Plantation fare such as okra gumbo, Hoppin' John, and Huguenot torte is available for lunch. Dinners feature fresh fish, fowl, and beef served overlooking America's oldest landscaped gardens. Entrées range from $10 to $20.

Poogan's Porch, 72 Queen St., 843/577-2337, serves daily lunch and dinner and Sunday brunch. Specialties are Creole fare, jambalaya, gumbo, quail, alligator, peanut-butter pie, and other lowcountry dishes. Paul Newman ate here and liked it. Lunch entrées are priced under $10; brunch and dinner under $15. (Poogan's is named after a dog who adopted the front porch of the 1888 house as his home and was tended by successive restaurant owners until his death.)

You'll find moderately expensive family dining for lunch and dinner offered at **Pusser's Landing**, 17 Lockwood Dr., 843/853-1000, at the City Marina. The fare blends Caribbean favorites, Old English pub specialties, Victorian raw bar items, and lowcountry classics. **The Trawler**, Coleman Blvd. on Shem Creek, Mt. Pleasant, 843/884-2560, offers waterfront dining daily for lunch and dinner. Entrées are $10 to $15.

If you tire of seafood and southern dishes, visit **Arizona Bar and Grill**, 14 Chapel St., 843/577-5090, where southwestern cuisine is served in an 1864 railroad warehouse. Lunch and dinner entrées cost less than $10.

Don't leave Charleston without sampling Chef Alice Warren's regional cuisine, including shrimp and grits, collard greens, deviled crabs, chops, and ribs, all priced under $10. **Alice's Fine Foods and Southern Cooking**, 468–470 King St., 843/853-9366, serves lunch and dinner every day.

LODGING

If you're in the mood to try something different, Charleston's islands have their own private resorts with rentals available. You can request a free guide to Charleston's beach resorts by calling these toll-free numbers: Kiawah Island, 800/845-3911; Wild Dunes Resort, 800/346-0606; Isle of Palms, 800/344-5105; Seabrook Island, 800/845-2233; and Sullivan's Island, 800/247-5050.

GREATER CHARLESTON

N

To A

701
17

703

COLEMAN BLVD

Sullivan's Island

JASPER BLVD

CENTRAL AV

MIDDLE ST

701
17

D

Mt. Pleasant

17A
701

J

E — Fort Sumter National Monument

★ Castle Pinckney National Monument

PATRIOT'S POINT RD

I

Charleston

Charleston Harbor

James Island

526

Wando River

Daniel Island

Cooper River

Drum Island

BAY ST

52

North Charleston

MORRISON DR

MEETING ST

KING ST

78

RUTLEDGE AV

CALHOUN ST

James Island

17T

River Av

52

26

To Ladson

B

7

171

17

700

M

RIVERLAND DR

526

To K

Ashley River

SAM RITTENBURG BLVD

7

642

61

H

SAVANNAH HWY

Stono River

RIVER RD

To Middleton Place

C

ASHLEY RIVER RD

F G

To F G

NEW BEES FERRY RD

To L

L

0 SCALE

3

KILOMETERS   MILES

3

—— ROAD   ★— PLACE OF INTEREST

—— DIVIDED HIGHWAY

You could spend a month or two of Sundays at Charleston's three- and four-star bed-and-breakfasts and historic inns and never repeat yourself. Representing more than 50 properties in and around the historic district is Historic Charleston Bed & Breakfast, 57 Broad St. 843/722-6606 or 800/743-3583.

Rates at the **1837 Bed and Breakfast**, 126 Wentworth St., 843/723-7166, range from $79 to $135 and include a full gourmet breakfast outside on the piazza or in the formal dining room. You'll get canopied beds, antiques, front porch rockers, and lots of southern hospitality.

Rates begin at $70 and include evening wine and sherry in the ballroom, a private bath, and parking at the **John Rutledge House Inn**, 116 Broad St., 843/723-7999. This intimate yet stately house is where Rutledge, a signer of the Declaration of Independence, lived. **Charleston Place**, 130 Market St., 843/722-4900, is historic Charleston's premier hotel, located minutes from historic homes, museums, and churches. Rates start at $126. The **Westin Francis Marion Hotel**, 387 King St., 843/722-0600 or 800/325-3535, is a recently restored landmark offering full-service elegance in a European-style hotel. Rates start at $160.

Middleton Inn at Middleton Place, 843/556-0500 or 800/543-4774, is a contemporary inn on a historic plantation overlooking a scenic bend in the Ashley River. Every room has a fireplace and a huge tiled bath. Outside are nature trails and opportunities for birding, kayaking, biking, tennis, croquet, and swimming. Rates start at $130 and include admission to the gardens and stable yards at Middleton Place.

Erected in the 1850s at Meeting and Queen Streets is **Mills House**

SIGHTS

- **A** Boone Hall Plantation
- **B** Charles Towne Landing
- **C** Drayton Hall
- **D** Fort Moultrie
- **E** Fort Sumter
- **F** Magnolia Plantation and Gardens
- **G** Middleton Place and Middleton Place House Museum
- **H** Old St. Andrews Parish Church
- **I** Patriots Point Naval and Maritime Museum

FOOD

- **G** Middleton Place Restaurant
- **J** The Trawler

LODGING

- **G** Middleton Inn at Middleton Place

CAMPING

- **K** Charleston KOA
- **L** Edisto Beach State Park
- **M** James Island County Park Campgrounds

Note: Items with the same letter are located in the same area.

Hotel, 843/577-2400 or 800/874-9600, where guests are greeted by top-hatted doormen and treated to marble floors, canopied beds, and southern hospitality in a four-star, four-diamond antebellum hotel. Robert E. Lee slept here, too. Rates begin at $126. At **Meeting Street Inn**, in the center of the historic district at 173 Meeting St., 843/723-1882 or 800/842-8022, you'll enjoy a "hunt" breakfast, afternoon socials, and a private courtyard with jet whirlpool. Rates begin at $99.

CAMPING

Among recommended camping facilities are **Charleston KOA**, 9494 Hwy. 78, Ladson, 843/797-1045 or 800/KOA-5812; **Edisto Beach State Park**, 50 miles southeast of Charleston off S.C. 174, 843/869-2156; and **James Island County Park Campgrounds**, 871 Riverland Dr., Charleston, 843/795-9884 or 800/743-PARK, a 125-RV site campground with full hookups, 10 furnished cabins, 24-hour security, recreation, wheelchair-accessible sites, and bathhouses within a 643-acre natural park setting.

NIGHTLIFE

Try to be in town for the internationally famous **Spoleto Festival**, held 17 days annually beginning the last week in May. For a free brochure, write Spoleto Festival U.S.A., P.O. Box 157, Charleston, SC 29402 or call 843/722-2764. Other times, you'll still find plenty of entertainment.

Acme-Downtown, 5 Faber St., 843/577-7383, is a neighborhood dance club open Tuesday through Sunday. **Chef & Clef Restaurant**, 102 N. Market St., 843/722-0732, offers live jazz and blues Monday through Saturday beginning at 6. **Dock Street Theater**, 133 Church St., 843/965-4032, presents more than 120 performances by the Charleston Stage Company each season, Thursday through Saturday at 8 and Sunday at 3. **Serenade at the Charleston Music Hall**, 37 John St., 843/853-2000, hosts a musical variety show nightly. **Tommy Condon's Irish Pub & Seafood Restaurant**, 160 Church St., 843/577-3818, has live Irish entertainment featuring singalongs and family fun every weekend.

HELPFUL HINT

Park and ride the DASH (Downtown Area Shuttle). The fare is 75 cents, exact change only. A one-day pass costs $2, a three-day pass costs $5, and a monthly pass costs $18. Children younger than six ride free with a paying adult.

10
MYRTLE BEACH AND
THE GRAND STRAND

Myrtle Beach is the sun and fun capital of coastal South Carolina's Grand Strand. But it wasn't always so comfortable here. The area's first inhabitants were the Waccamaw and Winyah Indians. The Spanish made the first known European settlement in North America on Winyah Bay, near present-day Georgetown, in 1526. Disease doomed the settlers, however, and it was not until 1730 that English colonists began to plan for the city of Georgetown.

Myrtle Beach tourism didn't begin until 1901, with the opening of its first hotel, the Seaside Inn. Early summer visitors had to deal with razorback hogs rooting under their cottages. Upscale resort building didn't begin until the 1920s, with the legendary Ocean Forest Hotel. Today the Grand Strand stretches 60 miles, beginning at Little River near the North Carolina line and ending at Georgetown; Myrtle Beach is its heart. This is the birthplace of the shag, the late 1950s dance craze that spawned "beach music." While the city's population is just over 28,000, it swells to 350,000 every summer. Golfers will find more than 90 superb courses; tennis lovers more than 500 courts.

A PERFECT DAY IN MYRTLE BEACH AND THE GRAND STRAND

You can start your day in one of two ways: Arise at dawn and scout the nearly deserted beach for shells or sleep late and grab lunch at one of many pancake

MYRTLE BEACH REGION

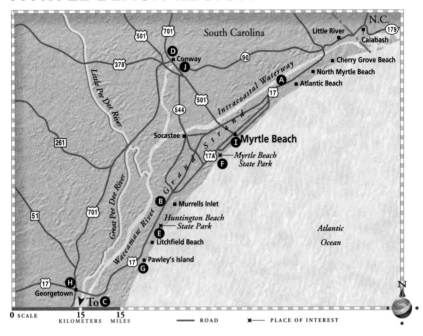

SIGHTS

- **A** Alligator Adventure
- **B** Brookgreen Gardens
- **C** Hopsewee Plantation
- **D** Horry County Museum
- **E** Huntington Beach State Park
- **F** Myrtle Beach State Park
- **G** Pawleys Island
- **H** Prince George Winyah Episcopal Church
- **I** Rice Museum
- **I** South Carolina Hall of Fame
- **J** Travelers Chapel

Note: Items with the same letter are located in the same area.

---

houses before staking out an umbrella and chair for a leisurely day in the sun. Beaches north and south of Myrtle offer less crowded shores, but all have the same vistas and pleasant temperatures. When the sun is high overhead, the fair-skinned will seek cover, perhaps with an outing to shaded Brookgreen Gardens. You can end the day by either enjoying the roar of waves at twilight on another nearly deserted beach or taking in Broadway at the Beach, an entertainment complex that promises never a dull moment—and delivers.

SIGHTSEEING HIGHLIGHTS

★★★★ BROOKGREEN GARDENS
1931 Brookgreen Gardens Dr., Murrells Inlet
843/237-4218 or 800/849-1931
The world's largest outdoor collection of American sculpture decorates the gardens, developed in the 1930s by Archer and Anna Hyatt Huntington on the site of a colonial rice plantation. More than 500 of America's finest nineteenth- and twentieth-century pieces by artists such as Frederic Remington, Daniel Chester French, and Anna Huntington are displayed, along with 2,000 plant species. A wildlife park and aviary also are on the grounds, which are handicapped accessible.
Details: Daily 9:30–4:45. $8.50 adults, $4 ages 6 to 12. (2 hours)

★★★★ HOPSEWEE PLANTATION
U.S. 17, 843/546-7891
This 1740s rice plantation was the home of Continental Congressman Thomas Lynch and the birthplace of his son Thomas Jr., a signer of the Declaration of Independence.
Details: U.S. 17, 12 miles south of Georgetown. Mar–Oct Tue–Fri 10–4. $6 adults, $2 ages 5 to 17. (2 hours)

★★★★ PRINCE GEORGE WINYAH EPISCOPAL CHURCH
301 Broad St., Georgetown, 843/546-4358
The church was established in 1721 by the Church of England to serve colonists.
Details: Mar–Nov Mon–Fri 11:30–4:30. Worship services Sun. Free. (30 minutes–1 hour)

★★★★ RICE MUSEUM
1842 Market Building, Front and Screven Sts.
843/546-7423
The story of rice and indigo, sources of wealth in colonial days, is told through dioramas and artifacts.
Details: Mon–Sat 9:30–4:30. $3 adults, $2 seniors, $1 ages 12 to 21. (2 hours)

★★★ SOUTH CAROLINA HALL OF FAME
21st Ave. N. and Oak St., Myrtle Beach, 843/448-4021
Interactive video displays honor outstanding South Carolinians, ranging

from John C. Calhoun and President Andrew Jackson to Mary McLeod Bethune, Joel Roberts Poinsett, Dizzy Gillespie, and General William C. Westmoreland.
Details: Mon–Fri 8–5. Free. (1–2 hours)

★★ ALLIGATOR ADVENTURE
Barefoot Landing, Hwy. 17, North Myrtle Beach
843/361-0789
This unusual research institute exhibits rare white albino American alligators, dwarf crocodiles, giant snakes, and other exotic wildlife. Live shows and demonstrations add to the educational experience.
Details: Hours and days vary according to season. Call for information. (2 hours)

★★ HORRY COUNTY MUSEUM
438 Main St., Conway, 843/248-1542
Located in Conway, "the Gateway to the Grand Strand," the museum offers archaeological and historic exhibits in an old post office building. Hint: The *h* is silent, so pronounce Horry "O-ree."
Details: Mon–Sat 9–5. Free. (1–2 hours)

★★ HUNTINGTON BEACH STATE PARK
U.S. 17 S., 843/237-4440
Named after the founders of nearby Brookgreen Gardens, the park features Atalaya, once the castlelike studio of famed sculptor Anna Hyatt Huntington. The 9,000-acre park has a visitor's center, boardwalk, nature trails, camping, picnicking, sunbathing, and nature programs.
Details: Open daily. $4 adults, $2 ages 6 to 12. (3–4 hours)

★★ PAWLEYS ISLAND
Once a refuge for colonial rice planters who sought escape from malaria, Pawleys Island is one of the oldest resorts on the Atlantic coast and consists mainly of beach houses. The original Pawleys Island Hammocks are handmade here and sold throughout the area.
Details: (4 hours)

★ MYRTLE BEACH STATE PARK
U.S. 17, 843/238-5325
This is one of the most popular parks in the state system, with cabins,

camping, pool and ocean swimming, pier fishing, picnicking, and year-round nature and recreation programs.
Details: *Open daily. $3 per car. (2–6 hours)*

★ TRAVELERS CHAPEL
U.S. 501, Conway
Approximately 12 by 24 feet, this unusual roadside building is open to everyone for meditation.
Details: *Daily 24 hours. (15 minutes)*

FOOD

Gullyfield Restaurant, 9916 U.S. 17 N., 843/449-3111, serves dinner every night. Specialties include lobster pie and oysters, with entrées priced from $15 to $24. **Joe's Crab Shack**, Barefoot Landing, Myrtle Beach, 843/272-5900, is the place to go for any kind of crab, from blue to stone to Alaskan. If you don't like seafood, other entrées include chicken and pasta. Open for lunch and dinner daily. **Sea Captain's House**, 3002 N. Ocean Blvd., Myrtle Beach, 843/448-8082, serves breakfast, lunch, and dinner daily and has a children's menu. Specialties are seafood, of course, but you also have a choice of steaks, pork chops, and chicken. **Back Porch**, U.S. 17 S. and Wachesaw Rd. at Murrells Inlet, 843/651-5263, serves dinner daily in a nineteenth-century farmhouse 15 miles south of Myrtle Beach (closed January and February). Moderately priced specialties include seafood and such lowcountry cuisine as Carolina cured ham, southern fried chicken, and homemade biscuits.

For a change of pace, try the oldest Italian restaurant on the Grand Strand, **Tony's Italian Restaurant**, 1407 U.S. 17, North Myrtle Beach, 843/249-1314. Its homemade pasta and veal dishes are a palate-pleasing change from all that wonderful fresh seafood. Complete dinner for two costs about $40; children's meals are less than $6. Open daily for dinner; closed December and January. Also recommended are **NASCAR Café**, Broadway at the Beach, 21st Ave. N. and the U.S. 17 Bypass, 843/946-RACE, and **Pink Magnolia**, 719 Front St., Georgetown, 843/527-6506, serving southern regional cuisine with entrées priced well below $10.

LODGING

More than 55,000 rooms are available here, in addition to a number of campsites. Lodgings range from early motel to luxury resort. Following are recommended Myrtle Beach facilities in a broad price range.

MYRTLE BEACH/THE GRAND STRAND

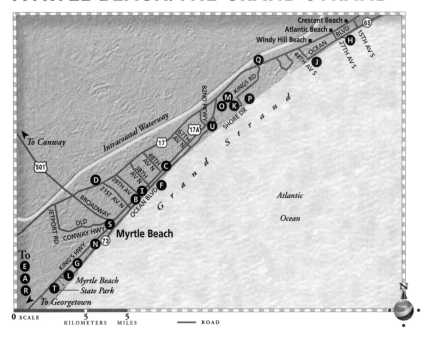

FOOD
- **A** Back Porch
- **B** Gullyfield Restaurant
- **C** Joe's Crab Shack
- **D** NASCAR Café
- **E** Pink Magnolia
- **F** Sea Captain's House
- **G** Tony's Italian Restaurant

LODGING
- **H** Atlantic Paradise Inn
- **I** Breakers Resort Hotel
- **J** Captain's Quarters
- **K** Caravelle Golf & Family Resort
- **L** Crown Reef Resort
- **M** Embassy Suites at Kingston Plantation
- **N** Myrtle Beach Polynesian Beach and Golf Resort
- **O** Ocean Creek Plantation Resort

CAMPING
- **P** Apache Family Campground
- **Q** Barefoot Camping Resort
- **R** Huntington Beach State Park
- **S** Myrtle Beach KOA Campground
- **T** Myrtle Beach State Park
- **U** PirateLand

Atlantic Paradise Inn, 1401 South Ocean Blvd., 843/444-0346 or 800/992-0269, is a low-price leader, with rooms starting at a very reasonable $30. **Breakers Resort Hotel**, 2006 N. Ocean Blvd., 843/626-5000 or 800/845-0688, has a wide range of amenities, including a summer children's program. Rates range from $32 to $425, depending on the accommodations. **Captain's Quarters Family & Golf Resort**, 901 S. Ocean Blvd., 843/448-1404 or 800/843-3561, has rates from $31 to $175, depending on accommodations. **Caravelle Golf & Family Resort**, 6900 N. Ocean Blvd., 843/918-8000 or 800/845-0893, features indoor and outdoor pools as well as a Lazy River and Kiddie Lazy River. Rates are $31 to $144, depending on season and accommodations.

Crown Reef Resort, 2913 S. Ocean Blvd., 843/626-8077 or 800/405-7333, is one of the newest on the Grand Strand. **Embassy Suites at Kingston Plantation**, 9800 Lake Dr., 843/449-0006 or 800/362-2779, away from the central beach area, has indoor and outdoor pools; tennis, squash, and racquetball courts; and a weight and fitness room. Rates range from $130 to $290. At **Myrtle Beach Polynesian Beach and Golf Resort**, 10th Ave. S. and Ocean Blvd., 843/448-1781 or 800/845-6971, rates run $30 to $115, depending on season and type of lodgings, **Ocean Creek Plantation Resort** is a 57-acre oceanfront resort at 10600 North Kings Hwy., 843/272-7724 or 800/845-0353, with seven tennis courts, beach club, the Four Seasons Restaurant, and a summer activity program for children. Barefoot Landing is just across the street. Rates range from $50 to $150.

CAMPING

Most tent sites at **Huntington Beach** and **Myrtle Beach State Parks** are rented on a first-come, first-served basis. Limited sites are available by reservation (see Sightseeing Highlights for addresses and phone numbers). Other sites are available at **Apache Family Campground**, 9700 Kings Rd., Myrtle Beach, 843/449-7323, a full-service facility where you can reserve sites year-round except for the week of July 4. Apache is home of the longest (half mile) fishing pier on the East Coast. **Barefoot Camping Resort**, 4825 Hwy. 17 S., North Myrtle Beach, 843/272-1790 or 800/272-1790, offers oceanfront and wooded sites, deluxe model and travel trailer rentals, a clubhouse, and a fitness center. **Myrtle Beach KOA Campground**, 613 Fifth Ave. S., Myrtle Beach, 843/448-3421 or 800/255-7614, sits on a secluded forest tract within walking distance of public beaches. **PirateLand Family Camping Resort**, 5401 S. Kings Hwy., Myrtle Beach, 843/238-5155 or 800/443-CAMP, is on 140 aces of mature oaks, private lagoons, and a half mile of beach. The campground offers furnished two- and three-bedroom vacation rentals and is open year-round.

NIGHTLIFE

At one time, the sun and sand were entertainment enough. But today's visitors want more, and they get it. **Alabama Theatre**, at Barefoot Landing on U.S. 17 N., 843/272-1111, offers Opryland's Celebration '99 and sometimes the famous music group (Alabama) that got its start at the Pavilion here. **Broadway at the Beach**, a brand-new 350-acre complex at 21st Avenue North and the U.S. 17 Bypass, 800/386-4662, includes live theater, a nightclub district with famous entertainers at the Palace, restaurants, specialty shops, and more. **Carolina Opry**, at the junction of U.S. 17 Business and the U.S. 17 Bypass, 800/THE-OPRY, offers a variety of music and comedy. **House of Blues**, Barefoot Landing, 4640 U.S. 17 S., North Myrtle Beach, 843/913-3740, offers live blues and regional cuisine. **Dixie Stampede**, at the U.S. 17 Business and Bypass junction, 800/433-4401, serves a four-course feast during the audience-participation show that focuses on friendly North/South rivalry. A finale features trick horseback riding and an Electric Parade. The club is handicapped accessible.

The **Crook and Chase Theatre**, 2901 Fantasy Way, 800/681-5209, hosts Broadway-style theater as well as cable television's *Crook and Chase* talk show. Call for show information and tickets. **Legends in Concert**, at 301 U.S. 17 S. (843/238-8888 or 800/THE OPRY), is a re-creation of performances by such superstars as Elvis Presley, John Lennon, Marilyn Monroe, Judy Garland, Nat King Cole, Michael Jackson, and Dolly Parton, using lookalikes and soundalikes.

GOLFING

Myrtle Beach started out with just a few golf courses but today it has more than 115. On Woodside Drive, **Pine Lakes**, 800/446-6817, called "the granddaddy," is Myrtle Beach's oldest and most prestigious course. Designed by Robert White, first president of the PGA of America, it's also the birthplace of *Sports Illustrated* and one of the 50 most historic courses in America.

North Myrtle Beach's **Tidewater Golf Club** (4901 Little River Neck Rd., 843/249-3829 or 800/446-5363) was named the best new public course in the United States in 1991 by *Golf Digest* and *Golf Magazine*. *Golf Magazine* named Tidewater and Myrtle Beach's **Heathland** course (1500 Legends Dr., 843/399-9318) two of the nation's top 10 new courses. Jack Nicklaus designed the **Long Bay Club** (Rt. 9 at Longs, seven miles west of Rt. 17,

843/339-2222), Arnold Palmer designed the **King's North at Myrtle Beach National** (U.S. 501, 843/448-2308), and Robert Trent Jones designed **Waterway Hills** (U.S. 17 Bypass, 843/449-6488 or 800/344-5590). In the past, the area has hosted the Senior PGA Tournament in November.

It was in Myrtle Beach that a group of hotel owners created the first "golf package," which introduced a whole new type of vacation. Today golf packages are offered throughout the year and are especially attractive from mid-November through early February, when motel rates and greens fees are at their lowest. For information on golf vacation packages, call 800/845-4653.

U.S. 17, which follows a precolonial Indian trail originating in Massachusetts, is the best way to see the oceanside communities that intersperse the sea oats from Little River to Georgetown. Get off the main highways and enjoy the vistas.

You'll see towns such as North Myrtle Beach (famous in some circles as the home of Vanna White), Atlantic Beach (once the only South Carolina beach where African Americans were welcomed), Myrtle Beach, Surfside, Garden City, Litchfield, and Pawleys Island. You can exit U.S. 17 to view matchless expanses of sandy shores or see small-town America up close. Of course, you'll also catch glimpses of championship golf courses and expensive resort communities.

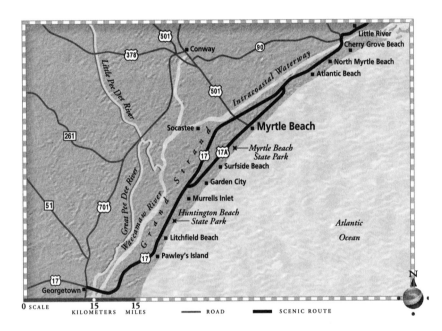

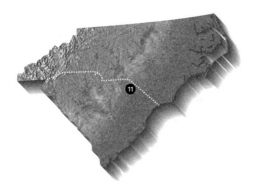

11
PEE DEE COUNTRY

People in other parts of the country may not immediately connect Pee Dee with South Carolina, but say "Darlington," and most, especially NASCAR fans, will recognize it. Darlington is the place to be on Labor Day weekend for the running of the Southern 500, one of NASCAR's most prestigious races and the biggest one-day tourist draw in the state.

The Pee Dee River has been dammed repeatedly for recreation and electric power and cuts through vast timberlands on its way to Georgetown and Winyah Bay. English gentry, the first European colonists along its banks, named the river after the Pee Dee Indians who lived in the area. The English were followed quickly by industrious French Huguenots, and plantations along the Pee Dee grew rice, indigo, and tobacco. By the end of the eighteenth century, King Cotton had taken over.

Today soybeans grow here along with corn, tobacco, cotton, and pecan trees. It is an area of small old cities—Florence, built in the 1880s, is among the most modern—and retirement communities, farms, golf courses, and, always abiding, the dark waters of the Pee Dee.

A PERFECT DAY IN PEE DEE COUNTRY

If you've never been to a NASCAR race, this is the place to view one. Darlington, home of the Southern 500, is synonymous with stock-car racing. So if you

PEE DEE COUNTRY

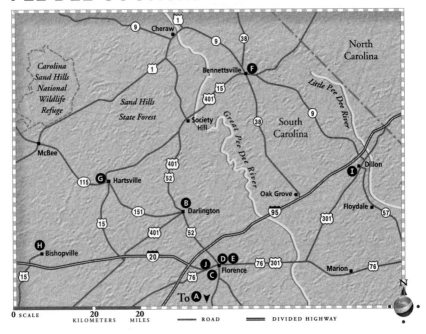

SIGHTS

- **A** Browntown Museum
- **B** Darlington Raceway
- **C** Florence Museum of Art, Science and History
- **D** Florence National Cemetery
- **E** Francis Marion University Planetarium
- **F** Jennings-Brown House and Marlboro County Historical Museum
- **A** Joe Weatherly NMPA Stock Car Hall of Fame
- **G** Kalmia Gardens
- **I** South of the Border
- **H** South Carolina Cotton Museum
- **J** War Between the States Museum

Note: Items with the same letter are located in the same area.

---

ordered your tickets as soon as they became available months ahead of time and have them in your hot little hands, pack up a "survival kit" and head to the track. Your kit should hold everything from earplugs—the noise is truly deafening—and sunblock to raincoats and ham biscuits. If the race is delayed for whatever reason, you can spend your time scoping out the crowd or reading a book.

You'll want to arrive early to find a parking place—parking can be a frustrating two-hour adventure if you get a late start—and find your seat. The crowds are always friendly, and drivers sometimes sign autographs.

SIGHTSEEING HIGHLIGHTS

★★★★ **FLORENCE MUSEUM OF ART, SCIENCE AND HISTORY**
558 Spruce St., 843/662-3351
You'll see African and Asian art, Native American pottery, and the Hall of South Carolina History. Also here are Timrod Park and Shrine, a one-room schoolhouse once presided over by Henry Timrod, poet laureate of the Confederacy.
Details: Tue–Sat 10–5, Sun 2–5. Free. (2 hours)

★★★★ **JOE WEATHERLY NMPA STOCK CAR HALL OF FAME**
1301 Harry Byrd Hwy. (S.C. 34), Darlington
843/395-8821
Located at the Darlington Raceway, one mile west of town on S.C. 34, the Hall of Fame holds the world's largest collection of stock-racing cars, including those of Richard Petty, David Pearson, Buddy Baker, Fireball Roberts, and Bill Elliott.
Details: Daily 8:30–5. $3 adults, under 12 free. (1 hour)

★★★ **BROWNTOWN MUSEUM**
Hwy. 341 between Johnsonville and Lake City
843/558-2355
Explore pioneer life at the Brown-Burrows House, an 1845 low-country farmstead listed on the National Register of Historic Places. The site includes an original cotton gin, a smokehouse, an outhouse and a corn crib.
Details: Apr–Dec Fri–Sun afternoons. $2 adults, 50 cents ages 6 to 12. Group tours are available. (2 hours)

★★★ **DARLINGTON RACEWAY**
1301 Harry Byrd Hwy. (S.C. 34), Darlington, 843/395-8499
NASCAR's TransSouth 400 is run in late March, and the Southern 500 is held on Labor Day weekend.
Details: Call for race times and admissions. (1–6 hours)

★★★ JENNINGS-BROWN HOUSE AND MARLBORO COUNTY HISTORICAL MUSEUM
119 S. Marlboro St., Bennettsville, 843/479-5624
The county's history, farming methods, and early businesses are detailed in the museum. It shares the grounds with the 1826 Jennings-Brown House, with its detached kitchen and period furnishings, and the Female Academy. The museum, built in the 1930s by the Works Project Administration, originally was the Women's Home Demonstration Club Market Building, where Marlboro County women sold farm produce and crafts. The Jennings-Brown House was built by one of Bennettsville's earliest physicians, and an upstairs bedroom has a handpainted and stenciled ceiling by an unknown artist. It was also used as headquarters for Major General Frank Blair, commander of the Seventeenth Army Corps, which captured and occupied Bennettsville in March 1865. The Bennettsville Female Academy, organized in 1830 by leading citizens, was a private school from 1833 to 1881 and is furnished to resemble a mid-nineteenth-century schoolroom.
Details: Mon–Fri 8:30–5. Admission to museum and academy free; guided house tour $2 adults, $1 children. (2 hours)

★★★ KALMIA GARDENS
1624 W. Carolina Ave., Hartsville, 843/383-8145
This 30-acre arboretum maintained by Coker College provides a nearly complete sampling of the state's terrain, flora, and fauna—a microcosm of the natural state, from the mountains to the ocean.
Details: Year-round daily. Free. (2 hours)

★★ FRANCIS MARION UNIVERSITY PLANETARIUM
U.S. 301 N., Florence, 843/661-1250
On the grounds of Francis Marion University, the planetarium offers programs free to the public two days each month.
Details: Second and fourth Sun at 3. (1 hour)

★★ SOUTH CAROLINA COTTON MUSEUM
121 W. Cedar Lane, Bishopville, 803/484-4497
Cotton was king for a long time in Pee Dee, and here is the place to learn its history in South Carolina. The museum is located in a brand new 12,000-square-foot building.
Details: Mon–Fri 10–5. $2 adults, $1.50 ages 65 and older, $1 students. (1 hour)

★★ SOUTH OF THE BORDER
843/774-2411 or 800/922-6064 (in South Carolina)
800/845-6011 (out of state)
You can't possibly miss it if you follow the billboards with the corny messages. It's huge, it's tacky, and it's fun. The complex offers food, lodging, gas, recreation, amusements, fireworks, and more.
Details: I-95 south of the South Carolina/North Carolina border. (1–2 hours)

★★ WAR BETWEEN THE STATES MUSEUM
107 S. Guerry St., Florence, 843/669-1266
Displays consist of relics and treasures, including flags, money, bayonets, and sabers, from the Civil War.
Details: Wed–Sat 10–5. $2 adults, $1.50 seniors and children. (2 hours)

★ FLORENCE NATIONAL CEMETERY
803 E. National Cemetary Rd.
This six-acre national shrine, frequently referred to as South Carolina's Little Arlington, holds the graves of the veterans of five wars.
Details: Year-round daily. (1 hour)

FITNESS AND RECREATION

The state parks in Pee Dee Country provide miles of boardwalks, hiking trails, and equestrian trails and great spots for fishing and bird-watching. In **Woods Bay State Park**, off U.S. 301 west of Olanta, you'll find a Carolina bay, an inexplicable shallow indentation in the earth filled with water and more than a few alligators. A boardwalk keeps your feet dry. **Lee State Park** and **Little Pee Dee State Park**, near Bishopville and Dillon respectively, provide some of the state's best bream fishing.

FOOD

So you wouldn't know a grit if one spit in your eye? Plan breakfast at **Grits Plus**, 200 W. Evans St., Florence, 843/667-8105, and order plain, buttered, cheese, or ham grits. Check out the "plus" menu, too. For an affordable adventure in fine dining, try the **Magnolia Restaurant**, I-95 and Hwy. 76, Florence, 843/669-4171, or **Two 31 South**, 231 S. Irby St., Florence, 843/664-0231.

Also recommended are **B.J.'s**, 1022 Pearl St., Darlington, 843/393-4957,

PEE DEE COUNTRY

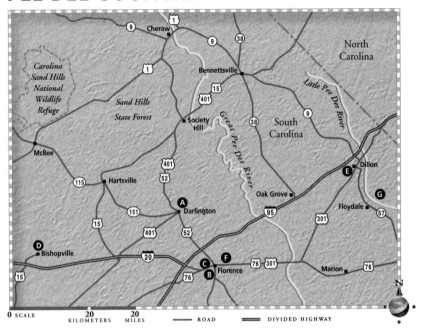

FOOD
- Ⓐ B.J.'s
- Ⓐ Country Barn BBQ
- Ⓑ Grits Plus
- Ⓐ Hong Kong Restaurant
- Ⓒ Magnolia Restaurant
- Ⓑ Two 31 South

LODGING
- Ⓐ Big Apple Inn
- Ⓐ Croft Magnolia Inn
- Ⓓ Fox Fire Bed and Breakfast
- Ⓑ Heritage Place
- Ⓔ South of the Border
- Ⓑ Youngs Plantation Inn

CAMPING
- Ⓔ Camp Pedro— South of the Border
- Ⓕ Florence KOA
- Ⓖ Little Pee Dee State Park

Note: Items with the same letter are located in the same area.

for great country cooking, the **Hong Kong Restaurant**, 608 Pearl St., Darlington, 843/393-3927, specializing in fine Asian cuisine, and the **Country Barn BBQ**, Hwy. 151, Darlington, 843/395-2257, with barbecue sliced (or chopped) any way you like it. All offer reasonably priced, really good food.

LODGING

Florence has more hotels and motels than any other area city. It's sprinkled with Econo Lodges and Days Inns, but these alternative accommodations are especially commended. **Heritage Place**, 309 S. Irby St., 843/662-0461, has moderate rates. Also offering good lodgings for your money is **Youngs Plantation Inn**, I-95 Exit 157 at U.S. 76, 843/669-4171. Amenities include a tennis court, and the inn is graced with the Magnolia Restaurant.

Big Apple Inn, 7056 Washington St. (Hwy. 52), Darlington, 843/393-8990, has one obvious attraction: It's near the race track. But the rooms are nice, and the service is good; rates range from inexpensive to moderate. Much more expensive and much more elegant is the **Croft Magnolia Inn**, 414 Cashua St., Darlington, 843/393-1908. This English-style inn serves a full breakfast as well as afternoon tea for guests of its six units. In nearby Bishopville, you'll find the cozy **Fox Fire Bed and Breakfast**, 416 N. Main St., 843/484-5643.

At **South of the Border**, I-95 Exit 1 at U.S. 301, Dillon, 843/774-2411 or 800/922-6064 in South Carolina, 800/845-6011 out of state, you'll find a variety of accommodations and prices to fit your pocketbook—in other words, as fancy as you want, as high-priced as you can afford. But all the conveniences are in the compound, and they range from restaurants to tennis courts, a post office, and a bank.

CAMPING

Camp Pedro at South of the Border has more than 100 sites. Call 843/774-2411 or 800/922-6064 in South Carolina, 800/845-6011 out of state. In Florence, try the **Florence KOA**, 115 E. Campground Rd., 843/665-7007 or 800/562-7807. If bream fishing is in your future, head for **Little Pee Dee State Park**, off S.C. 57 east of Dillon, 843/774-8872.

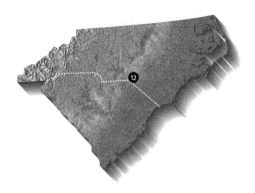

12
THE SANDHILLS

The area known as the North Carolina Sandhills was once part of a prehistoric ocean. Over the centuries, as the water retreated, it carved gracefully rolling hills that eventually would become the fairways of one of the world's greatest golf destinations. There is more to do here than golf, but if you have an avid linkster in the family, you'll never hear a word from him or her about horse shows, music festivals, or any number of other special events scheduled throughout the year.

Consisting of Pinehurst, Southern Pines, and Aberdeen, the Sandhills area hosts the PGA Tour, Seniors U.S. Open, U.S. Women's Open, and North and South Amateur Championship, to name a few. The 2000 U.S. Women's Public Links Amateur Championship is set for Legacy Golf Links, and the 2001 U.S. Women's Open Championship will be played at Pine Needles Lodge and Golf Club.

The Sandhills area consistently receives top honors for golf-course quality in *Golf Digest*'s "Places to Play Guide." What makes this location perfect for golf? It could be the sheer number of championship courses. But, more than that, the region embodies the golf tradition and conjures up golf's grandest era, when legends were born and grew.

For the non-golfer, the area provides quiet country lanes, friendly southern towns, and a diversity of activities. If you want to get out and about but not in a golf cart, you may opt for tennis, archery, water sports, bicycling, or croquet.

A PERFECT DAY IN THE SANDHILLS

If you stay at an establishment such as the Pinehurst Resort and Country Club and refuse to play golf, despite the shaking of heads over your quirk, start the day with an early swim in the pool and a light breakfast of croissants and fruit. Dress casually and head for Pottery Country, where potters don't mind if you watch them at work, but they will appreciate it if you buy their wares. Buy some and you won't be sorry—this pottery is reasonably priced and highly collectible. After lunch, head to Southern Pines to tour the Shaw House and its historic properties. Admire the handicrafts and be glad you have modern conveniences. Back at the resort, join other guests for cocktails before repairing to the incomparable Carolina Room, where an experience in fine continental dining awaits. A starlit stroll along the property prepares you for sweet dreams.

SIGHTSEEING HIGHLIGHTS

★★★★ NORTH CAROLINA POTTERY CENTER
250 East Ave., Seagrove, 336/873-8430

The entire Sandhills area is famous for its hand-thrown pottery and dishware, which are created before your eyes and offered for sale at reasonable prices. Typical standout features include salt-glazed stoneware, innovative designs, and wood firing in groundhog kilns. Most area potters, including Jugtown Pottery, Ben Owen Pottery, Whynot Pottery, Old House Pottery, and numerous independents, are open year-round.

Details: Tue–Sat 10–4. (3–4 hours)

★★★★ SANDHILLS HORTICULTURAL GARDENS AND SIR WALTER RALEIGH GARDENS
Sandhills Community College, Airport Rd., Pinehurst 910/695-3882

The gardens feature the Ebersole Holly Collection, a conifer garden, a formal English garden, and the Desmond Wetland Trail. The gardens are wheelchair accessible.

Details: Dawn–dusk year-round. Free. (2–3 hours)

★★★★ SHAW HOUSE
Morganton Rd. and SW Broad St., Southern Pines 910/692-2051

Three historic homes are located on this property, and another one

THE SANDHILLS

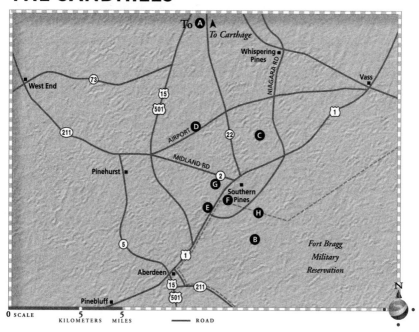

SIGHTS

Ⓐ House in the Horseshoe
Ⓑ Malcolm Blue Farm
Ⓒ Pottery Country
Ⓓ Sandhills Horticultural Gardens–Sir
Walter Raleigh Gardens

Ⓔ Shaw House
Ⓕ Taxidermy Hall of Fame
Ⓖ Weymouth Center
Ⓗ Weymouth Woods–Sandhills
Nature Preserve

(McLendon/Bryant Place) is about 30 minutes away. The antebellum Shaw House was built in the 1820s. The colonial-era Garner House is a log structure with wide-board heart pine paneling, original hand-forged hinges, and board doors. The Britt-Sanders Cabin, built around 1770, is a one-room pioneer home with a loft. The McLendon/Bryant Place, circa 1820, is a restored manor house with handmade window sashes and doors. Hand-molded chimney bricks were fired on the property.

Details: *Tue–Sun 1–4. McLendon/ Bryant Place open Sun 2–5. Admission by donation. (3 hours)*

FAYETTEVILLE

Slightly northeast of Pinehurst and exactly halfway between New York and Miami is Fayetteville, the first city named after the Marquis de Lafayette and the only one he actually visited. The city was formed in 1783 by the merger of two towns that had been settled early in the century by immigrants from the Highlands of Scotland.

Fayetteville was an inland port centrally located on the early plank road system of American highways. A great fire in 1831 destroyed more than 600 buildings in the city, which was rebuilt only to find itself in the destructive path of General William T. Sherman's Union troops. The city was again rebuilt.

Today visitors delight in touring many homes on the National Historic Register, historic churches, and the Museum of the Cape Fear. Adjacent are **Fort Bragg,** *America's second largest landmass military base with a daily population of 62,000, and* **Pope Air Force Base,** *home of the Flying Tigers. For more information contact Fayetteville Area Convention and Visitors Bureau, 245 Person St., Fayetteville, NC 28301-4911, 800/255-8217 or 910/483-5311.*

★★★ HOUSE IN THE HORSESHOE
Carbonton Rd., Carthage, 910/947-2051

Built around 1772, this plantation home has a gabled roof and large double-shouldered Flemish bond chimneys. Formerly a cotton plantation, the house shows bullet holes from a 1781 skirmish between Whigs and Tories. Special events include an annual reenactment of this Revolutionary War battle during the first weekend in August and a Christmas Open House and Candlelighting in early December.

Details: *10 miles north of Carthage. Hours vary seasonally. Free. (1–2 hours)*

★★★ MALCOLM BLUE FARM
Bethesda Rd., Aberdeen, 910/944-7558

On the National Register of Historic Places, this circa-1825 antebellum farm includes a farmhouse and barns, an old gristmill, and a wooden water tower. Annual events include the Historic Crafts and

---

Skills Festival the last weekend of September and the Christmas Open House on the second Sunday of December.
Details: *Hours vary according to season. Free. (1–2 hours)*

★★★ **WEYMOUTH WOODS AND SANDHILLS NATURE PRESERVE**
1024 Fort Bragg Rd., Southern Pines, 910/692-2167
The preserve has 571 acres of wildflowers, forest animals, and streams and ponds, plus 4.5 miles of hiking trails, a beaver pond, a museum with hands-on exhibits, and a full-time naturalist. Kids will love it and so will you.
Details: *Daily 9–6. Free. (3 hours)*

★★ **WEYMOUTH CENTER**
555 E. Connecticut Ave., 910/692-6261
This 1920s Georgian mansion, on 20 acres with extensive gardens, offers arts and humanities activities. The North Carolina Literary Hall of Fame offers information about North Carolina authors.
Details: *Mansion open Tue–Thu 10–2, by appointment only. Gardens open daily dawn–dusk. Free. (1–2 hours)*

★ **TAXIDERMY HALL OF FAME**
156 NW Broad St., Southern Pines, 910/692-3471
Every kind of wildlife native to North Carolina that is legally collectible is displayed here. You'll see state and national award-winning examples of taxidermy and the oldest rock on earth—or so they say.
Details: *Call for hours. (1 hour)*

FITNESS AND RECREATION

If you can exercise naturally anywhere in the world, you can do it here. Golfers enthusiastically walk the miles of courses day after day, while those who love and indulge them can limber up on the area's hiking and jogging trails, work out in various resort and commercial gyms, play tennis, fish, ride horseback, or go boating or swimming.

FOOD

All the usual restaurants are here, from Applebee's to Western Sizzlin', but in the Sandhills you will find some unique eateries. **Dugans**, on Market Square in

THE SANDHILLS

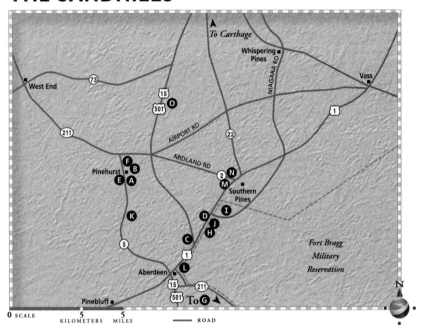

FOOD

Ⓐ Carolina Room
Ⓑ Dugans
Ⓒ John's Barbeque and Seafood Restaurant
Ⓓ Lob-Steer Inn
Ⓔ Magnolia Inn
Ⓕ Pine Crest Inn
Ⓖ Quewhiffle Seafood Restaurant
Ⓗ Thai Orchid Restaurant
Ⓘ Whiskey McNeill's

LODGING

Ⓙ Best Western Pinehurst Inn
Ⓚ The Golf Connection/CondoLodge
Ⓛ Inn at Bryant House
Ⓜ Mid Pines Inn and Golf Club
Ⓝ Pine Needles Lodge and Golf Club
Ⓐ Pinehurst Resort and Country Club

CAMPING

Ⓞ Pinehurst RV Resort

Note: Items with the same letter are located in the same area.

Pinehurst, 910/295-3400, is a continental restaurant open for lunch and dinner. Dinners average $17 or less per person. **John's Barbeque and Seafood Restaurant** is on U.S. 1 N., 910/692-9474. The food is good, and the prices are reasonable. John's is open lunch through dinner daily but closed Sunday. The **Carolina Room** at Pinehurst Resort and Country Club, Carolina Vista Dr., Pinehurst, 910/295-8434, serves breakfast, lunch, and dinner, specializing in continental dining. Allow more than $30 per diner. **Pine Crest Inn** on Dogwood Road in Pinehurst, 910/295-6121, is moderately expensive and features continental cuisine. Breakfast and dinner are served, and the inn offers a cocktail lounge with piano bar. Reservations are recommended.

The **Lob-Steer Inn**, U.S. 1 N., Southern Pines, 910/692-3503, is open for dinner only, serving . . . go ahead, guess. Expect to pay less than $30 per person, but don't plan too late a dinner: Closing time is 9:30 to 10 p.m. Moderately priced meals are also available at the **Magnolia Inn** in the village of Pinehurst, 910/295-6900. The inn serves lunch Tuesday through Saturday and dinner every day. Also recommended in Southern Pines is **Whiskey McNeill's**, 181 N.E. Broad St., 910/692-5440, where a good-time lunch or dinner can be had by all.

In Aberdeen, you might want to try the quaintly named **Quewhiffle Seafood Restaurant**, Rt. 211 E., 910/944-1619. It's open Tuesday through Saturday, with dinners at less than $15 per person. Also in Aberdeen is the **Thai Orchid Restaurant**, 1404 Sandhills Blvd., 910/944-9299. If you're tired of all the barbecue, steak, and seafood this area of North Carolina seems to call dinner, try this restaurant. It's inexpensive, open for lunch except Saturday, and open for dinner every day.

LODGING

Golf privileges come with accommodations at the **Best Western Pinehurst Inn**, 1500 Sandhills Blvd., Aberdeen, six minutes from Pinehurst, 910/944-2367 or 800/528-1234. Aberdeen's **Inn at Bryant House**, 214 N. Poplar St., 910/944-3300 or 800/453-4019, is a Historic Registry property that has been completely restored to its 1913 splendor.

The **Golf Connection/CondoLodge**, 650-C Page St., Pinehurst, 910/295-0003 or 800/255-4653, has 40 condos featuring, of course, golf privileges at the area's best courses. It also offers tennis privileges, swimming, picnicking, fishing, biking, horseback riding, and more.

Mid Pines Inn and Golf Club, 1010 Midland Rd., Southern Pines, 910/692-2114 or 800/323-2114, is a complete resort community with all that entails. Another excellent Southern Pines resort is **Pine Needles Lodge and Golf Club**, Midland Rd., 910/692-7111 or 800/747-7272.

Pinehurst Resort and Country Club, Carolina Vista Dr., Pinehurst, 910/295-6811 or 800/487-4653, has 525 rooms and condos with all the amenities you could wish. Non-golfers can enjoy themselves swimming, fishing, biking, playing tennis, canoeing, rafting, jogging, and exploring any of a dozen other activities that have nothing to do with getting teed off.

CAMPING

The year-round **Pinehurst RV Resort**, 251 Campground Rd., 910/295-5452 or 800/600-0705, has a lake with a beach area, fishing (no license required), biking, swimming, canoeing, golf, and, of course, trailer and tent sites with water and electric hookups. Pets on leashes are welcome.

GOLFING

The **Club at Longleaf**, 2001 Midland Rd., Southern Pines, 910/692-6100 or 800/889-5323, is a Dan Maples–designed course described by *Golf Digest* as "the most playable course in Pinehurst." Legends of the game have polished their skills for more than a century at **Pinehurst Resort and Country Club**, Carolina Vista Dr., Pinehurst, 910/295-6811 or 800/ITS-GOLF. The resort has eight championship courses and was the site of the 1991 and 1992 TOUR Championship, the 1994 U.S. Senior Open, and the 1999 U.S. Open. It also boasts the Pinehurst Golf Advantage School.

Legacy Golf Links, U.S. 15-501 S., Aberdeen, 910/944-8825, is the only public course in the area to receive four-star and great-value ratings from *Golf Digest*'s "Places To Play Guide." It blends the accessibility of a public course with a private club and a Jack Nicklaus II Golden Bear Design. **Mid Pines Resort**, 1010 Midland Rd., Southern Pines, 910/692-2114 or 800/323-2114, is ranked in the "Top 50 Courses" in the state by *Golfweek* magazine. Designed by Donald Ross and opened in 1921, this course is cited by those who have visited as "golf the way it was meant to be played." Also recommended is **Pine Needles Lodge and Golf Club**, Midland Rd., Southern Pines, 910/692-7111 or 800/747-7272. This site of the 1996 and 2001 U.S. Women's Open offers year-round golf schools and clinics.

For unusual caddying—done by llamas—in addition to the pleasure of a Rees Jones course, try **Talamore**, 1595 Midland Rd., Southern Pines, 910/692-5884 or 800/552-6292. It boasts a four-star rating from *Golf Digest*. **Whispering Woods Golf Club**, 26 Sandpiper Dr., Whispering Pines, 910/949-4653 or 800/224-5061, is one of the most peaceful and relaxing greens in the area. The Ellis Maples–designed course is a challenge to golfers of all ages and handicaps.

13
WILMINGTON

Wilmington, one of the East Coast's fastest growing deepwater ports, was founded before the Revolutionary War. It was in Wilmington that the first play written and produced in the colonies debuted in 1756. In 1788 Wilmington established the Thalian Association, a still-active amateur theater group. In 1841 it became a major rail center, and, during the Civil War, it was the last Atlantic port open to blockade runners.

Today Wilmington is home to a major movie-production studio and host to the North Carolina Jazz Festival in February, North Carolina Azalea Festival in April, Carolina Beach Music Festival in June, Cape Fear Rugby Tournament in July, Piney Woods Festival in September, and Carolina Beach Surf Fishing tournament in October. Seasons are mild in Wilmington, with 212 days of sunshine and a mean average temperature of 63.7 degrees. Temperatures usually reach the 80s in summer and drop into the 50s in winter.

A few interesting facts about the area: The Venus's-flytrap is found naturally only within a 100-mile radius of Wilmington. This perennial, which Charles Darwin pronounced "the most wonderful plant in the world," is both insectivorous and carnivorous. The loggerhead sea turtle, protected by the Endangered Species Act, visits the beach areas of the Cape Fear between mid-May and late August. The females weigh 200 to 500 pounds and lay an average of 120 eggs in the dunes closest to the ocean. Bald Head Island is the site of North Carolina's oldest standing lighthouse, "Old Baldy."

WILMINGTON AREA

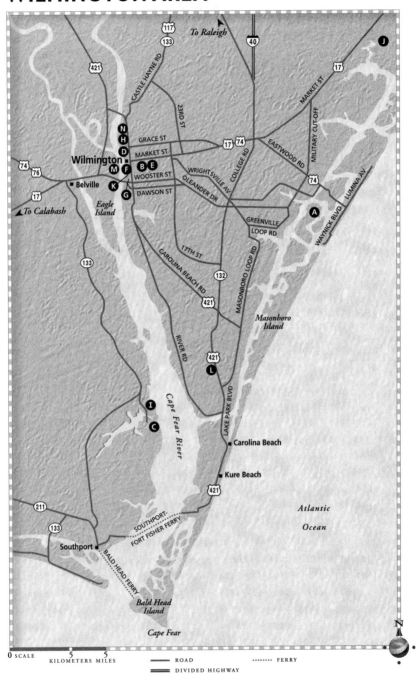

To Raleigh

To Calabash

Wilmington

Belville

Eagle Island

Cape Fear River

Masonboro Island

Carolina Beach

Kure Beach

Atlantic Ocean

Southport

Bald Head Island

Cape Fear

SOUTHPORT-FORT FISHER FERRY

BALD HEAD FERRY

CASTLE HAYNE RD
23RD ST
GRACE ST
MARKET ST
WOOSTER ST
DAWSON ST
WRIGHTSVILLE AV
OLEANDER DR
COLLEGE RD
EASTWOOD RD
MARKET ST
MILITARY CUT-OFF
LUMINA AV
WAYNICK BLVD
GREENVILLE LOOP RD
17TH ST
CAROLINA BEACH RD
RIVER RD
MASONBORO LOOP RD
LAKE PARK BLVD

0 SCALE
KILOMETERS MILES
5   5

ROAD
DIVIDED HIGHWAY
FERRY

N

A PERFECT DAY IN WILMINGTON

Start with a tour of the Cape Fear River on the *Captain J.N. Maffitt*, Wilmington's first tour boat. This is your basic open-air, sit-down-and-listen-while-the-breeze-refreshes-you tour. The 45-minute narrated cruise, which is really a river taxi to the USS *North Carolina*, leaves the foot of Market Street and follows a five-mile loop of the river. At the dock, disembark for a battleship tour.

For lunch, trek to the Fifth and Castle Streets location of Hall's Drug Store, a genuine old-fashioned soda fountain where you can sip fresh-squeezed lemonade or orangeade with a sandwich from the grill. Let your lunch digest during a sightseeing tour by horse-drawn carriage originating at Water and Market Streets. Your driver will tell you the stories behind the stately mansions and the historic riverfront. Afterward, shop Chandler's Wharf and take your pick of the dining opportunities afforded there.

MORE WILMINGTON HISTORY

Brunswick Town, some 16 miles from present-day Wilmington, was the site of one of the first incidents of armed resistance against English authority. It wasn't exactly a tea party, but the message was the same. In 1765, eight years before the Boston Tea Party, residents of Brunswick Town rallied against the Stamp Act, surrounding the home of royal Governor William Tryon and placing him under house arrest. They were successful in unloading and distributing unstamped goods from two ships in the harbor and forced the resignation of several officials. From that date, ships required no stamps on the Cape Fear.

Brunswick Town declined as Wilmington grew. Following destruction wrought by hurricanes and malaria-carrying mosquitoes, the town was deserted by the beginning of the Revolutionary War and was burned by the British in 1776. The town site was sold to the owner of Orton Plantation in the 1840s for $4.25.

SIGHTS

- Ⓐ Airlie Gardens
- Ⓑ Bellamy Mansion Museum of History and Design Arts
- Ⓒ Brunswick Town
- Ⓓ Burgwin Wright House and Garden
- Ⓔ Cape Fear Museum
- Ⓕ Cape Fear Riverboats
- Ⓖ Chandler's Wharf
- Ⓗ The Cotton Exchange
- Ⓘ Orton Plantation Gardens
- Ⓙ Poplar Grove Plantation
- Ⓚ St. John's Museum of Art
- Ⓛ Tote-'Em-In Zoo
- Ⓜ USS *North Carolina* Battleship Memorial
- Ⓝ Wilmington Railroad Museum

SIGHTSEEING HIGHLIGHTS

★★★★ CAPE FEAR MUSEUM
814 Market St., 910/341-4350

Hands-on exploration of southeastern North Carolina is possible here in the Michael Jordan (yes, that Michael Jordan) Discovery Gallery, where you can crawl through a beaver lodge, feed a Venus's-flytrap, build a tree, and move sand dunes. Changing exhibitions and weekend programs highlight the diverse environment and cultural history of the Cape Fear region.

Details: Mon–Sat 9–5, Sun 2–5. $4 adults, $3 seniors, $1 ages 5 to 18. (3 hours)

★★★★ ST. JOHN'S MUSEUM OF ART
114 Orange St., 910/763-0281
www.stjohnsart@wilmington.org

This museum is the primary visual arts center in southeastern North Carolina. It is housed in three restored, architecturally distinctive buildings—one is circa 1804—united by a sculpture garden. The museum houses an extensive collection of paintings, works on paper, sculpture, and Jugtown pottery from three centuries of "North Carolina masters." It also boasts one of the world's major holdings of color prints by Mary Cassatt. If you want something to take home, check out the Art Sales Gallery, which represents more than 80 contemporary North Carolina artists and craftspeople.

Details: Tue–Sat 10–5, Sun noon–4. $2 adults, $1 ages 6 to 17. (3 hours)

★★★★ USS NORTH CAROLINA BATTLESHIP MEMORIAL
Battleship Dr., Eagle Island, 910/350-1817 or
910/251-5797, www.city-info.com/ncbb55.html

One of the most popular tourist attractions in the area is this authentically restored World War II battleship. The USS *North Carolina* was part of the Pacific Fleet from 1941 to 1945 and took part in every major naval offensive in the Pacific, including Iwo Jima, Okinawa, Guadalcanal, and Tokyo Bay. It was the most decorated ship of the war. Portions of nine decks are open for touring.

Details: Sept 16–May 15 daily 8–5, May 16–Sept 15, 8–8. $8 adults, $4 ages 6 to 11. (3 hours)

★★★ **BELLAMY MANSION MUSEUM OF HISTORY AND DESIGN ARTS**
Fifth and Market Sts., 910/251-3700
One of the Cape Fear's newest museums, the Bellamy offers guided tours and exhibits featuring history, restoration, southern architecture, and regional design arts. The mansion is in an 1859 landmark.
Details: *Wed–Sat 10–5, Sun 1–5. $6 adults, $3 ages 5 to 12. (2–3 hours)*

★★★ **BRUNSWICK TOWN**
Winnabow, 910/371-6613
Brunswick Town was begun in 1726 as a port for exporting naval supplies and lumber to Europe and the West Indies, but most townspeople deserted it at the onset of the American Revolution. In 1862 the Confederate army built Fort Anderson here to protect the port of Wilmington. Today Brunswick Town is the site of more than 60 archaeological excavations that show the remains of the colonial town and the great earth mounds of Fort Anderson. Thousands of artifacts are displayed at the visitor's center.
Details: *Apr–Oct Mon–Sat 9–5, Sun 1–5; Nov–Mar Tue–Sat 10–4, Sun 1–4. Free. (2 hours)*

★★★ **BURGWIN WRIGHT HOUSE AND GARDEN**
224 Market St., 910/762-0570
www.geocities.com/picketfence/garden/4354
Wilmington's oldest restored house is a superb example of a colonial gentleman's townhouse. Dating to 1770, it contains a fine collection of eighteenth-century furniture and decorative arts. It also has a dungeon where Lord Charles Cornwallis, who headquartered here in 1781, was said to have kept his prisoners.
Details: *Feb–Dec Tue–Sat 10–4. $5 adults, $2 students. (1 hour)*

★★★ **ORTON PLANTATION GARDENS**
9149 Orton Rd. SE, Winnabow, 910/371-6851
Twenty acres of gardens feature live oaks, azaleas, camellias, and thousands of annuals. Take the walking tour and enjoy. Orton House, a private residence, was founded as a rice plantation in 1725 and may be seen from the garden paths.
Details: *Spring and summer daily 8–6, fall daily 10–5. $8 adults, $7 senior citizens, $3 ages 6 to 12. (2 hours)*

★★★ POPLAR GROVE PLANTATION
10200 U.S. 17 N., 910/686-9518
www.ego.net//us/nc/ilm/tts/pgrove.htm
Blacksmithing, textile, and basket-weaving demonstrations are regularly performed at this Greek Revival–style 1850 manor house/museum. It was originally a peanut plantation, just a short distance north of Wilmington. The plantation is open year-round, with a restaurant on the grounds.
Details: Mon–Sat 9–5, Sun noon–5. $7 adults, $6 senior citizens and active military, $3 ages 6 to 15. (2 hours)

★★★ WILMINGTON RAILROAD MUSEUM
Water and Red Cross Sts., 910/763-2634
This museum specializes in artifacts of the Atlantic Coastline Railroad.
Details: Mon and Tue, Thu–Sat 10–5, Sun 1–5. $3 adults, $2 seniors and military, $1.50 ages 6 to 11. (1 hour)

★★ AIRLIE GARDENS
Airlie Rd. (U.S. 76), 910/452-6393, www.airliegardens.org
These gardens once surrounded the home of a wealthy rice planter and are interspersed with trees and lakes with swans. Early spring, when the azaleas are in bloom, is the most colorful time to visit, but the gardens guarantee tranquil delight at any time of year.
Details: Apr–Oct Fri and Sat 9–5, Sun 1–5. Times vary the rest of the year. $8 adults, $5 children. (1–2 hours)

★★ CHANDLER'S WHARF
Ann and Water Sts.
Located on five acres of the Cape Fear River, Chandler's Wharf is a complex of restored historic buildings, cobblestone streets, picket fences, and spring-fed streams. It is also home to an elegant warehouse mall featuring one-of-a-kind stores.
Details: Open year-round. Free. (2–4 hours)

★★ THE COTTON EXCHANGE
321 N. Front St., 910/343-9896
Formerly the largest cotton exporting company in the world, this complex of eight historic buildings on the Cape Fear River houses 32 shops and restaurants.

Details: Mon–Sat 10–5:30, some shops open Sun 1–5, restaurants open evenings. Free. (1–3 hours)

★★ TOTE-'EM-IN ZOO
5811 Carolina Beach Rd., 910/791-0472

The five-acre forestlike environment and its residents—zebras, baboons, monkeys, exotic birds, a Siberian tiger, and Clyde the Camel—welcome the entire family.
Details: Mon–Fri 9–4, Sat and Sun 9–5. $5 adults, $3 ages 2 to 11. (2–3 hours)

★ CAPE FEAR RIVERBOATS
N. Water St., 910/343-1611 or 800/676-0162

Narrated sightseeing cruises and dinner cruises with entertainment are offered on this true stern-wheeler riverboat.
Details: Near the Wilmington Hilton Hotel. Apr–Dec. Call for times and prices. (2–4 hours)

FITNESS AND RECREATION

Fort Fisher State Recreation Area, U.S. 421 at Kure Beach, offers four miles of undeveloped shoreline to explore. **Jubilee Amusement Park** has go-carts and waterslides as well as amusement rides. It's also on U.S. 421, just over the bridge as you enter Carolina Beach. In Wilmington you'll find abundant jogging and biking trails, along with a YMCA, health clubs, and hotel fitness centers.

FOOD

Part of the ambiance of the Cape Fear coast comes from the shrimp boats lining the docks and the seafood markets close by. The fishing industry provides a livelihood for a number of residents, and area specialties include fried or boiled shrimp; fried, steamed, or raw oysters; steamed or sautéed Atlantic blue crab; King mackerel steaks cooked over charcoal; and grouper salad. OK, you could eat steaks, ribs, and fast food here, too, but why would you want to?

The **Bridge Tender**, 1414 Airlie Rd., Wrightsville Beach, 910/256-4519, may be a little pricey, but that's because of its reputation. Among other honors, it has received an award of excellence from *Wine Spectator* magazine and has been cited by several publications for its excellent seafood. Dinner for two will run about $50, but you can eat lunch for much less.

WILMINGTON AREA

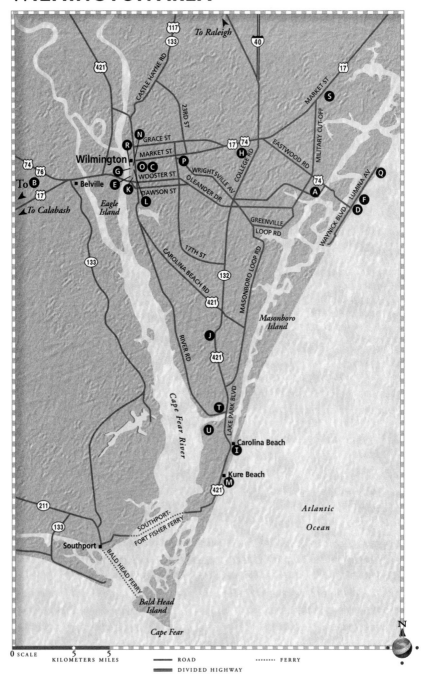

You can't find many old-fashioned soda fountains and grills in the country anymore, but **Hall's Drug Store**, on the corner of Fifth and Castle Streets, Wilmington, 910/762-5265, remains. Try the homemade soup, fresh-squeezed lemonade or orangeade, sandwiches from the grill, and real milkshakes.

King Neptune, 11 N. Lumina Ave., 910/256-2525, is an old-time seafood restaurant in the heart of Wrightsville Beach. It's informal, with dinner entrées ranging from $9 to $16. **Pilot House Restaurant**, 2 Ann St. in Chandler's Wharf, 910/343-0200, serves not only fresh seafood but also pasta and continental cuisine. The lunch crowd favors the grilled crab melt and Carolina seafood chowder, while the dinner crowd prefers more elaborate dishes, including filet au poivre. Lunch costs less than $10; dinner around $20. **Skinner & Daniels**, 5214 Market St., Wilmington, 910/799-1790, specializes in distinctive North Carolina barbecue—pork, chicken, beef, and short ribs—and Brunswick stew. You also get an amazing selection of veggies. Sandwiches cost less than $5; plates under $10. Open Monday through Saturday for lunch and dinner.

Also recommended are **Saxon's by the River** in Wilmington (138 S. Front St., 910/762-8898) and the **Raw Bar** in Wrightsville Beach (13 E. Salisbury St., 910/256-2974).

Just a few minutes' drive farther south on U.S. 17 is the tiny town of **Calabash**, where restaurants nearly outnumber residents. No matter which restaurant you pick, you'll be happy—with the food and the price. Other restaurants in other towns serve Calabash-style fish and chicken, but only here will you find the real thing.

FOOD

- Ⓐ Bridge Tender
- Ⓑ Calabash, N.C.
- Ⓒ Hall's Drug Store
- Ⓓ King Neptune
- Ⓔ Pilot House Restaurant
- Ⓕ Raw Bar
- Ⓖ Saxon's by the River
- Ⓗ Skinner & Daniels

LODGING

- Ⓘ Beacon House Inn Bed and Breakfast
- Ⓙ Beau Rivage Plantation

LODGING (continued)

- Ⓚ Catherine's Inn
- Ⓛ Curran House
- Ⓜ Docksider Inn-Oceanfront
- Ⓝ Inn at St. Thomas Court
- Ⓞ Inn on Orange
- Ⓟ Manor House Bed and Breakfast
- Ⓠ Shell Island Resort
- Ⓡ Stemmerman's Inn

CAMPING

- Ⓢ Camelot Campgrounds RV Park
- Ⓣ Carolina Beach Family Campground
- Ⓤ Carolina Beach State Park

LODGING

There's no lack of quality accommodations in Wilmington and on the Cape Fear coast. If you want something a little different, here are some suggestions. **Beau Rivage Plantation**, 6491 Rivage Promenade, Wilmington, 800/628-7080 or 910/392-9021, is open year-round with deluxe accommodations in one-bedroom suites; each has a private balcony with a golf-course view. Offering five rooms, a meal plan, and a waterfront location is **Catherine's Inn**, 410 S. Front St., Wilmington, 910/251-0863 or 800/476-0723. The **Inn on Orange** is a bed-and-breakfast at 410 Orange St., Wilmington, 910/815-0035.

Also in Wilmington are the **Manor House Bed and Breakfast**, with four rooms at 1417 Market Street, 910/763-3081; **Curran House**, with three rooms at 312 South Third Street, 910/763-6603; **Stemmerman's Inn**, with seven efficiencies at 132 South Front Street, 910/763-7776; and the **Inn at St. Thomas Court**, with 40 suites at 101 South Second Street, 910/343-1800 or 800/525-0909.

Beacon House Inn Bed and Breakfast offers nine rooms and two cottages at 715 Carolina Beach Avenue, Carolina Beach, 910/458-6244. **Docksider Inn-Oceanfront** offers 34 rooms and a fishing pier at Kure Beach, 910/458-4200. In Wrightsville Beach, you'll find **Shell Island Resort**, 2700 N. Lumina Ave., 910/256-8696 or 800/689-6765, with 160 suites (all with oceanfront views) and all the amenities you'd expect from a first-class facility.

CAMPING

Among recommended campgrounds are **Camelot Campgrounds RV Park**, 7415 Market St., Wilmington, 910/686-7705 or 800/454-7705, offering RV tent sites and a full range of amenities, including a store, nature trail, firewood, pool, and playground. **Carolina Beach Family Campground**, 9641 River Rd., Wilmington, 910/392-3322, has trailer and tent sites, water and electric hookups, and hot showers. Pets on leashes are welcome. **Carolina Beach State Park**, S.R. 1628, 910/458-8206, offers campsites, a marina, launching ramps, picnic areas, hiking trails, and group camping.

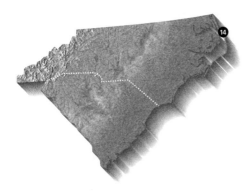

14
THE OUTER BANKS

The magic and mystery of the Outer Banks have not diminished with time. Four hundred years ago, with the 1587 arrival of the first English settlers, the history of European settlement in North Carolina began along this 130-mile stretch of barrier islands. The Outer Banks is also the site of the nation's oldest mystery: What happened to those colonists?

If history is a passion and slow-paced living and pristine beaches are preferences, the Outer Banks could provide the most satisfying vacation, or time-out, you have ever had. This is a family-oriented place, where younger children play in the sand while their more adventurous elders enjoy hang gliding and parasailing. Fishing is popular, as are biking, boating, and horseback riding.

Special events are held year-round and include regattas, golf and fishing tournaments, seafood and watermelon (not at the same time or place) festivals, kite contests, arts-and-crafts shows, and an annual Man Will Never Fly Memorial Society seminar and banquet. The latter is especially interesting because it was from Kitty Hawk that bicycle repair specialists Wilbur and Orville Wright made history with the first manned flight. The event is marked with the Wright Brothers Memorial, and a grand celebration already is being planned for the 100th anniversary of flight, December 17, 2003, at Kitty Hawk. For information about the weeklong series of events, call the First Flight Centennial Foundation, 919/715-0209.

THE OUTER BANKS

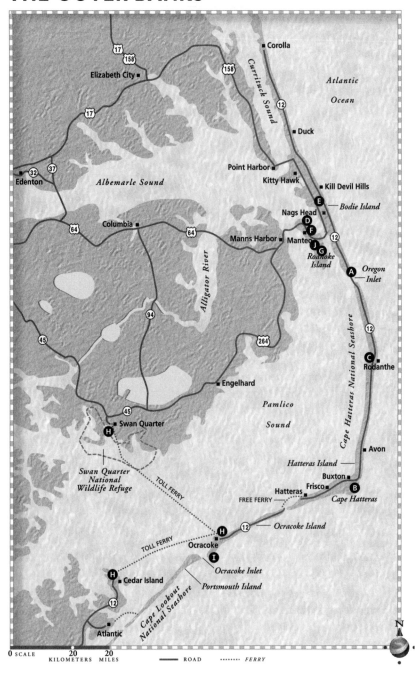

Corolla

Atlantic

Ocean

17
158

158

Currituck Sound

Elizabeth City

12

17

Duck

32
37

Point Harbor

Edenton

Albemarle Sound

Kitty Hawk

Kill Devil Hills

E

Bodie Island

Nags Head

D

64

Columbia

64

F

Manns Harbor

Manteo

12

J
G

Roanoke
Island

A
Oregon
Inlet

Alligator River

94

12

264

C
Rodanthe

45

Engelhard

Pamlico

45

Swan Quarter

Sound

H

Avon

Swan Quarter
National
Wildlife Refuge

TOLL FERRY

Hatteras Island

Buxton

Frisco

B

Hatteras

Cape Hatteras

FREE FERRY

Cape Hatteras National Seashore

12
Ocracoke Island

H

TOLL FERRY

Ocracoke

H
Cedar Island

I

Ocracoke Inlet

12

Portsmouth Island

Cape Lookout National Seashore

Atlantic

N

0 SCALE   20   20
KILOMETERS MILES   ——— ROAD   .... FERRY

A PERFECT DAY ON THE OUTER BANKS

One way to assure that your visit to the Outer Banks is different from any other day at the beach is to rent an off-road vehicle. Off-road driving is permitted along the Cape Hatteras National Seashore year-round, but each township has its own rules and regulations. No off-road vehicles are permitted in the Pea Island Wildlife Refuge or on the beaches at Southern Shores or Kitty Hawk. If in doubt, ask a park ranger or town official. But where permission is granted, look for the designated entrances and exits for off-road vehicles, then comb the beaches for that perfect surf-fishing spot or a place just to sit and watch the waves. Take a picnic and leave your cares, and the crowds, behind.

MORE OUTER BANKS HISTORY

Local legend has it that Nags Head, the largest resort in the Outer Banks, got its name from pirates who hung lanterns from the necks of ponies and walked them along the dunes at night. The lights lured unsuspecting ships aground, so the pirates could relieve them of their cargoes. A less colorful account says the area was named for the highest point of Scilly Island, the last view of their homeland seafaring English colonists saw. (There's no word on how that place got its name. Maybe it had similar pirates who practiced the same deception.)

SIGHTSEEING HIGHLIGHTS

★★★★ **CHICAMACOMICO LIFESAVING STATION**
Rodanthe, 252/987-2401
Chicamacomico, founded in 1874, was one of seven lifesaving stations established on the Outer Banks. Though it was the scene of many heroic shipwreck rescues, it was decommissioned by the U.S.

SIGHTS

Ⓐ Bodie Island Lighthouse
Ⓑ Cape Hatteras Lighthouse
Ⓒ Chicamacomico Lifesaving Station
Ⓓ Fort Raleigh National Historic Site
Ⓔ Jockey's Ridge State Park
Ⓕ The Lost Colony
Ⓖ North Carolina Aquariums
Ⓗ North Carolina Ferries
Ⓘ Ocracoke Island Lighthouse
Ⓙ Wright Brothers National Memorial

EDENTON

Most people visit the Outer Banks searching for the peace that comes from communing with nature and enjoying family activities such as fishing, swimming, sailing, and picnicking. But the Outer Banks can also provide an introduction to later colonial history if you visit nearby Edenton, just an hour's drive from Hatteras National Seashore.

Edenton was founded in the late seventeenth century and incorporated in 1722 on Edenton Bay at the head of Albemarle Sound. One of the city's residents signed the Declaration of Independence; another the U.S. Constitution. While Edenton was the second largest colonial port during the early eighteenth century, today its population is only 5,000. But its business district is thriving, and its waterfront is full of parks. It also has an extensive historic district with eighteenth-, nineteenth-, and early-twentieth-century buildings.

A visitor's center at 108 North Broad Street provides an audiovisual program and exhibits. From there you can take guided tours of five properties: the 1736 **Episcopal Church**, the 1758 **Cupola House**, the circa-1782 **Barker House**, the 1767 **Chowan County Courthouse** (a National Historic Landmark), and the early-nineteenth-century **Iredell House State Historic Site**. Tours are offered daily. Admission to the visitor's center is free; there are fees for the tours. Or you can devise your own self-guided walking tour after studying pamphlets from the visitor's center. For more information, call 252/482-2637.

Coast Guard (which evolved from the U.S. Lifesaving Service) in 1954. Today it is a museum.

Details: May–Oct Tue, Thu, Sat, 11–5 and by appointment; grounds open all year. Free. (1 hour)

★★★★ **THE LOST COLONY**
Waterside Theatre, 1409 Highway 34/264, Roanoke Island
800/488-5012, www.thelostcolony.org
America's premier outdoor drama is where television's Andy Griffith got his start and where you can learn the story of the first English colony in North America and ponder its mysterious disappearance.

Details: Mid-June–late Aug, nightly shows at 8 except Saturday. $16 adults, $11 seniors, military, and the disabled, $8 children under 12. (2 hours)

★★★★ WRIGHT BROTHERS NATIONAL MEMORIAL
Hwy. 158, Kill Devil Hills, 252/441-7430
www.nps.gov/wrbr/wright.htm
Wilbur and Orville Wright took their first successful flight in a heavier-than-air machine here on December 17, 1903. You can learn how they did it through daily presentations at the museum and the reconstructed hangar.

Details: Daily 9–5. $2 per person or $4 per car; seniors and under age 16 free. (2 hours)

★★★ BODIE ISLAND LIGHTHOUSE
N.C. 12, 252/441-5711
This horizontally striped structure, rising 156 feet above sea level, is what you expect to see when you envision an early American lighthouse. The base of the tower and the restored double keeper's quarters, with lighthouse exhibits, are open for viewing.

Details: Open year-round. Free. (1 hour)

★★★ FORT RALEIGH NATIONAL HISTORIC SITE
Hwy. 64/264, Manteo, 252/473-5772
www.nps.gov/fora
This north end of Roanoke Island is where Sir Walter Raleigh's explorers and colonists settled in 1585. You can trace their experiences through interpretive programs, then meander along the nature trail.

Details: Daily 9–5. Free. (2 hours)

★★★ JOCKEY'S RIDGE STATE PARK
W. Carolista Dr., Nags Head, 252/441-7132
The largest active sand dune on the Atlantic Coast would be an awe-inspiring sight even without the panoramic view afforded of the Outer Banks. But put them together, and the combination is unbeatable. Activities here include tumbling down slopes (go ahead, the kid in you wants to), hiking, kiting, hang gliding, and picnicking. Or you can access a beach.

Details: Open year-round. Free. (2–3 hours)

★★★ NORTH CAROLINA AQUARIUMS
North Carolina Marine Resources Center, Airport Rd.
Roanoke Island, 252/473-3493
Aquariums, a touch tank, and special events entice young and old alike into the undersea world of sharks, eels, sea turtles, and other marine life native to the North Carolina coast. Other North Carolina Aquariums are at Pine Knoll Shores, Atlantic Beach, and Fort Fisher, Kure Beach.

Details: Expected to reopen after rennovations in the spring of 2000. Call for hours and admission costs. (2–3 hours)

★★★ NORTH CAROLINA FERRIES
The Hatteras-Ocracoke Free Ferry links Hatteras and Ocracoke Islands with a 40-minute trip. Reservations are not accepted, and lines can get lengthy in summer, so allow yourself plenty of time.

Details: Ferries run year-round. $1 pedestrians, $2 bicycles, $10 motorcycles, cars, and combinations less than 20 feet, $20–$30 for longer combinations. For general North Carolina Ferries information, call 800/BY-FERRY. (40 minutes)

★★ CAPE HATTERAS LIGHTHOUSE
Buxton, Hatteras Island, 252/995-4474
The tallest brick lighthouse in North America is part of Cape Hatteras National Seashore, which preserves 75 miles along the Outer Banks and includes visitor's centers at Buxton, Bodie Island, and Ocracoke. The lighthouse will be closed until the spring of 2000 while it is being moved a half mile away from the shore. When opened, the lighthouse tower is open to the public on a seasonal basis. Take the challenge: Climb all 268 steps to the top and enjoy a breathtaking (if you have any breath left after the climb) view of the Cape Hatteras National Seashore.

Details: Call for hours. Free. (1–2 hours)

★★ OCRACOKE ISLAND LIGHTHOUSE
Point Rd., Ocracoke, 252/995-4474
The oldest lighthouse still in use in North Carolina serves as an entrance beacon to Ocracoke Inlet. The grounds are not open to the public, but you can get a great view of the lighthouse from nearby.

Details: (1 hour)

FITNESS AND RECREATION

More than five miles of hiking trails are offered in **Nags Head Woods Ecological Preserve**, a 1,400-acre maritime forest containing a rich diversity of wildlife. Kayak field trips are available in summer. Surf fishing is great at **Pea Island National Wildlife Refuge**, and free summer activities include bird-watching hikes and children's wildlife discovery. You can watch or try hang gliding at **Jockey's Ridge State Park**, Nags Head, and bike, windsurf, or play tennis at almost every location.

FOOD

No, seafood isn't on every menu in the Outer Banks, but where it's a specialty, it's out of this world. **Black Pelican Seafood Co.**, Milepost 4, 252/261-3171, is a legendary Kitty Hawk restaurant. It offers oceanfront deckside dining in a café-style setting with a raw bar and serves fresh seafood and wood-fired gourmet pizza. **Dock of the Bay Café**, 307 Virginia Dare Rd., Manteo, 252/473-6845, also offers outdoor waterfront dining and is recommended by *Gourmet* magazine. **Howard's Pub & Raw Bar**, Hwy. 12, Ocracoke Island, 252/928-4441, is open daily until 2 a.m. You can sit on the screened porch in a rocking chair and order from the area's widest selection of beer and wine; dine on fresh local shrimp, clams, and oysters; and enjoy live entertainment. Burgers, pizza, subs, and more are available for those who don't like seafood. **Miller's Waterfront Restaurant** at Milepost 16H, Nags Head, 252/441-6151, serves breakfast and dinner daily; fresh local seafood, prime rib, and steaks are specialties. **Owens' Restaurant** at Milepost 16H Beach Road, Nags Head, 252/441-7309, has been a tradition here for more than 50 years. Owens' serves the finest Carolina coastal cuisine: fresh seafood, shellfish, and lobster, as well as beef and pasta.

Barrier Island Inn on Currituck Sound, Duck Road in the Village of Duck, 252/261-3901, is open year-round for lunch and dinner and for breakfast during summer. You can enjoy great food, beautiful sunsets, and deck parties. Searching for a restaurant everyone will enjoy? **Anna Livia's Restaurant** at the Elizabethan Inn, Manteo (814 Hwy. 64, 252/473-2101), serves authentic Italian cuisine, fresh seafood, and international specialties.

An offshoot of a famous gourmet restaurant in Richmond, Virginia, **Millie's**, Milepost 9½ 2008 Virginia Dare Trail, Kill Devil Hills, 252/480-3463, is a restored 1940s diner offering contemporary gourmet fare in a casual atmosphere. It has a great jukebox and a full bar and serves brunch and dinner daily. **Weeping Radish Brewery and Restaurant**, with locations in Manteo (Hwy. 64/264, 252/473-1157), Corolla (817-A Ocean Trail, Monterey Plaza,

THE OUTER BANKS

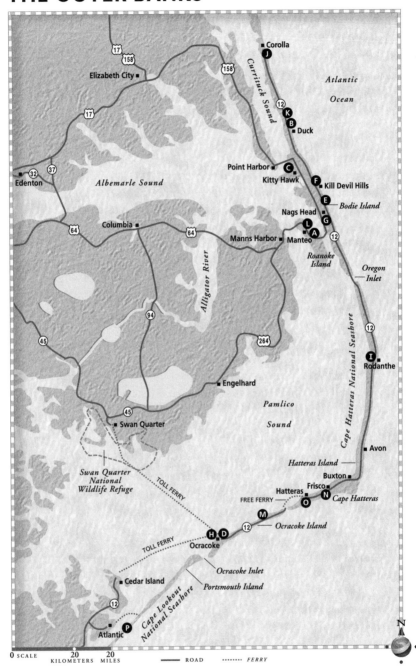

Corolla **J**

Atlantic
Ocean

Elizabeth City ■

17
158

158

Currituck Sound

12
K
B
Duck ■

Point Harbor ■ **C**
Kitty Hawk ■

F ■ Kill Devil Hills

32 **37**
Edenton ■

Albemarle Sound

E
Bodie Island

Nags Head ■ **G**
L
A

64
Columbia ■
64
Manns Harbor ■ Manteo ■

12

*Roanoke
Island*

*Oregon
Inlet*

Alligator River

94

264

45

12

I
Rodanthe

Engelhard ■

*Pamlico
Sound*

Cape Hatteras National Seashore

45
Swan Quarter ■

■ Avon

Hatteras Island

Buxton ■
Frisco ■
N *Cape Hatteras*

*Swan Quarter
National
Wildlife Refuge*

TOLL FERRY

Hatteras ■
FREE FERRY **O**

M
12 *Ocracoke Island*

H D
Ocracoke

TOLL FERRY

Ocracoke Inlet

■ Cedar Island
Portsmouth Island

*Cape Lookout
National Seashore*

12

P
Atlantic

N

0 SCALE   20   20
KILOMETERS MILES   ——— ROAD   ········ FERRY

252/453-6638) and Kitty Hawk (Milepost 1 1/2 , 252/261-0488), is an "authentic" Bavarian brewery and restaurant, open for lunch and dinner daily year-round. It has an outdoor beer garden, a pub room, and a kids' playground. Homemade desserts are a specialty. Also open year-round is the **Windmill Point Restaurant**, on Bypass 158 in Nags Head, 252/441-1535, serving seafood, steaks, and pasta on the waterfront. Its distinctive windmill was constructed from century-old trees by English craftsmen and transported from England. The restaurant also has the largest collection of memorabilia from the SS *United States*.

LODGING

You can find more and less expensive accommodations in Ocracoke, but recommended is the **Anchorage Inn and Marina**, Hwy. 12, 252/928-1101, with 35 rooms and a continental breakfast available. The **Inn at Corolla Light**, 1066 Ocean Trail, Corolla, 252/453-3340 or 800/215-0772, may be a little pricey, but this country inn offers a quiet, undiscovered, and romantic alternative to most other oceanfront lodgings. In addition to 41 luxurious rooms, complimentary amenities include a pool/restaurant complex, indoor sports center, tennis courts, bike paths, and jogging trails.

Hatteras Island Resort, Atlantic Dr., Rodanthe, 252/987-2345 or 800/331-6541, has all the above and more. Pets are even allowed, for a fee.

FOOD

- **Ⓐ** Anna Livia's Restaurant
- **Ⓑ** Barrier Island Inn
- **Ⓒ** Black Pelican Seafood Co.
- **Ⓐ** Dock of the Bay Café
- **Ⓓ** Howard's Pub & Raw Bar
- **Ⓔ** Miller's Waterfront Restaurant
- **Ⓕ** Millie's
- **Ⓔ** Owens' Restaurant
- **Ⓐ** Weeping Radish Brewery and Restaurant
- **Ⓖ** Windmill Point Restaurant

LODGING

- **Ⓗ** Anchorage Inn and Marina
- **Ⓔ** First Colony Inn

LODGING *(continued)*

- **Ⓘ** Hatteras Island Resort
- **Ⓙ** Inn at Corolla Light
- **Ⓕ** Ocean House Motel
- **Ⓔ** Owens' Motel
- **Ⓚ** Sanderling Inn Resort & Conference Center
- **Ⓛ** Tranquil House Inn

CAMPING

- **Ⓜ** Beachcomber's Campground
- **Ⓝ** Cape Hatteras National Seashore
- **Ⓕ** Collington Park Campground
- **Ⓞ** Hatteras Sands Camping Resort
- **Ⓟ** Salter Path Family Campground

Note: Items with the same letter are located in the same area.

NEW BERN

Ninety miles south of Edenton is New Bern, North Carolina's second oldest town. Founded by Swiss and German settlers in 1710 and named for Bern, Switzerland, it is the home of the **Tryon Palace Historic Sites and Gardens**, the eighteenth-century residence of the governor of both the colony and state of North Carolina. The site includes 14 acres of beautifully landscaped gardens, the Academy Museum (one of the oldest secondary schools in America), and three historic homes from the eighteenth and nineteenth centuries. These are the John Wright Stanly House, where George Washington was an overnight guest in 1791, the Dixon/Stevenson House, and the Robert Hay House. The palace itself burned in 1798 and was reconstructed in the 1950s from the original architect's plans. It is furnished with rare English and American antiques, selected to approximate an inventory of Royal Governor William Tryon's possessions made two years after he left New Bern to become governor of the colony of New York. This historic site is open year-round daily. Interior tours are led primarily by costumed interpreters. The palace is located at 610 Pollock Street in New Bern. For information, call 252/514-4900 or 800/767-1560.

New Bern also hosts the **Attmore-Oliver House Museum**, 510 Pollock St., which holds eighteenth- and nineteenth-century antiques, a unique doll collection, and a room full of Civil War memorabilia. Admission is free here and at the **Bellair Plantation and Restoration**, 1100 Washington Post Rd. An outstanding example of pre-Revolutionary Georgian architecture, this is the last eighteenth-century brick plantation country house standing in North Carolina. Also in New Bern is **Christ Episcopal Church**, 320 Pollock St., the third oldest church (founded in 1715) in the state. Here you will see the colonial communion silver given to the church by King George II in 1752.

You can opt for a guided tour of New Bern, including 90-minute trolley car tours through the historic downtown with a professional guide, or do it yourself. Either way, you'll be glad you added New Bern to your itinerary.

Sanderling Inn Resort & Conference Center, 1461 Duck Rd., 252/261-4111 or 800/701-4111, offers a restaurant, pool, golf and tennis privileges, fishing, and all the amenities you expect. **Ocean House Motel**, Milepost 9H, Kill Devil Hills, 252/441-2900, is an Outer Banks legend with its 45 designer rooms, swimming pool, and other conveniences.

The name fits the waterfront **Tranquil House Inn**, 405 Queen Elizabeth St., Manteo, 252/473-1404 or 800/458-7069. It offers 25 rooms, a restaurant, and a fishing pier. Reasonable rates include an evening wine reception and a continental breakfast. **First Colony Inn**, at Milepost 16, Beach Rd., Nags Head, 252/441-2343, is expensive (rates range from $75 to $160 in the off-season and from $135 to $250 in the high season). But it's a lovely National Historic Register property and justly famous. Here you can pamper yourself in a luxurious room filled with antiques (and a Jacuzzi) before getting back to nature on the beach.

For lodging in the famous "Old Nags Head Style," try **Owens' Motel** at Beach Road Milepost 16H, Nags Head, 252/441-6361. It features oceanfront efficiencies, an oceanfront gazebo from which to watch the waves, and a healthy dose of southern hospitality.

CAMPING

Camping on the Outer Banks provides peace and tranquility close to nature, in as much comfort as you require. **Beachcomber's Campground**, Ocracoke, 252/928-4031, has everything you could possibly need to hook up your trailer or pitch your tent. But don't plan to enjoy the ocean in the middle of winter here—the campground is open mid-March through December.

Cape Hatteras National Seashore has four National Park Service campgrounds at Oregon Inlet, Cape Point in Buxton, Frisco, and Ocracoke Island. Considered primitive (no electric hookups), all sites have bathrooms, water, unheated showers, grills, and picnic tables. For information, call 252/473-2111. **Hatteras Sands Camping Resort**, 252/986-2422, has trailer and tent sites and all the amenities, allowing your camp to be as luxurious or as primitive as you wish. It's open March through November. **Collington Park Campground**, 1608 Collington Rd., Kill Devil Hills, 252/441-6128, has trailer, shaded, and tent sites, a camp store, and all the amenities to make this year-round campground a pleasure to visit. **Salter Path Family Campground**, 1620 Salter Path Rd., Atlantic Beach, 252/247-3525, is a full-service campground with trailer, shaded, and tent sites. You can dig clams in Bogue Sound, among other activities.

Outer Banks Highways

U.S. 64 and 158 and N.C. 12 via the North Carolina ferry system lead to 130 miles of quiet, sun-kissed beaches, national parks, wildlife refuges, fishing, birding, kayaking, hang gliding, golfing, windsurfing, and more. Highway 158 approaches the Outer Banks from the north, and Highway 64 from the west. But it is Highway 12 that links the majority of the towns along these barrier islands.

The milepost marking system begins with Milepost 1 along Highway 12 at Kitty Hawk and extends south through Nags Head and links (with the help of the ferries) historic Roanoke, Hatteras, and Ocracoke Islands. Highway 58 runs north from Kitty Hawk to the villages of Duck and Corolla. In hurricane season, these islands may be evacuated, but the natives and tourists always return. The gulls, dunes, waves, and sense of history prove unbeatable lures. Drive slowly and view nature as it was—and should be.

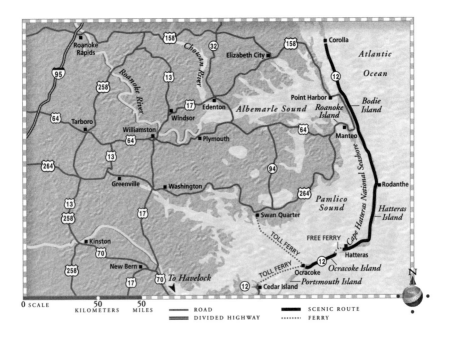

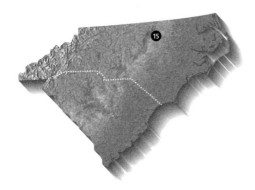

15
RALEIGH-DURHAM

Raleigh and Durham are part of what the science and business communities refer to as the Research Triangle (including Chapel Hill), but they still have individual identities. Raleigh, the capital of North Carolina, and its sister city are at the center of high-tech progress in the state, a position they have long enjoyed. After all, this is where the R. J. Reynolds plant first produced cigarettes rolled by machine instead of by hand. Commercial growth is booming, and the area, with a population of over a million, is consistently rated among the best places to live and work in the United States.

Greater Raleigh hosts three professional sports teams—baseball's Carolina Mudcats, hockey's Carolina Hurricanes, and soccer's Raleigh Capital Express. It offers the great college sports action that's made the Triangle famous—can you say ACC? The largest event in North Carolina happens here during 10 days in October, when the State Fair comes to town. More than 90 seasonal events are planned every year, November through December.

Durham, a small agricultural community until after the Civil War, quickly blossomed into an industrial city, thanks to the American Tobacco Company, founded here by Washington Duke. Today tobacco warehouses still ring with the chants of auctioneers from September through December. But the heart of the city is Duke University, which began as Trinity College. It changed its name in 1924 with the Duke family endowment of $40 million, and its medical center has subsequently become one of the best in the world.

RALEIGH

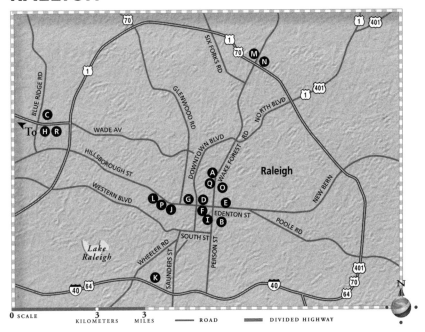

SIGHTS

- **A** Andrew Johnson Birthplace
- **B** Christ Episcopal Church
- **C** North Carolina Museum of Art
- **D** North Carolina Museum of History
- **E** North Carolina State Museum of Natural Sciences
- **F** State Capitol Complex

FOOD

- **G** 42nd Street Oyster Bar & Seafood Grill
- **H** Angus Barn
- **I** Big Ed's
- **J** Charlie Goodnight's Restaurant and Comedy Club
- **C** Museum Café
- **K** Seafood Restaurant

LODGING

- **L** Brownestone Hotel
- **M** Homestead Village
- **N** North Raleigh Hilton
- **O** Oakwood Inn
- **P** Velvet Cloak Inn
- **Q** William Thomas House Bed and Breakfast

CAMPING

- **R** William B. Umstead State Park

Note: Items with the same letter are located in the same area.

A PERFECT DAY IN RALEIGH-DURHAM

Begin with a guided tour of the capitol complex in Raleigh, then enjoy the unique shops that line the cobblestone streets of the City Market. At lunchtime, you're in the right place: Get in line at Big Ed's. Ignore the lawyers and other professionals in suits—your shorts are fine. Big Ed himself, and perhaps some of his grandchildren, will be seated in your midst, in the chair marked especially (and graphically) for him. After enjoying the fantastic food, head back to the hotel for a brief nap. Then, no matter what your stance on smoking, visit Durham for a tour of the Duke Homestead and Tobacco Museum. It offers a fascinating glimpse into earlier and very lucrative days. For dinner, try the French Quarter in Durham.

SIGHTSEEING HIGHLIGHTS

★★★★ DUKE HOMESTEAD AND TOBACCO MUSEUM
2828 Duke Homestead Rd., Durham, 919/477-5498
www.ah.dcr.state.nc.us/sections/hs/duke
This authentic living museum of tobacco history was the home of Washington Duke, an Orange County farmer whose chance discovery that Union troops were helping themselves to local bright-leaf tobacco prompted him to market the golden "weed." Durham's railroad proved an excellent means to market, and an industry was born.
   Details: Apr–Oct Mon–Sat 9–5, Sun 1–5; Nov–Mar Tue–Sat 10–4, Sun 1–4. Free. (2 hours)

★★★★ DUKE UNIVERSITY
919/684-5135, www.duke.edu/web/duma
Duke University Chapel is a magnificent Gothic-style chapel with beautiful stained-glass windows on the university's West Campus. Weekly worship services, concerts, and recitals are held here throughout the year. The Duke University Museum of Art, on the East Campus, exhibits medieval sculpture, stained glass, pre-Columbian art (extensive holdings), American and European paintings and sculpture, drawings and prints, Greek and Roman antiquities, and Chinese jade.
   Details: Free. (2–4 hours)

★★★★ NORTH CAROLINA MUSEUM OF ART
2110 Blue Ridge Rd., Raleigh, 919/839-6262

DUKE CHAPEL, DURHAM

More than 500 years of artistic heritage are displayed in this state museum. Call ahead for a schedule of special events, including family festivals, lectures, workshops, outdoor theater, and performing arts events.

Details: Tue–Thu 9–5, Fri 9–9, Sat 9–5, Sun 11–6. Admission is free. (3–4 hours)

★★★★ **NORTH CAROLINA MUSEUM OF HISTORY**
5 E. Edenton St., Raleigh, 919/715-0200
Innovative exhibits and programs beckon visitors just a few steps from the state capitol to a new state-of-the-art facility where North Carolina history can be explored. The Folklife and Sports Hall of Fame galleries showcase the state's heritage and sports heroes.

Details: Tue–Sat 9–5, Sun noon–5. Free. (3 hours)

★★★★ **NORTH CAROLINA MUSEUM OF LIFE AND SCIENCE**
433 Murray Ave., Durham, 919/220-5429
www.ncmls.citysearch.com
This 78-acre site has a 50,000-square-foot, hands-on science and technology center. Exhibits include aerospace technology, Carolina wildlife, a farmyard, and a butterfly house.

Details: Mon–Sat 10–5, Sun 12–5. $6 adults, $4 seniors and ages 3 to 12. (4 hours)

★★★★ NORTH CAROLINA STATE MUSEUM OF NATURAL SCIENCES
Bicentennial Place, Raleigh, 919/733-7450
www.naturalscience.org
The downtown museum's zoological collections were started in 1879 and today contain more than 500,000 specimens of fossils, invertebrates, fish, amphibians, reptiles, birds, and mammals. A brand new museum opened in 1999 next door to the current facility.
Details: Mon–Sat 9–5, Sun 1–5. Free. (3–4 hours)

★★★ ANDREW JOHNSON BIRTHPLACE
Mimosa St. and Wake Forest Rd., Raleigh, 919/834-4844
Also called Mordecai Historic Park, this sight features an antebellum plantation house museum, kitchen, and other historic structures grouped along a "village street" that provides a glimpse into eighteenth-century life in Raleigh. U.S. President Andrew Johnson's birthplace is preserved here.
Details: Mon and Wed–Sat 10–3, Sun 1–3. $4 adults, $2 students. (2 hours)

★★★ HISTORIC STAGVILLE
5825 Old Oxford Hwy., 919/620-0120
The former Stagville Plantation, once among the largest in the South, includes historic eighteenth- and nineteenth-century plantation buildings on 71 acres. The barn and original slave quarters at Horton Grove provide insights into plantation life and African American history, society, and culture.
Details: Call for hours and admission. (2 hours)

★★★ SARAH P. DUKE GARDENS
Anderson St., Durham, 919/684-3698
More than 1,500 plant varieties can be spotted on 55 acres of landscaped and woodland gardens. The site includes five miles of walks and pathways with bridges, courts, lawns, waterfalls, ponds, and pavilions. Also here are the Blomquist Garden of Native Plants and the Asiatic Arboretum.
Details: Daily 8–dusk. Guided tours are available. (2 hours)

★★★ STATE CAPITOL COMPLEX

The **Executive Mansion**, 200 N. Blount St, 919/733-3456, is an 1891 Victorian mansion that has housed North Carolina governors since it was built. Guided tours are available by reservation. The **Legislative Building**, 16 W. Jones St., 919/733-7928, is the meeting place of the state's General Assembly. The **North Carolina State Capitol**, a National Historic Landmark at 1 E. Edenton Street, 919/733-4994, was built in the late 1830s and is one of the best-preserved examples of a Greek Revival–style civic building.

Details: Free (3 hours)

★★ WEST POINT ON THE ENO

5101 N. Roxboro Rd., Durham, 919/471-1623

This 388-acre natural and historic city park offers picnicking, hiking, fishing, nature study, and environmental programs.

Details: Open year-round. Free. (1 hour)

★ CHRIST EPISCOPAL CHURCH

Wilmington and E. Edenton Sts., Raleigh, 919/834-6259

You can't miss it: Look for the rooster on the steeple rising over downtown Raleigh. Some claim it was the only fowl left in town after Sherman's troops marched through the city. The church is a historic structure that delights the eyes and lifts the soul.

Details: (30 minutes)

FITNESS AND RECREATION

Raleigh alone has 156 parks and lakes and a greenway system spanning more than 46 miles, enough to delight even the most committed fitness fan. If you insist on regimen, Raleigh and Durham both have professional gyms, health clubs, and YMCAs. **Eno River State Park**, 6101 Cole Mill Rd., Durham, offers hiking, fishing, backpacking, canoeing, picnicking, and nature programs in a setting that includes a fast-flowing river surrounded by rugged, forested hills. Best of all, admission is free.

FOOD

Whether you prefer blue jeans or black tie, you're sure to find the right dining experience in Raleigh-Durham. **Angus Barn**, Raleigh-Durham Hwy. at Airport Rd., Raleigh, 919/787-3505, serves some of the best steaks in the

DURHAM

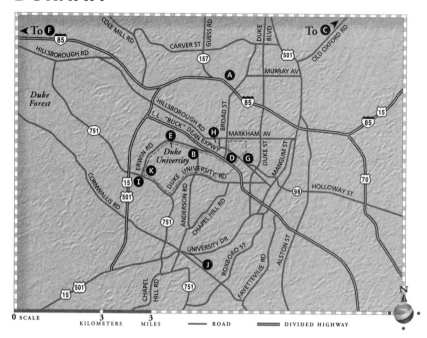

SIGHTS

- **A** Duke Homestead and Tobacco Museum
- **B** Duke University
- **C** Historic Stagville
- **D** North Carolina Museum of Life and Science
- **E** Sarah P. Duke Gardens
- **F** West Point on the Eno

FOOD

- **G** Anotherthyme
- **H** Blue Corn Cafe
- **I** Fairview Restaurant
- **J** Nana's Restaurant

LODGING

- **K** Washington Duke Inn and Golf Club

---

piedmont—heck, in the whole country. In fact, it has been named the third-best steakhouse in the United States by *Wine Spectator* magazine. The restaurant is open daily for dinner only. Dinner for two will exceed $50.

Charlie Goodnight's Restaurant and Comedy Club, 861 W. Morgan St., Raleigh, 919/828-5233, features theme nights and buffets with bar, dinner, and show specials. **Big Ed's City Market Restaurant**, 220 Wolfe St., 919/836-9909, keeps a chair reserved here for Big Ed, and most noontimes will find him in it. This family restaurant in downtown Raleigh serves reasonably priced home-style breakfast and lunch Monday through Saturday. **Torero's Mexican Restaurant**, 800 W. Main St., Raleigh, 919/682-4197, prepares authentic Mexican cuisine in a down-home atmosphere.

For an entirely different dining experience surrounded by fine art, eat in the **Museum Café**, North Carolina Museum of Art, 2110 Blue Ridge Blvd., Raleigh, 919/833-3548. Lunch is served Tuesday through Friday, dinner Friday only, and brunch Saturday and Sunday. The **Seafood Restaurant**, Highway 401 S., Raleigh, 919/772-9409, serves up scrumptious seafood—you can buy it fresh and eat it at home or have it cooked to order here. The **42nd Street Oyster Bar & Seafood Grill**, 508 W. Jones St., Raleigh, 919/831-2811, serves just what the name promises, from the city's largest selection of fresh seafood and shellfish. It's open for lunch and dinner weekdays and for dinner on weekends.

Anotherthyme, 109 N. Gregson St., Durham, 919/682-5225, is open for daily for dinner and late-night meals. This is a vegetarian/seafood restaurant with extremely reasonable prices. **Nana's Restaurant**, 2574 University Blvd., Durham, 919/493-8545, is open Monday through Saturday for dinner. It serves moderately priced southern food and continental dishes. It was named one of the best new restaurants in the country by *Esquire* magazine in 1993. Risotto is a specialty.

Fairview Restaurant at the Washington Duke Inn and Golf Club, 3001 Cameron Blvd., Durham, 919/493-6699, is a four-diamond place cited for its crab cakes and corn chowder. It overlooks the championship Duke University golf course and is open for dinner every day, lunch Monday through Saturday. **Blue Corn Cafe**, 716-B Ninth St., Durham, 919/286-9600, is open daily for lunch and dinner. Try Latin American dishes like the Cuban picadillo.

LODGING

For a change from the chains, try the **Brownestone Hotel**, 1707 Hillsborough St., Raleigh, 919/828-0811 or 800/331-7919. It is moderately priced and has an outdoor pool. **Homestead Village**, 3531 Wake Forest Rd., Raleigh, 919/981-7353, opened in 1998. Rates run from $60 to $80 per night. **North Raleigh Hilton**, 3415 Wake Forest Rd., Raleigh, 919/872-2323, charges $110 to $150 per night. Another option is **Oakwood Inn Bed and Breakfast**, 411 N. Bloodworth St., Raleigh, 919/832-9712 or 800/267-9712.

Velvet Cloak Inn, 1505 Hillsborough St., Raleigh, 919/828-0333, prides itself on timeless southern charm. It has 172 rooms and is located close to everything, including North Carolina State University, Research Triangle Park, and the Raleigh-Durham International Airport.

Washington Duke Inn and Golf Club, on the grounds of Duke University, 3001 Cameron Blvd., Durham, 919/490-0999 or 800/443-3853, boasts an AAA four-diamond rating and a Robert Trent Jones golf course, recently redesigned by his son, Rees Jones. You'll also find international fine dining and 171 luxurious guest rooms and suites. **William Thomas House Bed and Breakfast**, 530 N. Blount St., Raleigh, 919/755-9400 or 800/653-3466, is expensive but worth it. The circa-1881 house is near the capitol, City Market, and the Governor's Mansion.

CAMPING
William B. Umstead State Park, Hwy. 70, Raleigh, 919/787-3033, contains three small lakes in a 5,500-acre park. It offers hiking, biking, and horse trails, a campground, and a cabin and mess hall for groups.

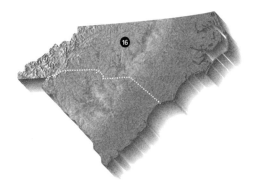

16
TRI-CITIES

Of North Carolina's Tri-Cities—Winston-Salem, Greensboro, and High Point—Greensboro is the largest. The city was named for General Nathanael Greene, who led the revolutionary forces in the nearby Battle of Guilford Courthouse, one of the decisive battles of the Revolution. Greensboro was the birthplace of Dolley Madison, William Sydney Porter (O. Henry), and Edward R. Murrow. This is where Charlotte Hawkins Brown helped pioneer education for southern African Americans and where the Woolworth Civil Rights sit-ins took place.

High Point, to the southwest, is billed as "the Home Furnishings Capital of the World." The small city hosts the International Home Furnishings Market each April and October, and it is headquarters for many of the nation's largest hosiery and textile manufacturers.

In the Blue Ridge foothills to the west of Greensboro, you can experience history every day in Winston-Salem. Stroll through an entire eighteenth-century town that its early settlers would still recognize, taste bread and cookies baked in a nineteenth-century brick oven, and ride a carriage over the same streets that George Washington walked.

But the area's attractions are not confined to history and industry. The Greater Greensboro Open has been played here for nearly 60 years at Forest Oaks Country Club. The North Carolina Shakespeare Festival at High Point Theatre, 336/841-2273, is held August through October, with performances also in Greenboro and Winston-Salem. The Oak Hollow World

GREENSBORO

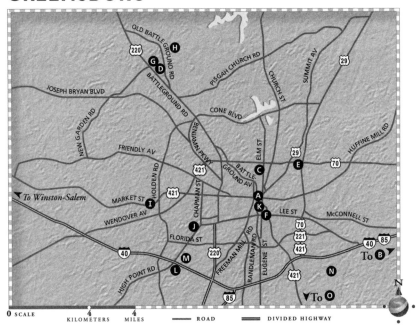

SIGHTS

- **Ⓐ** Blandwood
- **Ⓑ** Charlotte Hawkins Brown Memorial State Historic Site
- **Ⓒ** Greensboro Historical Museum
- **Ⓓ** Guilford Courthouse National Military Park
- **Ⓔ** Mattye Reed African American Heritage Center

SIGHTS (continued)

- **Ⓕ** Old Greensborough and the Downtown Greensboro Historic District
- **Ⓖ** Tannenbaum Park

FOOD

- **Ⓗ** Barn Dinner Theatre
- **Ⓘ** Giovanni's
- **Ⓙ** Staymey's

LODGING

- **Ⓚ** Biltmore Greensboro Hotel
- **Ⓛ** Holiday Inn Four Seasons
- **Ⓛ** Park Lane Hotel at Four Seasons

CAMPING

- **Ⓜ** Fields RV Campground
- **Ⓝ** Greensboro Campground
- **Ⓞ** Hagan-Stone Park

Note: Items with the same letter are located in the same area.

Championship Drag Boat Races at Oak Hollow Lake, 336/883-2016, are held the last weekend in July.

A PERFECT DAY IN THE TRI-CITIES

First visit the Greensboro Historical Museum, then head out to sights you can tour by yourself. The International Civil Rights Center and Museum is the site of the sit-ins in downtown Greensboro. The Walkway of History at February One Place chronicles six chapters in local African American history, ranging from the first fugitive slave on the Underground Railroad through the first African American state supreme court justice. There is a bronze likeness of O. Henry, a.k.a. William Sydney Porter, and his dog Lovey on the corner of North Elm and Bellemeade Streets and a bust of television commentator Edward R. Murrow on the southwest corner of Friendly Avenue and Murrow Boulevard. Drive to Old Salem for a scrumptious lunch, Moravian style, and spend a lazy afternoon in the historic neighborhood. At night, head for one of many restaurants in the vicinity of Four Seasons Town Center, one of the largest enclosed malls in the Southeast. After dinner, the mall offers 200 stores to explore, as well as a multiplex cinema.

MORE TRI-CITIES HISTORY

During the middle and late eighteenth century, land became expensive and scarce in and around the established coastal towns and cities of North Carolina. Thus, farmers and poor colonists began to move west. There were many conflicts with Indians in the area, and colonists pushed the local tribes into the mountains. Farms were begun on the fertile land, and a few towns sprang up.

From 1730 to 1780, thousands of settlers followed the Great Wagon Road south from Pennsylvania into this back country of North Carolina. The Moravians, a Protestant sect formed in a former province of Czechoslovakia, came to North Carolina in the 1750s after settling first in Savannah, Georgia, and then in Bethlehem, Pennsylvania. They founded Salem and Salem College, both of which exist today. In modern-day Winston-Salem, you can see first-hand the Moravian lifestyle with its Germanic influences. In Old Salem, costumed interpreters re-create late eighteenth- and early nineteenth-century life in a Moravian congregational tour. Historic Bethabara Park has a 1753 Moravian village, a 190-acre park, and a 1788 *gemeinhaus* (church). While you're in the area, be sure to sample the famous Moravian cookies (especially in demand at Christmas), which are baked here and shipped around the country.

SIGHTSEEING HIGHLIGHTS

★★★★ **ANGELA PETERSON DOLL AND MINIATURE MUSEUM**
101 W. Green Dr., High Point, 336/885-3655
Serious collectors and ordinary doll lovers alike will enjoy exhibits of more than 1,700 dolls, dollhouses, artifacts, and miniatures of all kinds—collected from 54 countries by one woman. The museum, which opened in 1992, has ten galleries of exhibits ranging from baby dolls to religious figures dating to 1490.
Details: Tue–Sat 10–5, Sun 1–5. $3.50 adults, $2 seniors and students over 15, $1 ages 6 to 15. (2 hours)

★★★★ **FURNITURE DISCOVERY MUSEUM**
101 W. Green Dr., High Point, 336/887-3876
There's a reason why North Carolina furniture is famous across the nation, and in this interactive, hands-on museum, you can see how it is made. An added reason to visit: It's located in the same building as the Angela Peterson Doll Museum, and combination tickets may be purchased.
Details: Mon–Sat 10–5, Sun 1–5. $5 adults, $4 seniors, $2 ages 6 to 15. (2 hours)

★★★★ **MUSEUM OF EARLY SOUTHERN DECORATIVE ARTS**
924 S. Main St., Old Salem, Winston-Salem
888/OLD-SALEM or 336/721-7300, www.oldsalem.org
This noted museum is the only facility dedicated to researching and exhibiting regional decorative arts of the early South. Guided tours take visitors through the 21 exhibit rooms and six galleries. Be prepared to leave your purse and camera in a locker at the site. All exhibition rooms are easily accessible to handicapped guests, and a wheelchair is available.
Details: Mon–Sat 9–5, Sun 1–4:30. $10 adults, $6 ages 6 to 16. (1 hour)

★★★★ **OLD SALEM**
Old Salem Rd. at Academy St., Winston-Salem
888/OLD-SALEM or 336/721-7300, www.oldsalem.org
The Cookie Monster would find heaven sampling the famous Moravian cookies made by Old Salem's Winkler Bakery. Your family

WINSTON-SALEM

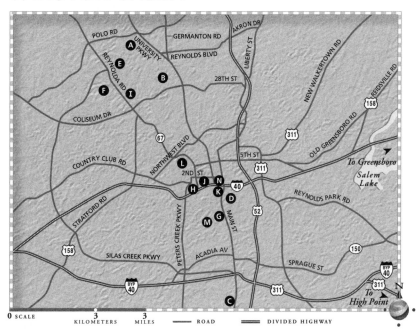

SIGHTS

A Historic Bethabara Park
B Museum of Anthropology, Wake Forest University
C Museum of Early Southern Decorative Arts
D Old Salem
E Reynolda House
F Southeastern Center for Contemporary Art

FOOD

G Old Salem Tavern Dining Room
H Rainbow News & Café
I The Vineyards

LODGING

J Adam's Mark of Winston-Salem
K Augustus T. Zevely Inn
L Colonel Ludlow Inn
M Henry F. Shaffner House
N Salem Inn

Note: Items with the same letter are located in the same area.

might be more interested in the costumed interpreters' re-creation of late-eighteenth- and early-nineteenth-century life in a Moravian congregational town.

Details: Mon–Sat 9–5, Sun 12:30–5. $15 adults, $8 ages 6 to 16. (2–3 hours)

★★★★ **REYNOLDA HOUSE**
2250 Reynolda Rd., Winston-Salem, 336/725-5325
www.reynoldahouse.org
The former home of the founder of R.J. Reynolds Tobacco Company has been transformed into a museum of American art, with extraordinary collections of eighteenth-, nineteenth-, and twentieth-century paintings, prints, and sculpture.

Details: Tue–Sat 9:30–4:30, Sun 1:30–4:30. $6 adults, $5 seniors, $3 students and children. (2 hours)

★★★★ **SOUTHEASTERN CENTER FOR CONTEMPORARY ART**
750 Marguerite Dr., Winston-Salem, 336/725-1904
www.scca.org
This museum grew from the 1929 English-style home of late industrialist James G. Hanes. Today it boasts a series of noted galleries on its 32 wooded acres and offers special events and activities.

Details: Tue–Sat 10–5, Sun 2–5. $3 adults, $2 senior citizens and students, under 12 free. (2–4 hours)

★★★ **GREENSBORO HISTORICAL MUSEUM**
130 Summit Ave., Greensboro, 336/373-2043
www.greensboro.lib.nc.us/museum
The role of piedmont North Carolina in the nation's history is illustrated here in 10 galleries and two restored houses. You will see the 1960 Greensboro Civil Rights sit-ins firsthand and view exhibits about First Lady Dolley Madison and author O. Henry. You'll also learn about piedmont furniture and military history.

Details: Tue–Sat 10–5, Sun 2–5. Free. (2 hours)

★★★ **GUILFORD COURTHOUSE NATIONAL MILITARY PARK**
2332 New Garden Rd., Greensboro, 336/288-1776
The Revolutionary War Battle of Guilford Courthouse was fought

on this site on March 15, 1781. You can trace the steps of the colonial forces at the visitor's center and on a tour road covering the 200-acre park with its 28 monuments.

Details: Daily 8:30–5. Free. (2–3 hours)

★★★ HISTORIC BETHABARA PARK
2147 Bethabara Rd., Winston-Salem, 336/924-8191

The Moravians built a village here in 1753. This 190-acre park, with a 1788 *gemeinhaus* and other historic structures, archaeological sites, and an eighteenth-century graveyard, shows the Moravian influence on daily life.

Details: Mon–Fri 9:30–4:30, Sat and Sun 1:30–4:30. Buildings closed Dec through Mar, but group tours are given by appointment all year. Free. (2 hours)

★★★ MATTYE REED AFRICAN AMERICAN HERITAGE CENTER
1601 E. Market St., Greensboro, 336/334-7847

The nation's largest collections of African art and artifacts are housed in the Mattye Reed African Heritage Center on the grounds of North Carolina A&T State University. Campus and community tours are available.

Details: Call for hours and tour information. Free. (2 hours)

★★★ TANNENBAUM PARK
2200 New Garden Rd., Greensboro, 336/545-5315

The 1778 Hoskins House and Kitchen, the 1820 Coble Barn, a blacksmith's forge, and the North Carolina Colonial Heritage Center are all in this eight-acre complex, which also hosts an annual colonial fair in September.

Details: Colonial Heritage Center open Tue–Fri 9–5, Sat 10–5, Sun 1–5. Park open Mon–Sat 9–5, Sun 1–5. Hoskins House open Sat 10–5, Sun 1–5. Free. (2–3 hours)

★★ BLANDWOOD
447 W. Washington St., Greensboro, 336/272-5003

The former home of Governor John Motley Morehead has been transformed into a house museum showing life in the mid-nineteenth century.

Details: Tue–Sat 11–2, Sun 2–5. (1 hour)

★★ CHARLOTTE HAWKINS BROWN MEMORIAL STATE HISTORIC SITE

Sedalia

North Carolina's first official historic site to honor an African American and a woman is the former location of the Palmer Institute, a black preparatory school established by Brown in 1902.

Details: 10 miles east of Greensboro, off I-85 at Exit 135. Winter Tue–Fri 10–4, Sun 1–4. Summer Mon–Sat 9–5, Sun 1–5. Free. (1 1/2 hours)

★★ MUSEUM OF ANTHROPOLOGY

Wake Forest University, Winston-Salem, 336/759-5282

You can explore cultures past and present at the only museum of its kind in the Southeast.

Details: Tue–Sat 10–4:30. Free. (2 hours)

★★ OLD GREENSBOROUGH AND THE DOWNTOWN GREENSBORO HISTORIC DISTRICT

447 Arlington St.

Self-guided and guided walking tours are available for these historic districts, where you'll see antiques, potters, and a historic theater, depot, drugstore, and country store.

Details: For information call Old Greensborough Preservation Society, 336/272-6617. (2 hours)

★ WORLD'S LARGEST BUREAU

508 Hamilton St., High Point, 336/884-5255

Built in 1926 to call attention to "the Furniture Capital of the World," this building, shaped like a huge chest of drawers, recently was restored as a beautiful nineteenth-century dresser. Drive-by tour only.

Details: Free. (5 minutes)

FITNESS AND RECREATION

You will find whatever type of recreation you desire in Tri-Cities parks. **Barber Park**, off Florida Street in Greensboro, 336/373-5886, has an indoor tennis and volleyball complex, walking trails, playgrounds, and horseshoe pits. It's open 8 a.m. to sunset. **Bryan Park Complex and Lake Townsend**, off Highway 29 North on Bryan Park Road, Browns Summit, 336/375-2222, offer two 18-hole championship golf courses, tennis courts, and soccer fields. You can sail,

THOMASVILLE

Nearby Thomasville features the World's Largest Chair, a 30-foot replica of a Duncan Phyfe design, situated in the center of town. Thomasville also houses the restored version of North Carolina's oldest railroad depot, built in 1870, and the North Carolina Vietnam Veterans Memorial, a 1.5-acre park whose monument honors the 1,607 North Carolinians killed or missing during the Vietnam War.

fish, and boat at the lake. **Bur-Mill Park**, on Owls Roost Rd. off U.S. 220 N., 336/545-5300, is open 8 a.m. to sunset and offers fishing, a par-three golf course, lighted driving range, volleyball courts, swimming, and hiking and biking trails. The park charges fees for some activities. **City Lake Park**, Greensboro/High Point Rd., High Point, 336/883-3498, has a 340-acre lake with boating, paddle-boat rentals, fishing, amusement rides, a train, a water-slide, and the largest outdoor swimming pool in the state.

But the most fun of all may be found at **Emerald Pointe Water Park**, Greensboro, or **Tanglewood Park** near Winston-Salem. Emerald Pointe, 336/852-9721 or 800/555-5900, is the Carolinas' largest water park with a giant wave pool, enclosed slides, drop slides, tube rides, cable glides, a children's area, and a drifting river. Call for seasonal hours. At Tanglewood, you can exercise your options and your body, too. At this year-round recreational facility on more than 1,100 acres, you can golf on two of *Golf Digest's* top-rated courses, play tennis, swim, ride horseback, fish, hike, and boat. The park is open daily, 7 a.m. to dusk. For admission fees, phone 336/778-6300.

FOOD
Barn Dinner Theater, 120 Stage Coach Trail, Greensboro, 336/292-2211, is the oldest continuously running dinner theater in the country, featuring popular Broadway plays following a hearty buffet. Try the roast top sirloin or baked Alaskan halibut. It's open Wednesday through Sunday, January through November, and daily in December. Less elegant is **Staymey's**, 2206 High Point Rd., Greensboro, 336/299-9888, a barbecue restaurant serving some of the South's best pork barbecue, chopped or sliced, accompanied by baked beans, coleslaw, and hush puppies on paper plates. The pork is cooked in modern pits in an adjoining building. Also in Greensboro is **La Spiedo di**

HIGH POINT

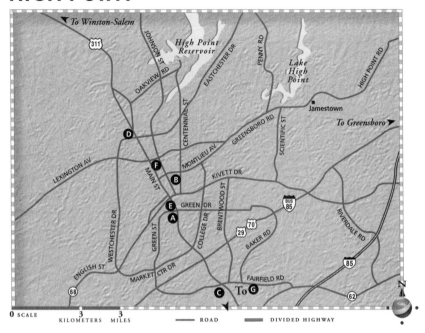

SIGHTS
- **Ⓐ** Angela Peterson Doll and Miniature Museum
- **Ⓐ** Furniture Discovery Museum
- **Ⓑ** World's Largest Bureau

FOOD
- **Ⓒ** Country Bar-B-Q
- **Ⓓ** Ham's
- **Ⓔ** Rosa Mae's

LODGING
- **Ⓕ** Premier Bed & Breakfast Inn

CAMPING
- **Ⓖ** Oak Hollow Family Campground

Note: Items with the same letter are located in the same area.

Noble, 1720 Battleground Ave., 336/333-9833, which serves Mediterranean and Tuscan dishes. Live jazz can be heard most nights. The restaurant is open for dinner daily. Entrées range from $10 to $25.

The Vineyards, 120 Reynolda Village, Winston-Salem, 336/748-0269, specializes in continental cuisine but also offers regional game dishes. It's expensive but always an excellent choice. The restaurant serves dinner Tuesday

---

through Sunday and is closed Monday and major holidays. Another fantastic choice, and more moderately priced, is the **Old Salem Tavern Dining Room**, 736 S. Main St., Winston-Salem, 336/748-8585. The staff, clothed in colonial costumes, serves lunch and dinner in a historic building. Chicken pie is a lunch favorite; veal and seafood are evening stars. For a good and inexpensive breakfast, lunch, or dinner, try **Rainbow News & Café**, 712 Brookstown Ave., Winston-Salem, 336/723-5010, in a house converted into a restaurant. The menu changes daily and offers vegetarian entrees. Closed Monday.

Also recommended in High Point are **Country Bar-B-Q**, 411 W. Fairfield Rd., 336/431-8978; **Rosa Mae's**, 106 N. Main St., 336/887-0556; and **Ham's**, 1807 N. Main St., 336/887-1556.

LODGING

Greensboro's **Holiday Inn Four Seasons**, 3121 High Point Rd., 800/242-6556 or 336/292-9161, containing the Joseph S. Koury Convention Center, is one of the largest hotels in the piedmont, with more than 1,000 rooms, an indoor pool, exercise room, golf and tennis privileges, jogging and nature trails, and always more than one meeting in session. It's adjacent to the upscale Four Seasons Mall and convenient to the airport. **Park Lane Hotel at Four Seasons**, 3005 High Point Rd., Greensboro, 336/294-4565 or 800/942-6556, is a smaller facility (161 rooms) but just as nice, with most of the same amenities, including a fitness center and complimentary breakfast. Much smaller (less than 30 rooms) but more intimate is the **Biltmore Greensboro Hotel**, 111 W. Washington St., Greensboro, 336/272-3474 or 800/332-0303.

The **Salem Inn**, 127 S. Cherry St., Winston-Salem, 336/725-8561 or 800/533-8760, has 129 rooms and offers a meal plan, pool, and jogging/nature trail. Bed and breakfast establishments and country inns abound in Winston-Salem and include the upscale **Augustus T. Zevely Inn**, 803 S. Main St., 800/928-9299, with 12 rooms; the **Colonel Ludlow Inn**, 434 Summit St., 800/301-1887, with 10 rooms and a Jacuzzi/exercise area; and the **Henry F. Shaffner House**, 150 S. Marshall St., 800/952-2256, with similar amenities.

Also recommended are the **Adam's Mark of Winston-Salem**, a medium-size hotel at 425 N. Cherry St., 336/725-3500; and the **Premier Bed & Breakfast Inn**, 1001 Johnson St., High Point, 336/889-8349.

CAMPING

Fields RV Campground, 2317 Campground Rd., Greensboro, 336/292-1381, supplies the major conveniences and is open year-round. You might also like the **Greensboro Campground**, 2300 Montreal Ave., Greensboro, 336/274-4143. **Hagan-Stone Park**, south of Greensboro off U.S. 421, Pleasant Garden, 336/674-0472, offers camping with trailer and tent sites, playgrounds, horseshoe pits, picnic shelters, softball fields, paddle boats, nature trails, and cross-country courses. **Outdoor Center YMCA**, 4924 Tapawingo Trail, 336/697-0525, has camping sites and cabins by the lake, including one that sleeps 15. **Oak Hollow Family Campground**, adjacent to Oak Hollow Marina and Tennis Center at 3415 N. Centennial, High Point, 336/883-3492, has more than 90 full-service campsites and features a modern bathhouse, country store, pool, and play area.

GOLFING

The Greater Greensboro Open is a regular PGA Tour stop in the spring, as is the PGA Senior Tour's Vantage Championship each October at Tanglewood Park, west of Winston-Salem. But golf is good everywhere in the Tri-Cities area. The following are recommended: **Bel Aire Golf and Country Club**, 1518 Pleasant Ridge Rd., Greensboro, 336/668-2413; **Heather Hills Golf Course**, 3801 Heathrow Dr., Winston-Salem, 336/788-5785; **Oak Hollow Golf Course**, 1400 Oak View Dr., High Point, 336/883-3260; **Blair Park Golf Course**, 1901 S. Main St., High Point, 336/883-3497; **Longview Golf Course**, 6321 Ballinger Rd., Greensboro, 336/294-4018; **Old Home Place Golf Club**, 4295 Wallburg Rd., Winston-Salem, 336/769-1076; and **Reynolds Park Golf Course**, 2391 Reynolds Park Rd., 336/650-7660.

APPENDIX

Consider this appendix your travel tool box. Use it along with the material in the Planning Your Trip chapter to craft the trip you want. Here are the tools you'll find inside:

1. **Planning Map.** Make copies of this map and plot out various trip possibilities. Once you've decided on your route, you can write it on the original map and refer to it as you're traveling.

2. **Mileage Chart.** This chart shows the driving distances (in miles) between various destinations throughout the region. Use it in conjunction with the Planning Map.

3. **Special Interest Tours.** If you'd like to plan a trip around a certain theme—such as nature, sports, or art—one of these tours may work for you.

4. **Resources.** This guide lists various regional chambers of commerce and visitors bureaus, state offices, bed-and-breakfast registries, and other useful sources of information.

PLANNING MAP: The Carolinas

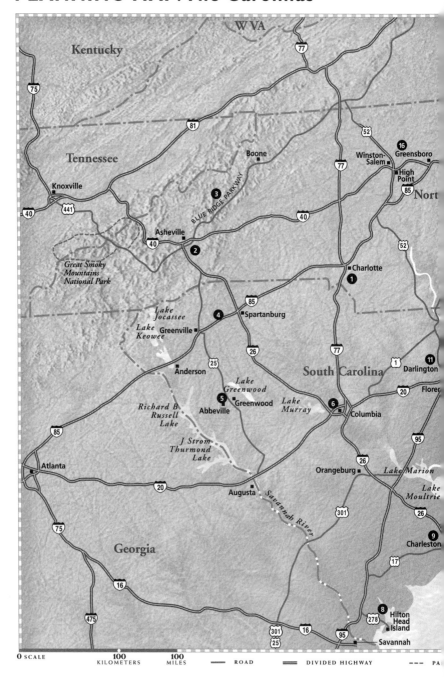

Kentucky

W VA

77

75

81

Tennessee

Boone

77

Winston-Salem

Greensboro 16

High Point

85 Nort

52

Knoxville

441

40

BLUE RIDGE PARKWAY

3

Asheville

40

2

Great Smoky Mountains National Park

Charlotte 1

52

Lake Jocassee

85

Spartanburg

4

Lake Keowee

Greenville

26

77

Anderson

25

South Carolina

Darlington 11

Florer

20

Lake Greenwood

Lake Murray

5

Greenwood

Abbeville

6

Columbia

Richard B Russell Lake

85

Atlanta

J Strom Thurmond Lake

26

Orangeburg

Lake Marion

Lake Moultrie

95

20

Augusta

Savannah River

301

26

75

Georgia

Charleston 9

17

16

8

Hilton Head Island

278

475

301

16

95

25

Savannah

0 SCALE   100 KILOMETERS   100 MILES   ROAD   DIVIDED HIGHWAY   PA

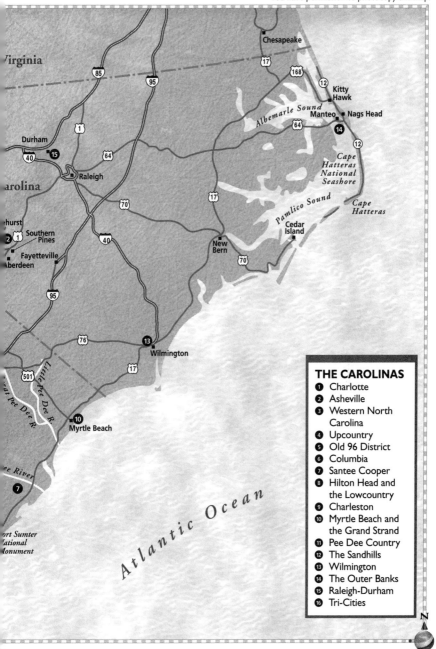

THE CAROLINAS
1. Charlotte
2. Asheville
3. Western North Carolina
4. Upcountry
5. Old 96 District
6. Columbia
7. Santee Cooper
8. Hilton Head and the Lowcountry
9. Charleston
10. Myrtle Beach and the Grand Strand
11. Pee Dee Country
12. The Sandhills
13. Wilmington
14. The Outer Banks
15. Raleigh-Durham
16. Tri-Cities

CAROLINAS MILEAGE CHART

	Charlotte, NC	Asheville, NC	Blowing Rock, NC	Greenville, SC	Abbeville, SC	Columbia, SC	Sumter, SC	Hilton Head, SC	Charleston, SC	Myrtle Beach, SC	Darlington, SC	Southern Pines, NC	Wilmington, NC	Kitty Hawk, NC	Raleigh, NC
Asheville, NC	114														
Blowing Rock, NC	91	86													
Greenville, SC	92	62	116												
Abbeville, SC	135	114	168	52											
Columbia, SC	91	157	182	101	89										
Sumter, SC	106	201	197	145	133	44									
Hilton Head, SC	307	370	398	300	195	216	210								
Charleston, SC	207	263	282	201	189	100	94	116							
Myrtle Beach, SC	179	291	270	244	230	147	97	210	94						
Darlington, SC	99	211	190	174	167	78	40	236	120	120					
Southern Pines, NC	104	218	185	198	220	116	112	308	192	80	72				
Wilmington, NC	220	327	306	296	304	198	177	290	180	120	137	121			
Kitty Hawk, NC	352	460	418	444	500	422	392	498	468	385	368	306	272		
Raleigh, NC	143	247	195	245	396	202	198	278	250	165	148	86	130	220	
Winston-Salem, NC	81	142	93	183	216	172	187	343	281	263	150	93	235	315	105

SPECIAL INTEREST TOURS

With *Carolinas Travel•Smart*, you can plan a trip of any length—a one-day excursion, a getaway weekend, or a three-week vacation—around any special interest. To get you started, the following pages contain six tours geared toward a variety of interests. For more information, refer to the chapters listed—chapter names are bolded and chapter numbers appear inside black bullets. You can follow a suggested itinerary in its entirety, or shorten, lengthen, or combine parts of each, depending on your starting and ending points.

Discuss alternative routes and schedules with your travel companions—it's a great way to have fun, even before you leave home. And remember: Don't hesitate to change your itinerary once you're on the road. Careful study and planning ahead will help you make informed decisions as you go, but spontaneity is the extra ingredient that will make your trip memorable.

BEST OF THE REGION TOUR

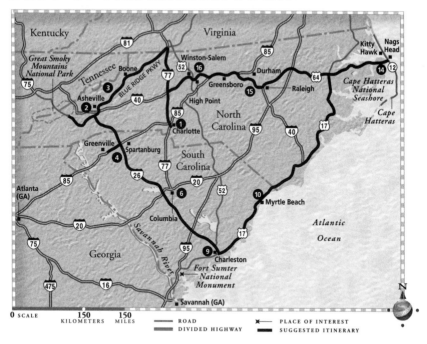

The "Carolinas' finest" tour crosses the states—from mountains to piedmont to beaches. Points of interest include America's most famous castle, the Biltmore House, lowcountry rice plantations, and giant research and development centers.

❶ **Charlotte**
❷ **Asheville**
❸ **Western North Carolina**
❹ **Upcountry**
❻ **Columbia**
❾ **Charleston**
❿ **Myrtle Beach and the Grand Strand**
⓮ **The Outer Banks**
⓯ **Raleigh-Durham**
⓰ **Tri-Cities**

Time needed: 2 to 4 weeks

NATURE LOVERS' TOUR

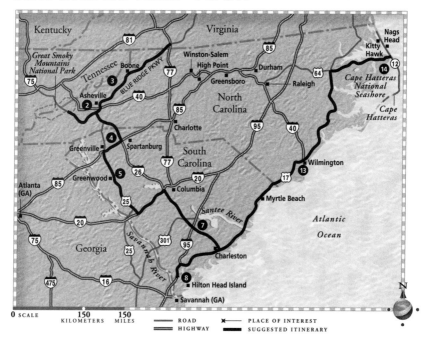

From mountains to piedmont, beaches to barrier islands, the Carolinas are a nature lover's paradise.

❷ **Asheville** (Biltmore Estate, Botanical Gardens)
❸ **Western North Carolina** (Appalachian Trail, Blue Ridge Mountains)
❹ **Upcountry** (Chattooga National Wild and Scenic River, Hatcher Gardens, Roper Mountain Science Center)
❺ **Greenwood and Abbeville** (Gardens of Park Seed Company, Lake Greenwood, Parsons Mountain Park)
❼ **Santee Cooper** (Lakes Marion and Moultrie)
❽ **Hilton Head Island and the Lowcountry** (Savannah National Wildlife Refuge, Tillman Sand Ridge Heritage Preserve)
⓭ **Wilmington** (Airlie Gardens, Orton Plantation Gardens)
⓮ **The Outer Banks** (Jockey's Ridge State Park)

Time needed: 1 to 4 weeks

FAMILY FUN TOUR

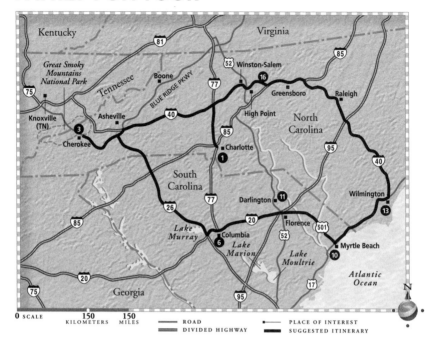

Family fun doesn't have to begin and end at theme parks, but if that is what you're looking for, you can find it in the Carolinas. You can visit Paramount's Carowinds, Tweetsie Railroad, Ghost Town in the Sky, water parks, battleships, beaches, NASCAR races, and more.

❶ **Charlotte** (Lowe's Motor Speedway, Discovery Place, Paramount's Carowinds)

❸ **Western North Carolina** (Cherokee, Ghost Town in the Sky, Tweetsie Railroad)

❻ **Columbia** (Lake Murray, Riverbanks Zoo and Botanical Garden)

❿ **Myrtle Beach and the Grand Strand** (Broadway at the Beach, The Pavilion)

⓫ **Pee Dee Country** (Darlington International Raceway)

⓭ **Wilmington** (USS *North Carolina, Henrietta II*)

⓰ **Tri-Cities** (Emerald Pointe Waterpark, Tanglewood Park)

Time needed: 2 weeks

ARTS AND CULTURE TOUR

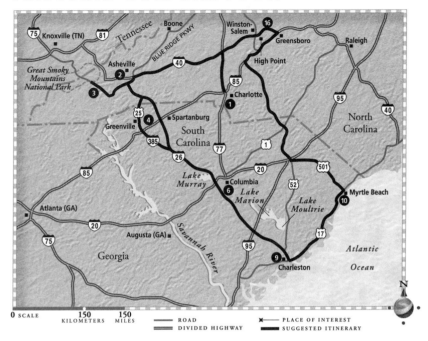

From bluegrass to beach, music reigns supreme in the Carolinas. Here you will also find world-famous fine artists, folk artists, and craftspeople.

❶ Charlotte (Mint Museum of Art, Spirit Square)

❷ Asheville (Asheville Art Museum, Folk Art Center)

❸ Western North Carolina (Oconaluftee Indian Village, Museum of North Carolina Handicrafts)

❹ Upcountry (Bob Jones University, Greenville Museum of Art, Spartanburg County Museum)

❻ Columbia (McKissick Museum, South Carolina State Museum)

❾ Charleston (Charleston Museum, Spoleto Festival)

❿ Myrtle Beach and the Grand Strand (Alabama Theater, Broadway at the Beach, Legends in Concert)

⑯ Tri-Cities (Museum of Early Southern Decorative Arts, Southeastern Center for Contemporary Art)

Time needed: 1 to 2 weeks

GOLFERS' TOUR

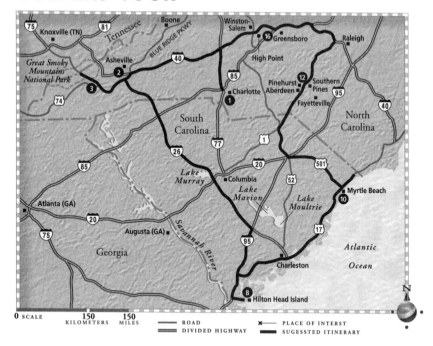

A dedicated golfer could spend the rest of his or her life in the Carolinas and never desire to leave. You will find championship courses designed by the top names in the sport in locations to boggle the mind and lift the spirit.

❶ **Charlotte** (Larkhaven, Oak Hill, Quail Hollow)

❷ **Asheville** (Biltmore Forest, Grove Park)

❸ **Western North Carolina** (Beech Mountain, High Hampton)

❽ **Hilton Head Island** (Ocean Course, Palmetto Dunes, Hilton Head National, Island West)

❿ **Myrtle Beach and the Grand Strand** (Pine Lakes, Tidewater, Long Bay)

⓬ **The Sandhills** (The Club at Longleaf, Pinehurst, Talamore, Legacy)

⓰ **Tri-Cities** (Bel Aire, Heather Hills, Oak Hollow)

Time needed: 2 to 4 weeks

HISTORY LOVERS' TOUR

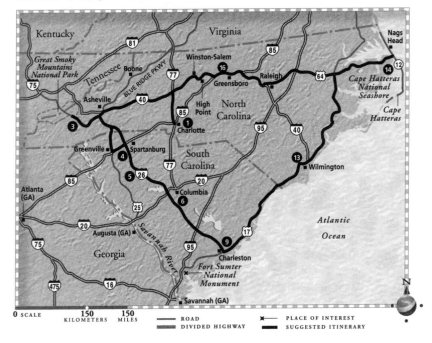

History buffs will find plenty to keep them busy here.

❶ **Charlotte** (Charlotte Museum of History, Kings Mountain Battlefield)

❸ **Western North Carolina** (*Horn in the West*, *Unto These Hills*, Oconaluftee Indian Village)

❹ **Upcountry** (Cowpens Battlefield, Walnut Grove)

❺ **Greenwood and Abbeville** (Burt-Stark House, Greenwood Museum, Ninety Six National Historic Site)

❻ **Columbia** (Hampton-Preston Mansion, Mann-Simons Cottage, Museum of African-American Culture, State House Complex)

❾ **Charleston** (Middleton House & Gardens, Drayton Hall, Fort Sumter)

⓭ **Wilmington** (Brunswick Town, Museum of the Cape Fear)

⓮ **The Outer Banks** (*The Lost Colony*)

⓰ **Tri-Cities** (Historic Bethabara, Mattye Reed African Heritage Center, Old Salem)

Time needed: 1 ½ to 2 weeks

RESOURCES

State Offices and Associations

North Carolina Campground Owners Association, 893 U.S. 70 W., Suite 202, Garner, NC 27529, 919/779-5709

North Carolina Hotel and Motel Association, P.O. Box 30457, Raleigh, NC 27622-0457, 919/786-9730

North Carolinas Ski Areas Association, P.O. Box 106, Blowing Rock, NC 28605, 828/295-7828

North Carolina Travel and Tourism Division, 301 N. Wilmington St., Raleigh, NC 27626-2825, 800/VISIT-NC, www.visitnc.com

South Carolina Department of Parks, Recreation and Tourism, 1205 Pendleton St., P.O. Box 71, Columbia, SC 29201, 803/734-0122, www.prt.state.sc.us/sc

South Carolina State Parks, 888/88-PARKS, www.sccsi.com/sc/Parks /index.html

Local Offices and Associations

Asheville Convention & Visitors Bureau, P.O. Box 1010, Asheville, NC 28802-1010, 800/257-1300

Charleston Area Convention and Visitors Bureau, P.O. Box 975, Charleston, SC 29402, 800/868-8118, charlestoncvb.com

Charlotte Convention & Visitors Bureau, 122 E. Stonewall St., Charlotte, NC 28202-1838, 800/231-4636, www.charlottecvb.org

Columbia Metropolitan Convention and Visitors Bureau, P.O. Box 15, Columbia, SC 29202, 800/264-4884, www.columbiasc.net

Greater Greenville Convention and Visitors Bureau, P.O. Box 10527, Greenville, SC 29603, 800/717-0023, www.greatergreenville.com

Greater Raleigh Convention & Visitors Bureau, P.O. Box 1879, Raleigh, NC 27602-1879, 800/849-8499, www.raleighcvb.org

Greensboro Area Convention & Visitors Bureau, 317 S. Greene St., Greensboro, NC 27401-2615, 800/344-2282, www.greensboronc.com

Lowcountry and Resort Islands Tourism Commission, P.O. Box 615, Yemassee, SC 29945, 800/528-6870, www.lowcountrytravel.com

Myrtle Beach Area Chamber of Commerce and Info Center, P.O. Box 2115, Myrtle Beach, SC 29578-2115, 843/626-7444 or 800/356-3016, www.myrtlebeachlive.com

Old 96 District Tourism Commission, P.O. Box 448, Laurens, SC 29360, 800/849-9633, www.old96.org

Pee Dee Tourism Commission, P.O. Box 3093, Florence, SC 29502,
    800/325-9005
Pinehurst Area Convention & Visitors Bureau, P.O. Box 2270, Southern
    Pines, NC 28388, 800/346-5362, www.homeofgolf.com
Santee Cooper Counties Promotion Commission, P.O. Drawer 40, Santee,
    SC 29142, 803/854-2131 or 800/227-8510, www.
    santeecoopercountry.org
Spartanburg Convention and Visitors Bureau, P.O. Box 1636, Spartanburg,
    SC 29304, 800/374-8326
Upcountry Carolina Association, P.O. Box 3116, Greenville, SC 29602,
    864/233-2690 or 800/849-4766, www.upcountry-sc.org

Publications

Access North Carolina: A Vacation and Travel Guide for Disabled Persons,
    800/VISIT-NC
North Carolina Official Travel Guide, 800/VISIT-NC
South Carolina Golf Guide, 800/682-5553
South Carolina Travel Guide, 803/734-0122

INDEX

Map Index

FRANCES CRESWELL HELMS

ABOUT THE AUTHOR

Frances Creswell Helms was born in South Carolina and grew up in North Carolina. She spent 15 years as a writer and editor for a daily South Carolina newspaper before beginning a seven-year stint as editor of *Richmond Magazine* in Richmond, Virginia. For five years she also wrote a weekly general interest column, distributed worldwide by the New York Times News Syndicate. Helms has won more than 100 state and national awards for writing, editing, layout, and design. In 1993 she earned a master's degree in journalism from the University of South Carolina. She and her husband, Vance E. Helms Jr., have five children and ten grandchildren.